Mapping the New World of American Philanthropy

Mapping the New World of American Philanthropy

Causes and Consequences of the Transfer of Wealth

SUSAN U. RAYMOND, PHD, AND
MARY BETH MARTIN, ESQ.

BICENTENNIAL
1807
WILEY
2007
BICENTENNIAL

John Wiley & Sons, Inc.

Library of Congress Cataloging-in-Publication Data:

ISBN: 978-0-470-08038-2

Printed in the United States of America

10 9 8 7 6 5 4 3 2 1

*To our expeditionary colleagues, who join us in the
exploration of the New World of American philanthropy.
And to Kate, Katharine, Josh, and Jennifer
for their tireless research assistance.*

Contents

List of Exhibits

About the Authors

Susan U. Raymond, PhD, is senior managing director of research, evaluation, and strategic planning for Changing Our World, a leading national philanthropic consulting firm. She has extensive experience in research, analysis, and planning, most recently with the prestigious New York Academy of Sciences. At the Academy, she created the first technology and public policy program, and then became director of strategic planning and special projects. Prior to this, Dr. Raymond was a project officer at the World Bank, and a senior consultant to the U.S. Agency for International Development, and to various private organizations, including the Carnegie Corporation, specializing in healthcare and international economic research.

Dr. Raymond is foreign policy and research advisor to the bipartisan congressional commission studying the effectiveness of public and private foreign assistance, the Helping to Enhance the Livelihood of People Commission. She is a member of the advisory board for the Center for Global Prosperity in Washington, D.C., and an associate research scientist at the Institute of Human Nutrition at Columbia University.

She is the author of *Philanthropy and the Future: Economics, Ethics, and Management,* published by John Wiley & Sons, Inc. in March 2004. She has published extensively in the areas of philanthropy, economics, healthcare, and corporate responsibility, in such journals as *Foreign Affairs, Development, Economic Reform Today, Annals of the New York Academy of Sciences, Journal of Healthcare Administration Education,* and *Technological Forecasting and Social Change.* Dr. Raymond was also a project team member for the Macroeconomics of Cardiovascular Disease project at the Center for Macroeconomics and Health of the Earth Institute at Columbia University, under Jeffrey Sachs.

Dr. Raymond earned her BA Phi Beta Kappa, from Macalester College, and her MA and PhD from the Johns Hopkins University School of Advanced International Studies. Her substantive focus was in the field of health and medical economics, and in international public health. She has worked on philanthropy and economic development projects throughout Africa, the Middle East, and Eastern Europe, as well as in Russia and Asia.

Mary Beth Martin, Esq., is a senior managing director at Changing Our World, Inc., overseeing the firm's Boston office. With nearly 20 years experience in the fundraising field, she has done extensive work in higher education, focusing primarily on planned giving, major gifts, and capital campaigns. Since joining Changing Our World, she has provided planned giving advice to numerous clients, in addition to providing fundraising strategy and capital campaign oversight. She has addressed both national and regional organizations, numerous nonprofit boards, and development professionals on the topic of planned giving.

Ms. Martin served for seven years as an adjunct professor of business law in the Carroll School of Management at Boston College, and taught introductory law courses for the American Institute of Banking. She received a BA from Boston College, Phi Beta Kappa, and a JD from Boston College Law School.

About the Contributors

Tamara Backer is a managing director at Changing Our World, Inc. Previously, Ms. Backer worked for EF Education, a leader in international exchange programs. At EF, she trained over 1,000 program volunteers and staff worldwide on nonprofit relationship building. She also participated in the start-up of the Academy of the Pacific Rim Charter School, and has provided counsel, and evaluated programs, for nonprofits such as Plimouth Plantation Museum in Massachusetts, Cancer Care Connection in Delaware, the University of Massachusetts–Boston, and Harvard University. Recent speaking engagements include the Greater D.C. Cares Business Volunteerism Council, and the National Restaurant Association's Community Relations Council. Ms. Backer holds an MA in education from Harvard University, with a concentration in administration, planning, and social policy, and a BA in East Asian studies from Bates College.

Maureen Baehr, after more than two decades of experience in the private sector as a human resources executive for American Express, and a management consultant to financial services clients including Lehman Brothers and Morgan Stanley, now consults on venture philanthropy, knowledge management, strategy, and capacity building for nonprofit organizations. Ms. Baehr is a member of the board of trustees for the AIDS Vaccine Advocacy Coalition and the Cabrini Mission Foundation. She has an MA in education from Harvard University and is committed to the mission to end AIDS as a significant part of her consulting and venture philanthropy work.

Nancy Nemecek Crume is an officer of Crume and Company, Inc., a Dallas-based business and marketing consultancy. After almost 20 years in positions at McCann Erickson, DDB Needham, and Omnicom Group, companies and seven years as a business and brand strategist in her own firm, Ms. Crume has built an extensive strategic planning track record. Ms.

Crume's clients have included corporations (MasterCard Worldwide, Texas Instruments, and Hallmark), advertising agencies (BBDO, The Integer Group, and TM), and nonprofit organizations (United Nations World Food Programme). Her focus continues to be the building and strengthening of businesses and their brands.

Steven DiSalvo, PhD, is a senior managing director working in the private philanthropy division of Changing Our World, Inc. Formerly, he served as executive director of the Joe Torre Safe at Home Foundation, which works to educate to end the cycle of domestic violence and save lives, and as the chief operating officer for Junior Achievement of New York, serving more than 150,000 students in the New York City area. Dr. DiSalvo has been a development officer at Fordham University and executive assistant to the president of Loyola University in Chicago. He completed his PhD in educational leadership from Fordham University, where he also holds a BS in psychology and an MBA in marketing. Dr. DiSalvo currently sits on two family foundation boards and is a member of the advisory board of the Center for American Catholic Studies at Fordham University.

Judith S. Giuliani is a managing director of Changing Our World, Inc., a national fundraising and philanthropic services company. Mrs. Giuliani is a registered nurse with an extensive medical and scientific background, particularly in infectious diseases. With her unique background, Mrs. Giuliani coordinated the efforts of the Family Assistance Center at Pier 94 in the aftermath of September 11. Also in response to September 11, Mrs. Giuliani became a Founding Member of the Board of Trustees of the Twin Towers Fund, which raised and distributed all of the $216 million to over 600 families and individuals. Contributions to the Fund also created the TTF Scholarship Fund and America's Camp. Mrs. Giuliani currently serves as the executive director of the Campaign for Saint Vincent Catholic Medical Centers in New York. In response to the possibility of nuclear, biological, and chemical acts of terrorism, the Campaign, chaired by her husband, the Honorable Rudolph W. Giuliani, focuses on emergency preparedness in the City of New York.

Anne F. Glauber is executive vice president and director of the Global Issues Communication Group at Ruder Finn, a leading public relations firm in New York City. In this capacity she is responsible for communications programs for a wide range of government agencies, global NGOs, and corporate responsibility programs for major corporations. She is the founder of the Business Council for Peace, bringing together women in the United States and enterprising women in war-torn countries, to build sustainable peace. Among the projects undertaken by the council is the development of handicraft businesses for women widowed by the Rwandan genocide. In 2003, she was named by Women's eNews as one of 21 leaders for the twenty-first century. Ms. Glauber holds her MA in international studies from the Johns Hopkins School of Advanced International Studies.

Eileen R. Heisman is president and CEO of the National Philanthropic Trust. She is a nationally recognized expert on philanthropy and planned giving, and has been a keynote speaker and panelist at many major philanthropic and estate planning conferences. Ms. Heisman was recognized as the 2003 Fundraising Executive of the Year by the Association of Fundraising Professionals, greater Philadelphia chapter, and received the 2003 Women of Distinction award from the *Philadelphia Business Journal*. Ms. Heisman is the co-author of *Your Guide to Donor Advised Funds,* published by Lightbulb Press.

Michael P. Hoffman is chairman and CEO of Changing Our World, Inc. Prior to forming Changing Our World, Mr. Hoffman was executive vice president for external affairs for the Franciscan Health Partnership, a Catholic healthcare system with assets of over $1.1 billion, and for the Franciscan Sisters of the Poor Foundation, a multimillion dollar healthcare foundation serving the poor around the world. Currently, he is a trustee for the College of Mt. Saint Vincent, the Catholic University of America, and the National Catholic Community Foundation. Mr. Hoffman is also chairman of the board of trustees of the Cabrini Center for Nursing and Rehabilitation, and serves on the board of the Rudolph W. Giuliani Center for Urban Leadership. He is a member of the Veterans of Foreign Wars and past chairman of the E-Philanthropy Foundation. Mr. Hoffman holds his BS from the United States Military Academy at West Point, and master's degrees from Webster University and the Embry Riddle Aeronautical University.

Howard Husock is director of the Manhattan Institute's Social Entrepreneurship Initiative, where he also serves as vice president for programs and research. He previously served as the director of case studies in public policy and management at Harvard University's Kennedy School of Government, where he remains an adjunct lecturer, and as a research fellow at the school's Taubman Center for State and Local Government. Mr. Husock is a prolific writer on housing and urban policy issues. He is author of *America's Trillion-Dollar Housing Mistake: The Failure of American Housing Policy.*

Katherine C. Jewell graduated from the University of Richmond with a BA in international studies, and is currently pursuing a law degree at St. John's University in New York.

Preston H. Koster joined Bessemer Trust in 1997, and is a senior client account manager, responsible for investment management and legacy planning for clients. He is also a team leader for New York–based client account managers and serves on the Officers Committee, Banking and Loan Committee, and Special Investments and Discretionary Distribution Committee. Mr. Koster has spent over 20 years with J. P. Morgan's Private Client Group. As a team leader in Morgan's Private Bank, he has extensive experience working with clients across generations, focusing on investment strategies, asset allocation, hedging, monetization of private assets, creative tax planning, and credit. As a banker, he was also the worldwide controller of Morgan's Private Bank. Mr. Koster received his BA from Westminster College and his MBA in finance from the Lubin School at Pace University.

The Very Reverend Dr. James A. Kowalski is dean of The Cathedral Church of Saint John the Divine in New York City, and is on the board of Leake and Watts, and an overseer for St. Luke's/Roosevelt Hospitals in New York. He was Rector of St. Luke's Episcopal Parish in Darien, Connecticut, where he served as President of the Fairfield County Economic Development Corporation and was a member of the Board of St. Luke's Lifeworks in Stamford, Connecticut. Dean Kowalski is a fellow of the American Leadership Forum and of the Henry Crown Aspen Institute Program. Dr. Kowalski holds his BA Phi Beta Kappa from Trinity College, his Masters in Divinity from the Episcopal Divinity School, and his Doctor of Ministry from the Hartford Seminary.

Glen Macdonald, founding president and partner of the Wealth and Giving Forum, spent most of his private sector career at PricewaterhouseCoopers, where he was a partner in the management consulting unit. Mr. MacDonald has been a lecturer in international politics at the University of North Carolina at Chapel Hill, and a special advisor to UNESCO in

Paris, on the technology policies in developing economies. He was a Ford Foundation Fellow at the Harvard Center for International Affairs, and a Fulbright scholar in Mexico. He holds a BA with highest honors and an MA from the University of North Carolina at Chapel Hill.

Deborah Maloy is a certified financial planner with over 20 years experience working with women and their families. She serves on the board of the Financial Planning Association of Massachusetts, as director of consumer awareness, working to promote financial literacy and fiscal responsibility. Deborah graduated from Emmanuel College in Boston, with a BA in economics; University of Rhode Island, with an MS in library science; Marywood College in Scranton, Pennsylvania, with an MBA in finance; and Boston University, with a diploma in financial planning. She also serves on the board of the YWCA of Malden, Massachusetts, working with others to further the YWCA mission of "eliminating racism, empowering women."

Antoinette M. Malveaux is director of strategic alliances at Casey Family Programs in Seattle, Washington. Previously, Ms. Malveaux was president and CEO of the National Black MBA Association. Under her leadership, the Association developed into a multinational organization and tripled its membership. Ms. Malveaux began her career with American Express Bank as director of global marketing and strategic planning. She has served on the board of trustees for the University of San Francisco, Seattle Central Community College, and the Girl Scouts USA Chicago Chapter. She has received the Rainbow PUSH Reginald Lewis Trailblazer Award and served as executive-in-residence at Howard University School of Business, teaching strategic management of nonprofit organizations.

Ms. Malveaux holds a BA in economics from the University of San Francisco, an MBA from the Wharton School of Business at the University of Pennsylvania, and a certificate in Executive Education for Leaders in Philanthropy from Stanford University.

Marc H. Morial is an attorney currently serving as president and CEO of the National Urban League. During his tenure, he has helped thrust the League into the forefront of major public policy issues, research, and effective community-based solutions. He is considered one of the nation's foremost experts on a wide range of issues related to cities and their residents. He has also been recognized by the *Nonprofit Times* as one of America's top

50 nonprofit executives, and has been named by *Ebony* magazine as one of the 100 Most Influential Blacks in America. Mr. Morial previously served two terms as mayor of New Orleans, and two years as a Louisiana state senator.

Rodney W. Nichols, former president and CEO of the New York Academy of Sciences from 1992 to 2001, was previously scholar-in-residence at the Carnegie Corporation of New York (1990–1992), and vice president and executive vice president of the Rockefeller University (1970–1990). He also served as a physicist, a manager in industry, and has worked for the federal government. An expert on national and international science policy, he has written extensively on these issues. He is on the board of advisors to *Foreign Affairs*, and *Technology in Society: An International Journal*. Appointed to the executive committee of the Carnegie Commission on Science, Technology, and Government (1989–1994), Mr. Nichols was principal author of the commission's January 1992 report, entitled *Science and Technology in U.S. International Affairs*. A member of the bilateral governing board of the U.S.-India Science and Technology Forum, he also currently serves on the boards of the Research Foundation of the City University of New York, the Eugene Lang College of New School University, the Irvington Institute for Immunological Research, the Manhattan Institute, and the ALS Association. He is a consultant to the Richard Lounsbery Foundation, the Simons Foundation, and other nonprofit initiatives.

Janice Schoos is a senior philanthropic advisor and senior managing director at Changing Our World, Inc. Ms. Schoos spent nearly 20 years at J. P. Morgan Chase. As part of J. P. Morgan Private Bank, she advised ultra-high net worth clients and their families on their philanthropic activities. In addition, Ms. Schoos was instrumental in building, managing, and training the sales staff of the J. P. Morgan Chase Charitable Giving Fund, the fourth-largest donor-advised fund sponsored by a financial institution. She has extensive experience advising clients in the areas of private foundation strategy and management, donor-advised funds, cause-related marketing, corporate sponsorships, as well as partnering with client intermediaries.

Sean Stannard-Stockton is a principal of Ensemble Capital Management in Burlingame, California, a registered investment advisor with a disciplined process and a unique specialty in investing and structuring assets for philanthropic purposes. He directs Ensemble Capital's tactical philanthropy service and manages client portfolios. He holds a BA in economics from the University of California at Davis, and has earned Chartered Financial Analyst (CFA) as well as Chartered Advisor in Philanthropy (CAP) designations. He can be reached through www.EnsembleCapital.com. You can read more by Sean Stannard-Stockton on his blog www.TacticalPhilanthropy.com.

András Szántó, PhD, is a visiting senior fellow at the Center for Arts and Culture, an independent think tank in Washington, D.C., a research affiliate of the Center for Arts and Cultural Policy Studies at Princeton University, and director of the NEA Arts Journalism Institute for classical music and opera writers at Columbia University. Until 2005 he was the director of the National Arts Journalism Program at Columbia, America's premier academic fellowship program and research center, devoted to the advancement of cultural journalism and public debate on the arts. Dr. Szántó has taught sociology at Columbia and Barnard College and has lectured extensively in universities and cultural institutions around the world. As a consultant, he has worked with the Pew Charitable Trusts, the Andy Warhol Foundation for the Visual Arts, the City University of New York, and has published a study about U.S. foundation support for international arts exchanges titled *A New Mandate for Philanthropy?* Dr. Szántó is co-author and editor of four books and numerous research reports, academic articles, and critical essays, including, most recently, *A Portrait of the Visual Arts: Meeting the Challenges of a New Era* (RAND, 2005).

Jenn Thompson is managing director for e-philanthropy at Changing Our World. Previously, she served as a senior director with the AOL Time Warner Foundation, where she managed the organization's e-philanthropy efforts. Ms. Thompson directed the Helping.org and NetworkforGood.org Web sites, leading e-philanthropy portals that raised more than $35 million for charities in the United States. Her work also covered the foundation's non-profit capacity–building efforts that provided strategic guidance to charities working to enhance their online presence. She also worked in AOL's member communications department, providing online help and information to 30 million AOL members. Ms. Thompson holds her BA from Pennsylvania State University.

Dennis Whittle is co-founder of GlobalGiving, which utilizes the Internet to enable more funding to reach projects around the globe. Before joining the World Bank in 1986, Mr. Whittle worked in the Philippines with the Asian Development Bank and with USAID. Until October 2000, Mr. Whittle was part of a troika that led the World Bank's Corporate Strategy and Innovation units. From 1992–1997, he led a variety of initiatives in the Bank's Russia program, including housing reform and energy efficiency projects. From 1987–1992, Mr. Whittle was an economist in the World Bank's Jakarta office, advising the Indonesian Ministries of Finance and National Development, and managing projects in the agriculture and forestry sectors. Mr. Whittle graduated with honors in religious studies from the University of North Carolina–Chapel Hill and did his graduate work in development studies and economics at Princeton University. Mr. Whittle has also completed the Advanced Management Program at Harvard Business School.

Nora Campbell Wood is a member of the board of trustees for the Campbell Family Foundation. She is also a senior director at Changing Our World, Inc. Previously, she worked in the corporate representation and sales departments for the International Management Group (IMG) in Australia and New York City. In addition, Ms. Wood has held various volunteer positions, providing support to abused and neglected children in Chicago and Connecticut. She holds a BA in psychology-based human relations from Connecticut College.

Barbara Yastine is a senior advisor to Changing Our World, Inc. and the leader of the Changing Our World philanthropy business. Barbara has 20 years' executive experience in major global financial institutions. Most recently, she served as CFO for Credit Suisse's Corporate and Investment Bank (formerly Credit Suisse First Boston). Prior to joining Credit Suisse in 2002, Barbara was with Citigroup and its predecessors for 15 years in a variety of financial and executive roles. Her last position at Citigroup was as CFO of its Corporate and Investment bank, which included Smith Barney at the time, and she served on the company's 30-person management committee.

The Defining Legacy
of Our Generation

JUDITH S. GIULIANI

*I believe that every human mind feels pleasure in doing good to
another . . .*

—Thomas Jefferson to John Adams, 1816

Most things start small. My own experience with philanthropy and
volunteerism began that way, as a teenage "candy striper" at a hospital in
my hometown. Giving of oneself was a core value in my family, and volunteering at the hospital was thus an expression of who I was, as a person, and
what my family stood for.

Most small things that are vibrant grow. Once we become wage earners,
our volunteerism becomes not only the investment of our time, but the
donation of our financial resources. As I became an adult, my involvement
turned to managing volunteer efforts, especially in healthcare—which is
where, as a nurse, my heart was—as well as to philanthropic giving.

As small things grow, they also expand. I watched as programs that I
nurtured in a single institution spread across other institutions. Almost
two decades ago (can it have been that long?) I co-chaired the Festival of
Clowns at the Babies' Hospital (now Morgan Stanley Childrens' Hospital
of New York-Presbyterian Hospital), which brought circus clowns of the
Big Apple Circus into the hospital, to teach children how to inject themselves with life-saving medications. This model was gradually replicated, and
now many hospitals use clown volunteers to remove the fear from children,
who must learn to adjust to disease and therapy.

This process—the single seed, growing then spreading—is very much at the heart of the transfer of wealth that is addressed in this volume. The Baby-Boomer generation finds itself in possession of three resources—money, education, and experience—that have rarely been combined at such levels. Thanks to the beauty of an open society and an open economy, economic prosperity has enabled unprecedented levels of wealth to spread across unprecedented numbers of people. Those people are more highly educated than ever in the nation's history. And they have traveled more extensively than any generation of American ever has.

These three capacities now open an opportunity for our generation to leave a defining legacy. That legacy can be the permanent enrichment of American philanthropy, with significant resources carefully managed and continually targeted at a range of social needs with reach that spans the globe. Ours is a generation of thousands, even hundreds of thousands, of business and community leaders who seek to express their own commitment to community through their philanthropy, and to do so in their lifetimes, bringing their own personal capabilities to the table along with their money. Philanthropy will be the expression of our generation's values.

This is a defining legacy indeed. But its most important result will not be financial, it will be the message we are sending to our children—a message of commitment to community.

In traveling to more than 30 countries in the last five years, I have seen two elements that will make this legacy particularly unique as it passes to our children.

First, it will be a global message. When I pushed the magazine cart through the halls of the hospital as a candy striper, I did not think in global terms. Most of us in our youth could not conceive in any practical way of the cultural, economic, and political globe of which we were a part. Today, our children think globally as a matter of course. The world outside America's borders permeates every part of their lives, from the nationalities of their schoolmates, to the sources of their music, to the food in the cafeteria. Philanthropy and volunteerism will be naturally global for them, as it increasingly will be for us.

Second, technology has provided, and will continue to provide, a booster rocket for philanthropy in three ways. First, it has made the knowledge of social needs nearly instantaneous and widespread. The tragedies of the tsunami and hurricane Katrina were not only played out on television news, they were on the Internet around the world, even as the winds howled and the waters consumed human lives. Electronic communication speeds and spreads knowledge as never before.

Technology enables equally quick and broad flows of resources. Philanthropy can respond to need immediately, and from hundreds of thousands of households, with the click of a mouse.

Finally, technology improves management, and improved management builds donor trust, which in turn reinforces the flow of funds. In sorting files recently, and trying to make sense out of years of accumulated paper, I found a tattered piece of graph paper which served as our "spreadsheet" for the Festival of Clowns. Penciled in neatly arranged columns were the amounts of checks donated, the names of donors, and the little tick marks of the arithmetic to total income. All tidily written next to the coffee stains from the committee's weekly meetings. Technology has made such pencil marks prehistoric.

In enabling the management of finances and the tracking of programs, sophisticated technology has given our philanthropy and nonprofits the tools that build competence and efficiency in resource management, and hence allowed us to create trust in nonprofit institutions. That trust will span the next generation.

The transfer of wealth will be the defining legacy of our generation, one of which our children can be proud and will seek to emulate. As a result, we as a nation, we as a community that spans oceans and weaves myriad cultures into a single purpose of human betterment, can only become stronger. This strength is our legacy.

Being All That We Can Be

MICHAEL P. HOFFMAN

I am extremely proud to provide the introduction for this volume of essays, written by some of the most thoughtful and forward-thinking opinion leaders in American philanthropy. I salute Susan Raymond and Mary Beth Martin, colleagues and friends, for creating this volume. I thank all of the authors who have contributed their thoughts. The range of their expertise and the scope of their experience is humbling, and their collaboration is a reason for deep gratitude. That gratitude is born both in recognition of their time and in recognition of the importance of the times in which we live. This work is important because much is at stake.

These are truly historic times.

For decades, perhaps for centuries, philanthropy has been a cottage industry in America. Small or large, philanthropies have operated in a relative organizational vacuum. Every foundation developed its own priorities, quite independent of the actions of other philanthropies, and quite apart from the actions of government (often in the very same areas of interest), or the actions of corporations or other commercial entities. Indeed, philanthropies often selected nonprofits for support less on the basis of a deep understanding of the range of nonprofit activity in its area of interest, or the relative merits of alternative nonprofits, than on personal connections. Who was in your foursome or what was on the nightly news was more likely to define a philanthropic portfolio than was research that actually indicated social priorities and the probability of impact.

In short, private philanthropy was often an afterthought, a transfer of resources that was *ad hoc* and informal, carried out to respond to needs of the moment, pleas of the "crise du jour," personal interests, or networks of close friends with favorite causes. For the most part, it was not characterized by purposeful decision making, strategic analysis, or 360-degree scans of either problem or nonprofit environment.

This cottage industry approach has served America well. As is well documented in the essays included in this volume, private philanthropy, indeed the entire nonprofit sector, is alive and well in America. A record number of nonprofits now benefits from a record level of philanthropic giving. Government increasingly recognizes, and even encourages, these resource transfers. Communities realize the advantages of having private philanthropic commitments expended close to the community, to reflect community priorities.

So, all is well. Or is it?

When a cottage industry grows to represent a third of a trillion dollars of value, questions need to be asked, and opportunities need serious consideration. *Opportunity* is the operative term.

With the growth in recognition of the importance of private philanthropy, the proliferation of nonprofit endeavors, and the growing importance of corporate social responsibility comes the opportunity—nay, the imperative—to seek both efficiency and effectiveness. What is increasingly important is coordination. Every philanthropy "doing its own thing" results in duplication of effort and disjointed resource allocation. However amazing the growth of philanthropy, there is no ceiling on social need. Hence, inefficiency and spottiness of coverage exacts a social price, especially when people have come to expect solutions from private philanthropy that they once expected from government.

What is to be done? We need to redefine philanthropy. We need to see the actions of private philanthropy, not as the expression of passing predilections, but as the product of purposeful understanding of social issues and as the means to building coalitions of *all* actors on the social stage. We need to see philanthropy as an expression of partnership. If the problem is foster care, for example, the solution is not random injections of money from random philanthropists today, with another issue diverting their attention tomorrow. The answer is to understand the issue deeply, and then use private philanthropy as the center of gravity for the solution, attracting and sorting through the broad range of nonprofits steeped in the issue, attracting a critical mass of foundations and philanthropists to an acknowledged approach to the problem, and adding in government and corporate interests in ways that serve both their interests and the needs of foster care.

This is but one example. It is illustrative only. The point is that random scattershot approaches to philanthropy undervalue the true importance of philanthropy in America. Strategic cooperation is critical. With such cooperation will come leverage—the ability to attract to important issues resources from all manner of public and private organizations. We must be purposeful, collaborative, strategic, and discriminating.

Let us be clear. This is not an argument for the revivification of the Central Committee of the Supreme Soviet. America does not need a Central Committee for Philanthropic Allocations. Coordination and communication must come from within the sector itself, embodied in networks and leadership communication, not from some grand central plan. But, the alternative requires that philanthropic and nonprofit leadership begin to communicate and cooperate across institutional lines. The advantage, of course, is that the sector has no SEC sanctions against such coordination (at least, not yet).

The only barrier to such cooperation is history. This is no small statement. If the trend of organizational change is any measure, history is a formidable opponent of change. Looking back to what worked yesterday promises us the safe and secure. We seek comfort in the familiar, when what we may actually need is the bold and brash. But the safe offers only the illusion of security.

As trillions of dollars of wealth change hands in America, we have the opportunity to transform American philanthropy from a cottage industry to an engine of progress. Let us not fail to seize this moment. Let us not fail, if not for ourselves, then for our children.

July 2006   MICHAEL P. HOFFMAN
                                               Chairman
                                               Changing Our World, Inc.

The Causes: Social and Economic Pressures Forming the New World

OVERVIEW OF THE ISSUES

We live in a rapidly changing world. In the last two decades, the global economy has grown by as much as five percent a year. Total global gross world product, in purchasing power parity terms, is now over $70 trillion dollars, and has grown by over $10 trillion in the last five years alone. The United States now accounts for only 20 percent of the world economy, with much higher rates of economic growth characterizing many emerging economies, especially those of Asia.

> Just as the American continent was created by the pressures of geological tectonic plates, so the new world of American philanthropy is a product of the pressures of the tectonic plates of economic and social change. Understanding the new world of philanthropy that is emerging—from the pressures of economic progress, changes in wealth and income distribution, social conflict, technological change, and globalization—requires understanding the dimensions of the pressures themselves.

World economic growth has been accompanied by a range of other changes that both serve and challenge America. As a nation, we have seen immigration and diversity grow rapidly. We are part of a global environment unlike any other in the history of the planet. In 1960, only 1.6 million Americans traveled abroad; in 2000 that number had increased 16-fold, to nearly 27 million travelers. The American economy is premised on technology and services; indeed, services now account for 64 percent of all economic value in the world. That means that individual economic advancement is ever more a product of brains, not brawn. Education and continual learning are the basis for success.

Economic success in America has been striking. There are now between 7.5 and 9 million millionaire households in the United States (depending on whether the measure is net worth or financial assets), compared to fewer than 1 million just two decades ago. This represents seven percent of total households. Importantly, from the perspective of the transfer of wealth, half of all millionaire households are headed by retirees.

While this economic success has provided fuel for the growth of philanthropy, the philanthropic outcome will be a result, not only of wealth creation, but of the nature of the economic and social change within which it is seated. Areas of change, like the geological tectonic plates beneath the earth's crust, are pressing against one another. And, just as the American continent was created by the pressures of geological tectonic plates, so the new world of American philanthropy is a product of the pressures of the tectonic plates of economic and social change. Understanding the new world of philanthropy that is emerging—from the pressures of economic progress, changes in wealth and income distribution, social conflict, technological change, and globalization—requires understanding the dimensions of the pressures themselves.

The essays in this section address changes in such areas as demographics, ethnicity, wealth-holding, and technology, which are giving rise to the contours of the new world of American philanthropy.

Demographic Trends: America the Old

SUSAN RAYMOND, PHD, AND
MARY BETH MARTIN, ESQ.

"Old age," Bette Davis once quipped, "is no place for sissies." If that is so, then America is well on its way to being a nation of Bravehearts.

For we are aging. A century ago, just over 4 percent of the American population was over the age of 65. Today, those over 65 represent 12.4 percent of the population, and by 2020, that portion will rise to 16 percent. By 2030, one in five Americans will be between the ages of 65 and 84. By 2030, the number of Americans aged 85 to 99 will increase to five million, two and a half times the number today.

> Demographic changes pose challenges to strategies posited on the transfer of wealth among generations, and to philanthropy. There is little to be done to avoid those challenges because life is linear.

The aging of the population knows only a few geographic exceptions. Exhibits 1.1 and 1.2 depict the sharp increase in the elderly population, in virtually every state, between 2005 and 2025. Only where immigration is a major portion of population growth—New York, California, and Texas—is the relatively young age of the foreign-born population offsetting the aging of the native population.

EXHIBIT 1.1   PERCENT OF THE POPULATION OVER
AGE 65 (2005)

● 14.1–23   ⬢ 10.1–14   ○ 5–10

Source: This is a map created by the author from raw data of the U.S. Bureau of the Census using commercial MapPoint software.

The forces underpinning these trends are both natural and behavioral. The Baby Boomer generation of post World War II is naturally surging through the population age pyramid. Life expectancy at birth is now nearly 30 years longer than it was in 1900 and, on average, women can expect to live to over 80 years of age. More strikingly, however, America is not simply living longer on average, it is living longer at older ages. In 1990, a person aged 65 could expect to live only 11.3 more years; today, someone who reaches age 65 can, on average, expect to live another 19 years—nearly twice the expectancy of a century ago. Those who make it to age 75 can expect to live almost 12 more years. The force of that surge is fueled both by improved economics and improved health. Neither is likely to change anytime soon.

The poverty rate of Baby Boomers is just over seven percent lower than any other segment of the American population. Those born between 1946 and 1955 represent an estimated $1 trillion in annual spending, with average spending per household of over $46,000. In most, probably all, societies

EXHIBIT I.2 PERCENT OF THE POPULATION OVER AGE 65 (2025)

● 14.1–23 ○ 10.1–14 ○ 5–10

Source: This is a map created by the author from raw data of the U.S. Bureau of the Census using commercial MapPoint software.

there is a correlation between wealth and health. The wealthier a society becomes, the healthier it becomes. Economics and health go hand in hand.

It is not surprising that the health of the elderly is also improving. In 2006, the U.S. Centers for Disease Control and Prevention found that in 2004, the United States showed the sharpest drop in deaths in 60 years. In part, that is because the nature of disease and disease management is changing. Innovations in pharmaceuticals and new understandings of disease progress, have converted previously fatal conditions into chronic diseases, which are annoying and expensive, but manageable for many years.

As education rises and communications expand, the elderly are more and more aware of the lifestyle changes that can extend their healthy years. In 1965, 28.5 percent of men over the age of 65, and 27.7 percent of women over the age of 65, smoked. Today, smokers comprise only 10.1 percent of men in that age group, and only 8.3 percent of women. These are the lowest smoking percentages of any age group, and they represent the steepest decline in smoking of any age group. The consequent benefits in cardiovascular and cerebrovascular health have contributed to the increasing life expectancy of the elderly.

Mammography provides another striking example. In 1987, only 22 percent of women over the age of 65 had regular mammograms. Today, over three-quarters of women over 65 do. And the rates are nearly the same for Hispanic, African American, and white women over the age of 65. In the last decade, hospital visits for injuries and falls among those 65 and older have fallen by 20 percent.

Similarly, those over age 65 have lower rates of obesity, higher rates of exercise, and higher rates of fruit and vegetable consumption than do American adults under age 65. In short, the elderly are healthier than in the past. As a consequence, life expectancies will continue to rise. The consequences, however, are doubled-edged.

On one hand, this means that the assets of the elderly will continue to appreciate over their longer lifetimes, pushing up in value—but out in time—the transfer of wealth to their children, grandchildren, and philanthropy. Resources may have higher values, but they may not be soon in coming.

On the other hand, the social costs of aging will challenge both the timing and size dimensions of the transfer. Obviously, the older Americans become, the more expensive their longevity. While it is true that older Americans are healthier than their forebears, the costs and consequences of their illnesses are also higher. Although the over 65 population represents 12 percent of the entire population, it accounts for over a third of all hospitalizations. Net of Medicare, those over the age of 65 have healthcare expenditures four times those of adults under age 65.

Furthermore, the lengthened timeframe of the transfer also poses challenges because inflation is an economic fact of life. A comparison of healthcare cost escalation and the growth of healthcare philanthropy, provides an illustration of the point. As noted in Exhibit 1.3, cost increases in healthcare have far outstripped the rate of inflation consistently over the last two decades. Philanthropy allocated to healthcare has more than doubled in the last four decades. Still, on a year-over-year basis, the rate of increase of philanthropic dollars in healthcare has exceeded the rate of cost escalation in only a handful of years in the past two decades. As a result, healthcare philanthropy now accounts for only two percent of healthcare resources. The longer it takes for the increase in philanthropic dollars to reach healthcare institutions, the greater the difference between costs and resources, and the less powerful the philanthropic dollar.

EXHIBIT I.3   CHANGES IN HEALTH EXPENDITURES VERSUS HEALTH PHILANTHROPY

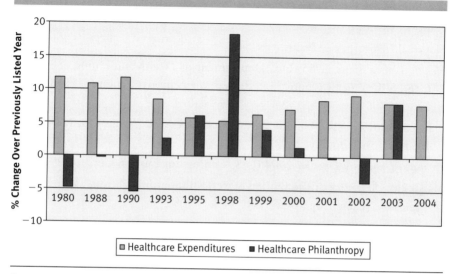

Source: Giving USA 2006, and U.S. Department of Health and Human Services.

There is an irony here, of course. Health costs escalate because we are getting older, and the older we get, the longer it takes to transfer philanthropic resources. And the longer it takes, the greater the difference between rising costs and declining resources.

An additional challenge is the relationship between the pace of aging and geography. Rural areas are aging more rapidly than the rest of the nation. Yet, significant philanthropic institutions are largely missing from rural America, and the vast majority of U.S. foundations do not have any focus on rural issues. The social challenges of aging in rural America, therefore, will likely not attract rising levels of philanthropy, nor will philanthropy in the rest of the country rise fast enough to be siphoned to such areas, even if a rural focus could be crafted. Beyond the wealth already present in rural areas, the transfer of wealth overall in America may come too late to be of social benefit in America's heartland. This discontinuity could reinforce the economic divide between rural and urban America.

Demographics pose challenges to strategies posited on the transfer of wealth among generations and to philanthropy. There is little to be done to avoid those challenges because life, as far as anyone knows, is linear. But the difficulties are best kept in mind when considering the overall social and economic implications of the passing of the torch among generations.

■ SOURCES

U.S. Bureau of the Census.

National Institute on Aging.

National Institutes of Health.

Health, United States, 2005 (U.S. Department of Health and Human Services, Centers for Disease Control and Prevention, National Center for Health Statistics: 2006).

"Hospitalization in the United States," *Fact Book No. 6* (Agency for Healthcare Research and Quality: 2002).

Deaths: Preliminary Data for 2004 (U.S. Centers for Disease Control: 2006).

"Historical Statistics of the United States, Millennium Edition," *Volume One: Population* (Cambridge University Press: 2006).

Ethnic Philanthropy in the Face of Major Demographic Change in the Twenty-First Century

The Honorable Marc H. Morial

Over the course of the twentieth century, the face of America changed profoundly. In 1900, one out of every eight Americans was a person of color, according to U.S. Census Bureau statistics. By 2000, that had increased to three out of ten.

By 2015, it is projected that minorities will make up 37 percent of the U.S. population. By 2050, roughly one of every two Americans is likely to be a race other than white, or a combination of races, making the United States the first nation in history without a majority ethnic group.

In 1900, only two, nonsouthern states—Nevada and Arizona—had a nonwhite population of more than 10 percent. That level of diversity spread to 26 states by 2000. And three states, California, Hawaii, and New Mexico, and the District of Columbia, had more than 50 percent minority populations.

> Over the past few decades, much of the growth in population among minorities occurred in younger age groups. The future of ethnic minorities lies in the hands of the young. Philanthropies and nonprofits must keep this generation in mind.

The twentieth century featured a great movement for equal rights and a great movement of technology. It gave the world airplanes, automobiles, electric lights, microphones, cameras, movie cameras, television, Internet, and cell phones. It saw the world united to overthrow Adolph Hitler.

It's a history of demographic change. It's a history of millions of European immigrants, from countries all over Europe, fleeing famine, economic strife, and all sorts of difficulty, finding their way through Ellis Island, to the shores of the United States.

Behind the movements were people who exhibited bravery, courage, ingenuity, innovation, and sacrifice, because they wanted to see their children and their children's children, have it better than they did.

Not a lot knew English or "American culture" for that matter. It's a similar story to that of African Americans, who fled the South for better economic and political prospects. Disenfranchisement in the South caused massive numbers of blacks—three million or so—to flee to the North. Their population in the South fell, from 32 percent of the population at the turn of the century, to only 19 percent by 2000.

Black migrants and European immigrants formed the backbone of the working class in northern cities, such as Philadelphia, New York, Washington, D.C., Cleveland, Detroit, and many more. They worked on Henry Ford's assembly line. They made the rubber, pressed the steel, and molded the glass. They built planes and constructed bombs in World War II. They engineered the Industrial Revolution that made America a world power.

The way the United States dealt with immigration and black migration in the early twentieth century is not necessarily the perfect prescription for the twenty-first century. However, it should be recognized that a great deal that was positive came out of it.

Toward the end of the century, Latin America and Asia fueled much of the nation's immigration. From 1980 to 2000, the Asian and Pacific Islander population tripled, while the Hispanic population doubled. For the first 60 years of the twentieth century, nonblack minorities made up less than one percent of the nation's population. By 2000, their share skyrocketed to 12.5 percent. And much of that growth occurred in younger age groups: By 2000, 39 percent of Americans under 25 were of a race other than white, compared to 16 percent of people 65 and older.

The increased numbers have set off alarms among certain sectors of American society. There's no debate that diversity and changes that have occurred over the last 50 years have made this nation better and stronger, and positioned it well for its next century to be its greatest. But into the twenty-first century, the nation faces a dramatic transformation. In less than 50 years, there will be no majority ethnic group: the United States will become a nation that is not only diverse, but diverse within diverse.

The Hispanic community, for example, is not singular and monolithic. It is comprised of people from Mexico, Costa Rica, Nicaragua, Guatemala, Ecuador, and Puerto Rico. There are people from many different countries and nationalities. In New York City, fully one-third of the black community is not African American. There are people with roots in the Caribbean, East and West Africa.

By 2010 or 2015, it is expected that non–African American blacks will outnumber African American blacks in New York City. And since the fall of the Berlin Wall, and the collapse of the old Iron Curtain countries, the nation is also seeing a surge of immigration from Europe, Russia, Poland, and Romania.

Over the past three decades, minorities in the United States have made substantial progress politically and economically. From 1973 to 2004, the per capita income of blacks increased 70 percent, from $2,521 ($9,284 in 2004 dollars) to $15,758; Hispanics' income rose 56 percent, from $2,454 ($9,037 in 2004 dollars) to $14,106; By contrast, the income of whites increased nearly 57 percent, from $4,361 ($16,060 in 2004 dollars) to $25,203 (see Exhibit 1.4).

Increased incomes have spurred more philanthropy. According to a 1999 survey by the Roper Center for Public Opinion Research, 54.4 percent of blacks, and 57.4 percent of Hispanics, gave money to charity from 1988 to 1996, compared to 75.2 percent of whites.

EXHIBIT 1.4   PER CAPITA INCOME CHANGE

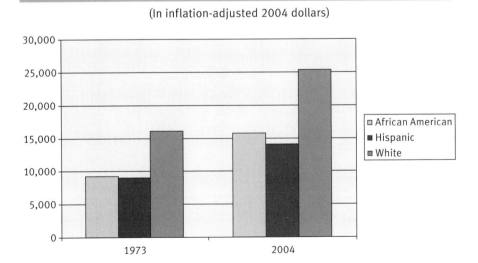

(In inflation-adjusted 2004 dollars)

Source: U.S. Bureau of the Census.

African Americans also earned the highest index of civic engagement in a 1997 National Survey of Philanthropy and Civic Renewal, followed by whites, and then Hispanics. Blacks scored highest in every category regarding spirit of volunteerism and active citizenship. The exception was "giving climate," in which whites scored the highest. Hispanics scored below blacks on all categories, but scored above whites in spirit of volunteerism and active citizenship.

Minorities consider education, social justice, and economic empowerment as their top charitable causes, according to a 2004 survey of 166 New York City–based minority philanthropists by the City University of New York's Center on Philanthropy and Civil Society.

Education, to them, provides the "best hope for ameliorating community conditions, and for making structural changes" in that it opens up gateways for success for the talented and ambitious, and helps create a new social order, the report concluded.

Social justice is seen as a way to remedy past injustices and lack of equal access. Minority donors are not merely satisfied with preventing history from repeating itself, they want to attack the root causes of inequities.

Economic empowerment and participation in the marketplace is viewed as the best way to impact the nation's economic, social, and political policies, especially by the younger generation.

Where minorities are the least involved is in contributions to political causes and candidates. Just because they supported advancing social change did not translate into support for political candidates and campaigns. Older donors tend to be disillusioned with the political system, while their younger counterparts preferred direct engagement and individual solutions.

Among minority donors, philanthropy begins young. They begin volunteer work during college and go from there. They often take on leadership roles in organizing events and joining boards. The ability to make contributions is often combined with a willingness to leverage money through fundraising events, matching gifts, donations from firms, and the like.

Members of communities of color tend to prefer direct, informal support of children and elderly groups that they have personal ties to, rather than institutions or organized philanthropies.

The Center on Philanthropy and Civil Society also found African Americans were more likely to give to their church, Hispanics to community-based organizations, and Asian Americans to ethnic cultural institutions. The purpose of their philanthropy is to "create pathways" for people excluded from access and opportunity. Where significant differences arise is between generations. The targets of philanthropy by older minorities differed from that of their younger counterparts.

Older African Americans, Hispanics, and Asian Americans tend to reinvest their philanthropy back into organizations that serve their own ethnic community, while their younger counterparts give back to organizations that "emphasize individual attainment," such as educational training, and employ a business model of operation.

Because the younger generation represents an emerging pool of future philanthropists, such differences have major implications for the future of giving and fundraising efforts.

According to the Center on Philanthropy, the majority of older African Americans (55 percent) tend to give to their churches, followed by organizations serving the black community (21 percent). By contrast, their younger counterparts are likely to donate to educational programs (60 percent), followed by schools or colleges (30 percent), and their churches (30 percent).

Older Hispanics are likely to focus their philanthropy on organizations serving their own ethnic community (66 percent), followed by schools or colleges (26 percent). The younger generation preferred to give to education programs (61 percent), followed by their churches (28 percent), and then their own ethnic community (22 percent).

From multiple alternatives, the majority of older Asian Americans tended to support organizations in their own ethnic community (74 percent), followed by schools and colleges (24 percent), and their churches (21 percent). Their younger counterparts favored schools or colleges (38 percent), educational programs (33 percent), organizations serving their own communities (33 percent), and then their churches (24 percent).

Over the past few decades, much of the growth in population among minorities occurred in younger age groups: In 2000, 39 percent of Americans under 25 were of a race other than white, compared to 16 percent of minorities over 65. The future of ethnic philanthropy lies in the hands of young minorities, who have very contrasting views about where to give their money than older generations.

Philanthropies and nonprofits must keep this generation in mind. These future contributors consider entrée on Wall Street and into financial networks as the key to their empowerment, rather than marches on Washington. Essential to empowerment of minorities in this nation is mining these sources of new philanthropy to fund programs designed to narrow the wealth gap that exists between whites and minorities.

There is no doubt that the twenty-first century is going to challenge and test us as a nation, but it also gives a special opportunity to make this the greatest nation on earth. This generation lives in a great time of influence and affluence. Americans make up six to eight percent of the world's population, and hold 50 percent of its wealth.

The reaffirmation of a commitment to diversity in the twenty-first century, and to eliminating disparities between members of American society, is an absolute requirement to make the United States strong. Without it, our nation cannot expect to survive, much less thrive, if half of the population is left behind educationally, economically, and politically.

Women and the Wealth Transfer

DEBORAH D. MALOY, CFP®

As the first wave of Baby Boomers turns 60 this year, they are being bombarded with birthday wishes for a happy, healthy, prosperous, and meaningful life. Approaching retirement, these Americans—born between 1946 and 1964—now account for 25 percent of the population. Companies have thrived, and individuals have made fortunes, catering to the wants and needs of this population since they were born. The amount that will be changing hands during the next 50 years is estimated at anywhere from $40 to $110 trillion.[1] As today's recipients become tomorrow's donors, businesses, bank accounts, stocks, bonds, art collections, automobiles, and homes will be willed to heirs, gifted to charities, taxed by governments, and placed in trusts for future generations.

> The number of women-owned businesses increased from 2.6 million in 1982 to 10.6 million in 2004, the result of government policies to promote affirmative action in the awarding of contracts, as well as the determination of women to create more flexibility, balance, and control over their work. Nearly half (48 percent) of all privately held businesses in the United States are at least 50 percent owned by women.

There is a considerable wealth gap; it is estimated that two-thirds of the transferring assets will be allocated to only seven percent of the population. Eighty percent of the population is in line to receive the remaining one-third of the wealth transfer.

To what extent will gender play a role in this wealth transfer? How have the financial resources and habits of women changed over the years, and how will the upcoming wealth transfer affect how these resources are deployed? What trends will emerge as women Baby Boomers receive their inheritances?

It started back in the 1920s. Women wore aprons back then, and sent their husbands off to work in the morning, then stayed home to cook, clean, sew, and watch children. These women lived in a time when listening to the radio was family entertainment, and they raised their children during the Great Depression. Stories the children (now elderly) of these families tell are from a time when families experienced financial hardship. Tales of stretching dollars and dimes, of unemployment lines and bread lines, of not being able to pay the rent are valued memories of childhood years of today's elderly.

The little girls of that day learned the value of money; having money meant that they were fed, had a place to live, and had shoes to wear. Women who were young during the Depression learned to save for a rainy day, and saw what happened to people who didn't. They witnessed the desperation of their parents, and it would have a deep impact on how they would handle their own finances later in life. Today, they have fears about aging and out-living their money; many are concerned about becoming a "burden" on family members, not wanting to be "bag ladies."

The wealth of the women of the Greatest Generation has been something of a surprise, especially to them. Most of them did not really inherit large wealth from their parents. Back then, when they were due to inherit, the values of real estate and financial assets were relatively low compared to today's values, even with inflation factored in. People typically invested in safe, low-yielding vehicles that did not have much potential to increase in value. Pension benefits were given in the form of monthly payments until death, and women were generally entitled to survivor benefits, upon the death of their husbands. Stock options, profit-sharing plans, and IRAs were not assets generally held by the average person.

With lessons learned during the Depression, these individuals have a healthy fear of borrowing or using credit cards. As a result, this thrifty generation has excellent saving habits and little debt. This is the generation that will leave behind significant assets to their children, their causes, their churches, and alma maters.

The inheritors are the Baby Boomers. The women's liberation movement—fueled by unprecedented numbers of college-educated women entering the workforce, encouraged by affirmative action initiatives—expanded the choices available to women during the last three decades. The woman of the twenty-first century is no longer predominantly a stay-at-home mother, nurse, teacher, or librarian, although she is certainly free to become any one of those. This woman grew up in the Age of Aquarius, against the backdrop of the Vietnam War. She wanted to make a difference back then, whether it was ending the war, fighting for women's rights, picketing for the rights of migrant workers, or alleviating poverty, and this has not changed.

What is the landscape now, and what financial concerns does she have as she prepares to participate in the largest transfer of wealth in history, either as a wealth transferor or as an inheritor?

ISSUES SURROUNDING LONGEVITY

Medical advances have increased our lifespans dramatically over the last century. At the beginning of the twentieth century, the average person lived to be 47 years old. Today, a 65 year old white female has a life expectancy of 85 years. Imagine all the medical breakthroughs that have not been discovered yet and how long we will be able to be kept alive in the future. The cost of custodial care has risen beyond the ability of many seniors to pay, and they are spending down assets to continue living in the family home or to pay nursing home costs.

Women live longer than men. Today, the population is almost evenly divided between men (49.3 percent) and women (50.7 percent), but women still outlive men by six years, on average. In the over-75 population, women outnumber men, 62 to 38 percent. In the over-85 population, the fastest-growing age group, women account for 70 percent of the group.[2] Married women, who have outlived their husbands and inherited the marital assets, will make the final decision on the disposition of those assets.

With increased life expectancy, there is an increased possibility that a woman might outlive her assets. Since fixed incomes do not always keep pace with inflation, she may be forced to cut back on her standard of living. Fears of living too long, and of not having the resources to maintain lifestyle, is a common concern of women approaching their later years. And since women now over 65 are living longer, their beneficiaries may have to wait longer than they had expected for their inheritances.

ISSUES SURROUNDING HEALTHCARE NEEDS

Health insurance coverage is an extremely valuable employee benefit, and many women work at companies specifically to obtain medical coverage for their families. But the benefit is tied to employment, and if employment is terminated, the (former) employee has four choices: find another job with health insurance benefits, pay for continued coverage for 18 months under COBRA provisions, obtain private health insurance, or go without any insurance at all. In 2004, there were 44 million Americans without health insurance.[3]

Medicare only covers seniors starting at age 65, giving rise to a multitude of scenarios in which people in their late fifties and early sixties are scrambling for coverage. For example, the employed husband with insurance turns 65 and retires from his job, leaving his 62-year-old spouse with no health insurance. Or a 58-year-old woman who is head of household, caring for her elderly mother, loses her job when her position is downsized; she is having a difficult time finding a new position with health benefits. Private health insurance is extremely costly, especially if prescription drug coverage is included.

If having health insurance coverage is of major importance prior to age 65, long-term care insurance is as quickly becoming the cornerstone of an estate plan. Women overwhelmingly prefer to be cared for at home, by home health aides, and the cost of services in the home ranges from $75,000 to $100,000 per year, depending on where you live. State-funded Medicaid services do not pay for in-home services, and taxpayers in all states are no longer willing to pay for nursing home services for people with assets. Nursing home costs run from $5,000 to $9,000 per month.

In addition to the normal reticence to address the issue of what specifically happens if they become unable to care for themselves as they age, women exhibit an aversion to paying the annual premium. The cost of insurance becomes more expensive each year; it is typically recommended for people in their fifties and early sixties. Coverage can be denied if certain medical conditions are present, which is another reason to purchase this type of policy before major medical issues turn up. It is reasonable to expect that the wealth transferors may need to use some of their accumulated wealth for healthcare expenses.

ISSUES SURROUNDING FAMILY MEMBERS

Women have traditionally taken on the role of family caregiver. Whether taking care of children or of aging parents, women have often let their careers, aspirations, and personal needs take a backseat to taking care of family members; on average, 15 percent of a woman's working years are spent caring for others.[4] The result is lower or no accumulated pension, smaller Social Security checks, and less time to accumulate benefits as a participant in an employer's retirement plan.

In one survey of female Baby Boomers, more than 60 percent of participants predicted that they ultimately would be financially responsible for an adult child and/or an aging parent.[5] The actual numbers back up the predictions; another study of affluent 60-year-olds found that 62 percent were financially contributing to either an aging parent or an adult child.[6]

Caught squarely in the Sandwich Generation, older Baby Boomers may have elderly parents who require more care and attention, may not be able to live independently any longer, and may not have the financial resources to pay for their own needs. At the same time, the adult children are taking longer to leave the nest, due to the high price of striking out on their own. Many carry high student loan debt, incurred to pay for an education during a time when college costs were increasing at twice the rate of inflation.

In the role of caregiver, it would appear that women forgo some of the financial rewards that come from having longer work histories, such as accumulation of assets in retirement plans or pension benefits. At the same time, they are often vulnerable to requests for financial assistance from family members in need. Both wealth transferors and inheritors have the needs of their families and loved ones in mind when decisions are made to transfer assets.

INCREASING FINANCIAL CLOUT OF WOMEN

The number of women-owned businesses has increased, from 2.6 million in 1982 to 10.6 million in 2004, the result of government policies to promote affirmative action in the awarding of contracts, as well as the determination of women to create more flexibility, balance, and control over their work. Nearly half (48 percent) of all privately held businesses in the United States are at least 50 percent owned by women (see Exhibit 1.5).[7]

Women influence 80 percent of the spending decisions in U.S. households.[8]

Since 1984, the number of widowed and divorced women has increased, from 7.8 percent to 10 percent widowed, and 7.3 percent to 11.5 percent divorced. Women who have never married remain at just over 21 percent of the population, while the percentage of married women has decreased, from 63 to 57 percent.[9]

Women account for 46 percent of the total civilian workforce, and 60 percent of the female population was in the labor force in 2005 (see Exhibit

EXHIBIT 1.5   OWNERSHIP OF PRIVATE FIRMS (2002)

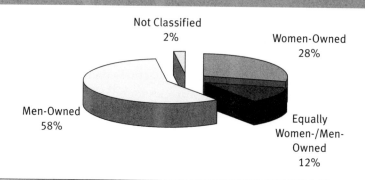

Source: U.S. Small Business Administration.

1.6).[10] In 1975 only 40 percent of the labor force was female. The income of women has steadily risen in comparison to the income of men. In the early 1970s, women's incomes were, on average, 59 percent of men's; the gap has since closed to 80 percent. A compelling study of the pay gap by Warren Farrell, PhD, suggests that this gap is misleading, and that the pay differential

EXHIBIT 1.6   PERCENTAGE OF WOMEN IN THE LABOR FORCE BY ETHNICITY (2005)

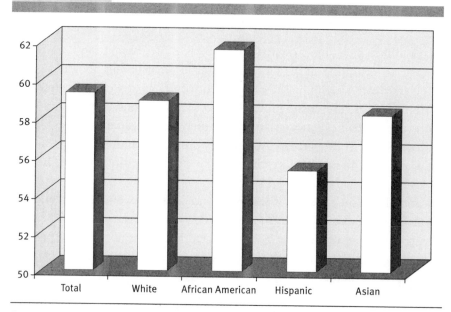

Source: U.S. Bureau of Labor Statistics.

is due to factors related to career choices and the wide range of working conditions that a specific job demands.[11] While the idea that there is no longer a pay gap can be debated, it's hard to ignore that women are accepted, welcomed, listened to, and often preferred in the workplace.

Women control 60 percent of the nation's wealth and have more economic clout than at any other period in history.[12] It is estimated that 80 to 90 percent of women will be responsible for their own finances at some point in their lives.[13] The number of women earning $100,000 or more tripled in the last decade.[14]

To summarize the above statistics, today's women make more money, control a majority of the nation's wealth, own more businesses than ever before, make most of the household spending decisions, and typically outlive the men in their families, ending up with their assets as well. Women want assurances—that they have sufficient resources to live on for the rest of their lives, that family members are provided for, and that their health-care needs are met.

Resources and Fiscal Habits of Women

There are many paths to financial security, and women today have discovered a variety of savings vehicles and resources to make the journey comfortable. Women acquire resources by inheriting them, acquiring them through marriage or divorce, or through employment earnings. Depending on a woman's situation, the wealth transfer could be many things—a lifesaver, enabling her to pay off accumulated debt; a safety net, providing an income stream for retirement; a legacy, in the form of donations to worthy causes; a chance to discover, through travel, art lessons, or starting a business. Wealth recipients can struggle with windfall inheritances, and many people who are not used to having money can lose large sums of it within a very short time.

For many women, the most important financial resource is the ability to earn an income through work; 60 percent of all women were in the labor force in 2005.[15] Building a salaried work history entitles a woman to receive Social Security benefits at retirement, to contribute to employer-sponsored retirement plans with pretax dollars, and to receive a variety of paid fringe benefits, such as car allowance, sick leave, and life insurance. The biggest challenge for Baby Boomer women approaching retirement is how to replace the income they now receive from employment. Contrary to the popular notion that expenses are reduced to 70 percent of preretirement expenses, the actual experience is that retirees spend differently, rather than less.

Women have become savvy investors and want to be certain that their assets are working for them. They are receptive to learning about investment strategies, asset allocation, tax reduction techniques, and aligning their money with their values. Women are open to working with financial advisors and move cautiously but with conviction once they have explored all the options. Women who were comfortable investing in bank certificates of deposit and U.S. Treasury obligations are now inquiring about hedge funds, exchange-traded funds, and real estate investment trusts (REITs).

There are some observable trends that illustrate how women today are using financial resources:

- Savings rates have declined, from 6 percent of income in 1984, to negative .5 percent in 2005—the lowest rate since the Great Depression.[16] The average 401K balance was $56,878 at the end of 2004, far short of the amount needed to retire with a decent income.[17]

- Credit card use is increasing. In 1989, only 56.4 percent of the population held at least one major credit card. By 2004, the figure was 76 percent. More than 25 percent of cardholders report never paying off the entire balance.[18]

- The use of home equity debt to fund home improvements, consolidate debt, and pay for college, cars, and vacations is on the rise.

- Today, there is a vast array of retirement vehicles. With the demise of the company pension, the low salary replacement rate of Social Security checks, and a general unease about the solvency of the Social Security system, it is up to the individual to make use of all available vehicles designed to accumulate retirement assets. These include IRAs, Roth IRAs, SEP-IRAs, 401Ks, 403Bs, 457 plans, and tax-deferred annuities.

- The number of debt and mortgage options has increased, (e.g., fixed or variable rates and terms, reverse mortgages, and home equity loans). The 40-year fixed mortgage and the six-year auto loan are foreign concepts to the older generation.

When combined, the trends of low rates of savings and increased borrowing using credit cards and home equity should be alarming to an aging population whose working years are almost over. It is probable that many Baby Boomers will continue to work beyond normal retirement age; and the issues of longevity, healthcare, and needs of family members will continue to weigh in when Baby Boomers make decisions, especially financial ones.

Although it will be many years before the full impact of the wealth transfer can be felt and analyzed, some broad observations can be made today. The wealthiest population group (the top seven percent) will continue to live well, make annual gifts to charity, and leave legacies. The majority of the population (80 percent) is expected to receive 33 percent of the wealth transfer, and will have some roadblocks to financial security in the form of retirement and longevity, spending, family needs, healthcare, and debt.

▪ NOTES

1. John J. Havens and Paul G. Schervish, "Millionaires and the Millennium: New Estimates of the Forthcoming Wealth Transfer and the Prospects for a Golden Age of Philanthropy" (report from the Boston College Social Welfare Research Institute, released October 19, 1999).

2. U.S. Bureau of the Census, "Table 1: Annual Estimates of the Population by Sex and Five-Year Age Groups for the United States: April 1, 2000 to July 1, 2005."

3. U.S. Census Bureau, "Health Insurance Coverage in the United States: 2002," September 2003, www.census.gov/prod/2003pubs/p60223.pdf.

4. Women's Institute for a Secure Retirement, and National Center for Women's Retirement Research.

5. "Women and Investing," a study by Oppenheimer Funds, 2005.

6. "Retirement Attitudes: Affluent 60-Year-Olds Neglect Managing Their Assets," *Pension Benefits,* Lincoln Financial Group, October 2005: 11–12.

7. Center for Women's Business Research, "Top Facts About Women-Owned Businesses," 2005.

8. Preston R. Speece, "Wising Up to the Women's Market," *National Underwriter,* February 2006: 19–20.

9. U.S. Department of Commerce, "Statistical Abstract of the United States," 1986 and 2006.

10. U.S. Department of Labor, "Employment Status of Women and Men in 2005," *Monthly Labor Review,* Bureau of Labor Statistics, November 2005.

11. Warren Farrell, PhD, "Why Men Earn More: The Startling Truth Behind the Pay Gap—and What Women Can Do About It," American Management Association, 2005.

12. "Women and Investing: Make It Happen," Oppenheimer Funds, Inc., 2006.

13. Ibid.

14. Preston R. Speece, "Wising Up to the Women's Market," *National Underwriter,* February 20, 2006: 19–20.

15. U.S. Department of Labor, *Monthly Labor Review,* Bureau of Labor Statistics, November, 2005.

16. U.S. Department of Commerce, "Statistical Abstract of the United States," 1986 and 2000.

17. Employee Benefit Research Institute.

18. U.S. Department of Commerce, "Statistical Abstract of the United States," 1986 and 2000.

Philanthropy with Less Than Nine Zeros: The Philanthropic Participation of the Middle Class and the Next Generations

SUSAN RAYMOND, PHD, AND BARBARA YASTINE

To judge by the headlines, the "transfer of wealth" is less about America than it is about a few economic titans. One could be forgiven for concluding that, short of those with a billion dollars to put on the table, nothing much has changed in the nation's philanthropic capacity. It is certainly true that much philanthropy flows in large gifts. In 2005, nonprofits received 2,197 philanthropic gifts in excess of $1 million each. Of these, 796 (36 percent) were made by individuals. At the very top of that giving group, gifts from those individuals who gave $50 million or more in a single gift totaled $2.6 billion in giving. Even this significant sum, however, represented just 1.3 percent of all individual giving in 2005.[1]

> While it is true that the wealth that has washed over America in the last two decades has been particularly beneficial to the wealthiest Americans, it is also true that increasingly the middle class holds significant financial assets.

The truth about individual philanthropy appears to be more nuanced, both in terms of the growing capacity of America's middle class (which comprises 60 percent of all households) to enter the philanthropic arena, and in terms of the propensity for the nation's coming generations (popularly known as "X" and "Y") to find themselves on the societal commons both as volunteers and as donors. Understanding the status of both elements of nonbillionaire America is important in appreciating the philanthropic robustness of the future.

MIDDLE CLASS WEALTH: "NO LONGER AN OXYMORON"

The Federal Reserve Bank has found that the increase in net worth over the last decade has been clearest in the middle income group. That increase, driven in part by real estate values, has resulted in a 25.4 percent increase in the median family net worth (the difference between a family's gross assets and its liabilities) of families whose income is in the 40–55.9 percentile of the nation, and a 70.9 percent increase in those in the 60–79.9 percentile.[2] The mean (average) has risen more rapidly, but the median, a more cautious measure (half of the households in the category have more wealth than the median, and half have less), also shows significant growth (see Exhibit 1.7).

EXHIBIT 1.7   FAMILY NET WORTH: 40–79.9 PERCENTILES

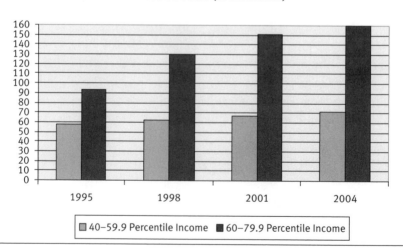

2004 Dollars (in thousands)

1995   1998   2001   2004

■ 40–59.9 Percentile Income   ■ 60–79.9 Percentile Income

Source: U.S. Bureau of the Census and Historical Statistics of the United States, Millenium Edition.

The median of the upper two percentile categories more than doubled in that same time period, but the wealth increase was also present in the middle class.

It is also true that, by and large, America is not a nation of savers. The Federal Reserve Bank, however, found that those who do save are saving more. The importance of saving for purchases has fallen over time, and the most significant increase has been in saving for retirement, an indication that more and more Americans are looking toward the future. Furthermore, there may be more saving going on than meets the eye. Dresdner Bank speculates that people are saving not by "not spending" but by investing (in housing as well as the financial market) and then counting on that rising wealth as a form of savings.[3]

As Stan Davis and Christopher Meyer of Harvard Business School have noted, "Middle class wealth is no longer an oxymoron."[4]

PROLIFERATING PHILANTHROPIC MODELS AND MECHANISMS

What does this have to do with philanthropy? At least two important elements are relevant.

The Importance of New Tools

First, the middle class is building wealth. There is evidence that at least some of that wealth, although admittedly not Gatesonian in size, will flow to philanthropy. New tools are available to enable it to do so.

Take, for example, the rise of community foundations. The number of community foundations has more than doubled in the last 15 years, and their giving has more than tripled in inflation-adjusted terms. While these foundations represent only one percent of all grant making foundations, they represent 10 percent of all grant dollars. The South accounts for nearly 30 percent of all community foundations, and the Midwest for 28 percent.[5] In these two regions, community foundations represent a wellspring of philanthropy, fueled by the giving of the middle class.

Such mechanisms, including donor advised funds, permit relatively small gifts (e.g., $15,000) to build value over time, as well as to serve as a mechanism for the giving of all members of a family to flow into a common pool. The result can be significant. A decade or more of small gifts can result in tens of thousands of dollars in a community foundation fund, enough to throw off thousands of dollars in annual donations.

The Internet provides another example of a giving mechanism that is both open to all yet scaled to the level of gifting appropriate to the non-megawealthy. The Internet is a boon to relationship building between citizens and nonprofits on many levels. First, the technology has brought unprecedented efficiency to the solicitation and collection of small donations, enabling and motivating more institutions to pursue the modest donor. Second, its convenience and 24/7 availability helps turn intentions into contributions often lost in the process of seeking out addresses, writing checks and cover letters, and licking stamps. Third, interest has spawned new online models that appeal especially to younger generations, and those outside the philanthropic mainstream. For example, look at the many microfinance sites that post requests for funding from would-be entrepreneurs in the developing world. Funders select the individual recipient, lending as little as $25—making philanthropy about as personal as it can get. Fourth, the Internet is a powerful means of communication between nonprofits and donors, albeit one that most nonprofits do not yet use to full advantage. More frequent, fulsome, and personalized communication helps to address one of the most common reasons people stop giving to a cause: They don't feel informed or involved enough.

A final example of the proliferation of mechanisms is the use of philanthropic giving as a substitute for commercial gifts. Weddings, funerals, birthdays, anniversaries, and religious ceremonies are now commonly accompanied by family encouragement to make contributions to a favorite charity in lieu of gifts. As such giving becomes common and accepted, the entire world of philanthropy is opened, not just to middle-class adults, but to children who learn that charity can be an expression of their love for, and joy in, family and friends.

RISING RECOGNITION

Second, as the middle class becomes more invested in philanthropy, and the nonprofits it supports, its families will pay more attention. And there is plenty to pay attention to, and a growing willingness on the part of the media to shine the light of a free press on philanthropy and nonprofits. A Changing Our World, Inc. survey of newspaper articles on nonprofits and philanthropy reveals that the current news coverage is many multiples of what it was 30 years ago. For example, in the period 1970–1975 the *Wall Street Journal* carried fewer than two dozen articles on either topic; from 2000–2005 that total was more than 1,000. In effect, *Wall Street Journal* readers went from reading about the sector less than twice a month, to reading about it nearly three times a day (see Exhibit 1.8).

Nonprofits and philanthropies might have been able to make mistakes in 1970 and not be noticed; the probability that they will be able to do so in 2015 is approaching zero.

Hence, by virtue of its involvement, the middle class will not only become an active participant in philanthropy, but will be constant judge of the sector. The philanthropic and nonprofit sectors would ignore that attention at their own peril.

THE NEXT GENERATION OF SOCIAL INVESTORS

What of the young? Certainly they do not command wealth, even in the tens of thousands of dollars, let alone the billions. Are they then outside the scope of attention of the transfer of wealth? Does one have to be old to be relevant? Let us first pause to examine the numbers.

Together, Generation X (ages 27–40) and Generation Y (ages 18–26) represent nearly half the U.S. population. In general, these two groups are

EXHIBIT 1.8   NEWSPAPER ARTICLES ON NONPROFITS OR PHILANTHROPY

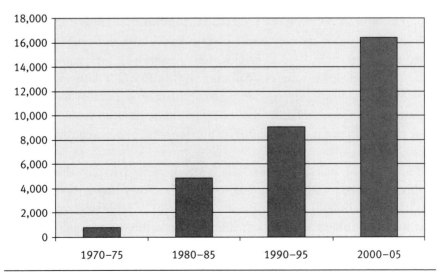

(*Wall Street Journal*, *New York Times*, and *Washington Post*)

Source: Changing Our World, Inc., 2006.

more diverse than any previous American cohort, better educated, and more technologically savvy.

It is estimated that Generations X and Y volunteer more than the Baby Boomer generation at equivalent points in their lives. In 2005, 12 percent of Yale's graduating class, 11 percent of Dartmouth's, and 8 percent at both Harvard and Princeton applied, not to Wall Street's investment banks, but to Teach for America.[6] The commitment to giving to social needs is alive and well among America's youth.

Volunteering is closely associated with the propensity to donate to philanthropic causes. Those who volunteer are much more likely to become financial supporters of nonprofits.

However, there is also evidence that the X and Y generations will not "give" in traditional ways. Indeed, a national survey of over 7,000 households found that only 53 percent of Generation X households made donations of $25 or more, compared with 75 percent of Baby Boomers.[7] However, a survey of 1,800 young people (aged 13–25) by Cone and AMP Insights found that 89 percent of 13 to 25-year-olds say they are likely to switch brands (given equal price and quality) to support a cause, and 69 percent say they consider a company's social commitment when deciding where to shop.[8] Giving is woven into the everyday consciousness and actions of these cohorts. They don't show up as generous donors because their financial support is reflected in the contributions of the companies they patronize.

There is also growing evidence that the increased community orientation of the X and Y generations will have even longer lasting effects through their children. A 2005 survey indicated that, unlike previous generations, 82 percent of teens say they have "no problems" with their parents, compared to 48 percent in 1974.[9] The closeness of teens with their parents means that the philanthropic values of parents will find an easier pathway into the lives of their children, strengthening the philanthropic sector irrespective of how much money a family has. The portion of children who give when their parents do not is 48 percent. The portion who give when their parents do is 71 percent.[10]

Furthermore, in Generation X, it is not inherited wealth that is most highly correlated with giving. Those who give from earned wealth tend to give proportionally more for every increment of increased wealth than do those who inherit their wealth.[11] In this sense, the Internet is a powerful tool for high-engagement philanthropy among these new, technology-savvy donors. As their earned incomes increase and e-philanthropy becomes a common part of the transfer of wealth, this generation will have the opportunity to become more constantly and consistently involved in philanthropic giving.

The future of philanthropy, then, is not denominated merely in the billions upon billions of retiring national economic titans. It is premised very deeply on the behavior of the great middle class, and its future is rooted in the young.

▦ NOTES

1. Gifts as listed by The Center on Philanthropy at Indiana University; total individual giving as published by Giving USA 2006.

2. B. K. Bucks, A. B. Kennickell, and K. B. Moore. "Recent Changes in U.S. Family Finances: Evidence from the 2001 and 2004 Survey of Consumer Finances," Federal Reserve Bulletin, 2006: A1–A38.

3. D. F. Milleker, "America's Savings Renaissance?" *USA Update,* Frankfurt: Dresdner Bank, April 2002.

4. S. Davis and C. Meyer, *Future Wealth* (Cambridge: Harvard Business School Press, 2002).

5. *Key Facts on Community Foundations* (Foundation Center, September 2006).

6. T. Lewin, "Top Graduates Line Up to Teach to the Poor," *New York Times,* October 2, 2005: A1.

7. P. Panepento, "Connecting with Generation X," *Chronicle on Philanthropy,* March 31, 2005.

8. "Up Front," *Business Week,* November 6, 2006.

9. N. Howe and W. Strauss, "Generation Give and Give and Give," *USA Weekend Magazine,* April 27, 2005.

10. R. Steinberg and M. Wilhelm, *Giving: The Next Generation—Parental Effects on Donations* (Indiana University Center on Philanthropy, 2003).

11. Ibid.

The Next Generation Takes the Controls: Philanthropic, Structural and Investment Considerations for Establishing Foundations for the Wealthy Individual

PRESTON H. KOSTER

As huge transfers of wealth take place, now and over the next several decades, the question that has to be addressed is "how will these events translate into an opportunity for both family and philanthropy?" A very popular television show that focuses on current political issues highlighted this very question. One of the lead characters was asked by a very wealthy individual to help him set up and run a major impact foundation. The wealthy entrepreneur said that his family could never spend all the money he created, and he needed to feel good about his success.

The following represents a series of observations, trends, and situations that I have noted, over the last decade, in working with clients and their families, in the ultra-high end of the personal wealth market. First, however, we have to make the assumption that money has only three purposes: to maintain your lifestyle, to provide for your family, and to contribute to causes important to the individual. The creator of the wealth has to make the initial decision as to where the family is on that continuum and what social values are already in place. Another question that goes through the minds of many, very successful, first-generation individuals is perhaps more subtle: "How do I preserve my name and ego?" That question can lead to the next thought: *In order for me to complete the American financial success story, should I make a material impact on society, either locally or globally, by giving away money?*

> The first generation must really think beyond their lifetimes before they create a legacy that the next generation has to manage.

A century ago, a number of the extremely wealthy, first-generation, Robber Baron–era families took a socially responsible approach to their wealth. Wealth is still highly concentrated in the United States, and the tendency toward charity at that level remains. The recent actions of Warren Buffett and Bill Gates are but illustrations of the fundamental role that philanthropy continues to play in the thinking of many of America's wealthiest families. The challenge today, however, is impact. Many of the socially responsible projects of today are so vast in scope that it becomes a real challenge to make a material impact (see Exhibit 1.9).

The first generation must really think beyond their lifetimes before they create a legacy that the next generation has to manage. If a foundation is the agreed upon structure, there are many considerations.

One consideration is what to name the foundation. If the name of the grantor is given to the foundation, it could create a problem for a child with

EXHIBIT 1.9   DISTRIBUTION OF MONEY
INCOME (2004)

Percent of Wealth Controlled by Household Income Quintile

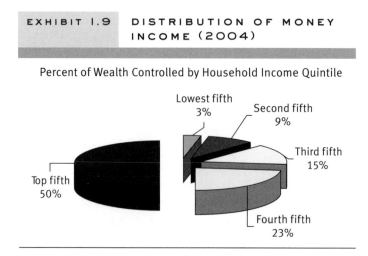

Lowest fifth
3%

Second fifth
9%

Third fifth
15%

Top fifth
50%

Fourth fifth
23%

Source: U.S. Bureau of the Census.

the same name, especially if that child has taken a different career or lifestyle path that is different from that of the grantor. Also, now that tax returns are on the Internet, the name could create a potential security risk for the children. It could also increase dramatically the number of solicitations flowing to the foundation, and hence create an administrative burden for the foundation. Since the foundation can be used as a vehicle to supplement the income of the second generation, there is the issue of whether the children will perform the level of work required to justify the compensation. Finally, leaving the management of a foundation to children could create a point of conflict among siblings, as well as create issues for relatives who have not been as successful.

A good alternative to a foundation is a National Gift Fund or Community Trust structure. The following scenarios discuss several approaches I have seen taken by clients. One cannot ignore the tax savings opportunities that can be realized by gifting huge amounts to charity, regardless of the structure. The form and valuations of the gifts are also very relevant when it comes to tax savings.

SCENARIO 1: GROWING PAINS OF A FAMILY FOUNDATION

Background

A certain family foundation was initially funded with $10 million, and over time, it built up to several hundred million within a corporate structure. It was designed to be totally controlled by the family. All the major charitable programs were directed by the family, with outside directors acting as financial planning resources or in administrative roles. As time progressed, the principal determined that his children should have a more meaningful role in the charitable direction and management. The foundation also began to serve as a vehicle for the principal to pass along his business skills and network of contacts, to the charities chosen for support.

Challenges

As the foundation grew in size, the family members realized that the time commitment that went into giving away five percent in small increments was too great of a challenge. Therefore, while the overriding mission remained constant, the number of grants grew smaller, but more significant in size, and the big "impact'" grant program was put into place. The principal also realized that a foundation with hundreds of millions of dollars in assets might drift away from its intended mission, if he were not around to keep a firm hand on the wheel. Without his direction, a foundation of such size could be taken over by non–family members, and the bylaws and mission could change. This structure, therefore, was considered a weak link, and a new structure was created.

Solution/Conclusion

After considerable review by financial advisors and attorneys, it was decided to collapse the existing foundation into a trust, governed by an irrevocable trust agreement. The trust was designed with a maximum degree of flexibility, but with a limited life. It would last through the life of grandchildren and then would dissolve, paying out to predetermined nonprofit entities or their successors. The trust also prevented family members from abusing the foundation for personal benefit, once the principal was not around. This carefully crafted trust document became the solution, to achieve the principal's goals of keeping the mission in place, and keeping family members as the key decision makers.

SCENARIO II: FLEXIBILITY OF A NATIONAL GIFT FUND

Background

Two separate clients had very clearly defined charitable intentions, and wanted to complete the gifts during their lifetimes. Both clients decided they did not want to establish foundations. Their balance sheets offered unique opportunities to execute their gifting program and make thoughtful tax and investment decisions. Their children were not to be engaged in the process. The magnitude of the gifting programs ranged from $10,000 to $2 million, and it was decided that a National Gift Fund would be used as the vehicle for contributions.

Challenges

Due both to their wishes and a series of delayed pledges they had made, the gifting challenge was to make some gifts at later points in time and some gifts over a number of years. The financial challenge was to separate the investment decision from the timing of the charitable decision.

Solutions/Conclusion

In one case, the funding mechanism was a large block of a very successful stock. The owner, who wasn't legally obligated to hold the stock, felt it could decrease in value. The investment decision was to sell the stock while it was at a high value, then park the funds in the National Gift Fund, to realize the tax advantages of the gift, and let the Fund give away the proceeds later. The stock did subsequently drop, but by then the proceeds had been put into a balanced portfolio, which continues to grow with lower volatility than would have been the case with one stock. While that transaction isn't unique, it is a good lesson in separating the investment decision from the charitable decision. The client and their financial advisor made the investment decision, and the client, through the National Gift Fund, manages the charitable program.

The second client's portfolio had a series of hedge fund investments that had a significant long-term gain. The financial advisors wanted to sell the funds that were not part of the client's substantial IRA, or the family's investment LLC. The advisors were able to convince the administrators of the National Gift Fund to accept the hedge fund investments, and redeem the investment based on the hedge fund manager's payout schedule. While a little cumbersome for the National Gift Fund, the transaction provided the needed liquidity to make the charitable gift, was very tax efficient, and gave the financial managers the ability to redirect the client's asset allocation.

Wealthy individuals should consider gift funds (or community trust funds) if they do not want their family members actively involved in decision making on future gifts. Working with financial advisors, these funds can be sufficiently flexible, to help separate the gifting from the client's investment decision, to help all parties diversify, or make more prudent investment decisions.

Scenario III: Provisions in Foundations and Wills to Meet Client's Objectives

Background

A wealthy individual decided to focus his major charitable giving programs at a very local level, in a relatively small community. Over the years, he had established a major scholarship fund for local students, and provided the funds to build a community center. In addition, he had set up a foundation, and a trust, to continue to help fund these and other community activities.

Challenges

Although the community had a number of financially sophisticated citizens, many of them came from outside the community. The donor's main concern was to ensure that certain of these local initiatives, including the community center, would continue to be funded beyond his lifetime, since the community did not have the financial depth to do so. At the same time, the donor wanted to have continued family input into disbursement of these funds beyond his life.

Solutions/Conclusion

Within the foundation established for continuing his initiatives, a subaccount was established, with the sole purpose of supporting the future cash flow of the community center. This was done by projecting a future budget, including maintenance, depreciation, and cash flows in and out of the center. Funds were set aside, to be managed through an asset-allocation model similar to the foundation's asset allocations.

With regard to family input into future disbursements, the local community required that board members be local citizens. Since none of the extended family was local, their input could only continue through the foundation itself, and not directly at the local level. This same client has also used funding stipulations in his will to ensure that other community groups he has funded receive additional funds from the estate, only if they support their operating budget with income and not use principal for that purpose. Thoughtful wording of a client's will or trust agreements can be used as a method to help ensure that long-term goals and financial discipline are preserved.

AUTHOR'S NOTE

The preceding scenarios are fictional in nature, but are derived from commonly encountered circumstances in the wealth management industry. The above conclusions are preliminary and general in nature, and clients should always consult with their investment and legal advisors before taking action.

The Evolution of the Tactical Philanthropist

SEAN STANNARD-STOCKTON

> Americans . . . constantly form associations. They have not only commercial and manufacturing companies, in which all take part, but associations of a thousand other kinds, religious, moral, serious, futile, general or restricted, enormous or diminutive. The Americans make associations to give entertainment, to found seminaries, to build inns, to construct churches, to diffuse books, to send missionaries to the antipodes; in this manner they found hospitals, prisons, and schools. If it is proposed to inculcate some truth or to foster some feeling by the encouragement of a great example, they form a society.
>
> —Alexis de Tocqueville on the role of American philanthropy

CREATING A PHILANTHROPIC UNIVERSE

In the beginning was strategy, and it was good. Strategy helps philanthropists to select the targets of their generosity—the churches, hospitals, schools, and every other imaginable form of nonprofit seeking financial encouragement. Strategic philanthropy means many different things to many different people, but generally refers to the concept of giving to nonprofit entities in a way that strategically advances the donor's interests. Strategic Philanthropy provides an invaluable framework for the philanthropic impulse, answering the "who" and the "why" of a plan to give, but omitting one key question: How? The term *strategic philanthropy* originally referred to corporate initiatives intended to serve a company's business interests, such as sponsoring charitable events to gain visibility among influential audiences. But over time, the phrase has grown to encompass much more, culminating in four core principles:[1]

1. Addressing root causes
2. Establishing a theory of change
3. Deciding on a focus
4. Measuring outcomes

FROM STRATEGIC TO TACTICAL PHILANTHROPY

Too often, Strategic Philanthropy results in a virtuous and admirable plan that addresses a family's core values and beliefs—a plan that could potentially result in real impact, if not for a single drawback: the plan is never implemented. The creation of today's philanthropic universe requires a leap beyond strategy into tactics. How will this world be built? What will be its tools, its raw materials, its building blocks, its points of intersection? To practice Tactical Philanthropy is to organize, optimize, and transfer philanthropic capital in ways that maximize the impact of the donor's strategic plan. It is the practice of transforming philanthropic strategy into reality. Philanthropy is at its core a series of financial transactions. Just as a well-designed financial plan is valuable only if the correct savings vehicles are selected, created, and funded, a great Strategic Philanthropy plan is valuable only if the right tactics are discovered, or created, and finally implemented. Tactical Philanthropy concerns itself with structuring these transactions in ways that are efficient and mutually advantageous to donors and nonprofits.

PHILANTHROPY'S UNIQUELY AMERICAN HERITAGE

The opening epigraph by Alexis de Tocqueville, the nineteenth-century author of *Democracy in America,* reminds us that organized philanthropy has a long and multifaceted history in the United States. But it was the publication of the 1889 essay "Wealth," by Andrew Carnegie, that ignited American philanthropy as we know it today. Carnegie went against the grain of the time by stating his unorthodox view that, for wealthy Americans, philanthropy was not a discretionary choice but rather a fundamental moral responsibility. He called for prosperous families to administer their surplus assets to help their communities. Philanthropy was the *only* appropriate use of surplus funds, Carnegie insisted, and the wealthy man who died without giving would die disgraced. Carnegie's influential essay was widely read and is still published today. Carnegie's call to action led his peers in the early twentieth century to create America's first private foundations. Established by some of the nation's richest families, these foundations in many ways duplicated the large institutions in place at the time, building hospitals, libraries, and doing other works that the government would ordinarily do today (see Exhibit 1.10).

In 1914 the Cleveland Foundation became the nation's first community foundation, when it was founded to focus on grant making for the charitable assets held by the Cleveland Trust Company. The trend took hold, and over the next decade dozens of new community foundations sprang up around the country. Today, community foundations direct more than $30 billion in assets and make annual grants of over $2 billion.

The evolution of vehicles for American philanthropy expanded with the arrival of charitable trusts. Although these unique fiduciary entities began in England and have existed for several hundred years, their American incarnation was codified into law in the 1969 Tax Reform Act.

EXHIBIT 1.10   THE NUMBER OF FOUNDATIONS HAS TRIPLED

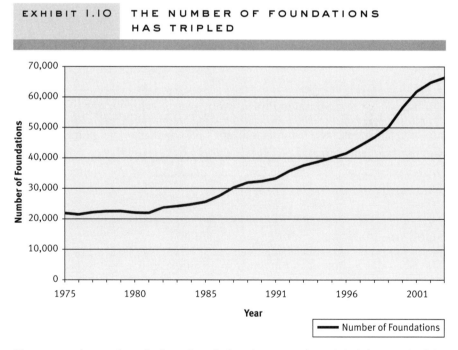

Since 1975, the number of private foundations has more than tripled, but much of the growth has occurred in foundations of smaller size. In 2004, nearly two-thirds of all private foundations held total assets of less than $1 million.

Source: The Foundation Center.

THE EVOLUTION CONTINUES

Americans have always been attracted to philanthropy, supporting a variety of philanthropic vehicles that have flourished, with the support of the nation's wealthiest families and individuals. Now these vehicles are becoming more and more useful to those of more earthbound means.

Donor Advised Funds

In 1991 Boston-based Fidelity Investments launched their Charitable Gift Fund, the first national donor advised fund affiliated with a financial services company. By marketing the concept to their captive base of financial service customers, the Fidelity Charitable Gift Fund has become a considerable philanthropic force. In 15 years the fund has grown significantly, making over $5 billion in grants to over 95,000 nonprofit organizations. Competing financial providers such as Charles Schwab and Vanguard have since launched their own successful charitable gift funds.

Charitable Trusts

Financial service professionals have extolled the virtues of charitable trusts to clients since the vehicle was codified in 1969. Charitable trusts allow donors to keep an income interest in assets placed in trust for a charity, allowing those assets to support a donor's personal financial plan, as well as their philanthropic plan. Like the marketing of donor advised funds by the financial services industry, the continual marketing of charitable trusts has dramatically increased awareness of them.

Small Foundations

The latest development in philanthropic vehicles is the spectacular drop in the costs of operating a private foundation. Just as technology has lowered expenses for some financial services, such as trading commissions, mutual fund fees, and money transfer costs, it has also led to declining costs for private foundations. Today, a private foundation can operate out of a centralized data processing facility, with the foundation's managers remotely accessing information, directing grants from any location via an Internet interface.

More and more people are learning about the variety of philanthropic vehicles available, from the financial services industry, or by word-of-mouth within the philanthropic community. At the same time, a few high-profile donors have placed the whole idea of philanthropy right in the center of the world's field of attention (see Exhibit 1.11). In June 2006, the richest person in the world, Microsoft founder Bill Gates, made an extraordinary decision. At the relatively young age of 50, Gates declared that he would retire from his position at Microsoft to focus on running his private foundation. Shortly afterward, the second-richest person in the world, legendary investor Warren Buffett, announced his intention to bequeath the bulk of his fortune—some $30 billion[2]—to the Gates Foundation. The symbolic significance and cultural implications of business leaders as visible as Gates and Buffett, moving so forcefully from the world of profit into the world of philanthropy, cannot be overstated.

Whether other corporate executives will follow the lead of Gates and Buffett—as the two billionaires clearly hope they will—remains to be seen. But even as it echoes the substance of the beliefs Andrew Carnegie outlined

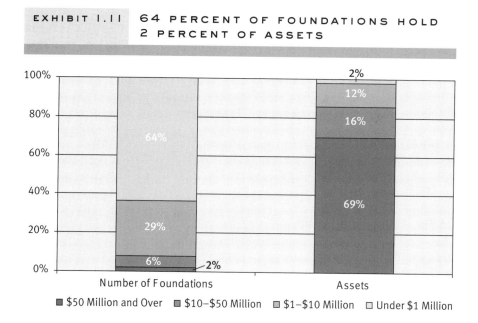

EXHIBIT 1.11   64 PERCENT OF FOUNDATIONS HOLD 2 PERCENT OF ASSETS

■ $50 Million and Over   ■ $10–$50 Million   ▨ $1–$10 Million   □ Under $1 Million

The top two percent of all foundations, those with $50 million or more, held 69 percent of all private foundation assets. And yet 64 percent of all foundations held just two percent of assets demonstrating that, in their sheer numbers alone, small foundations are very much alive and well.

Source: The Foundation Center, 2006.

more than a century ago, their decision demonstrates the continued and growing importance of philanthropy to successful Americans.

Preparing for Trillions

Even as awareness and practical usability of philanthropic vehicles has increased, so too has the available pool of assets to fund them. The pace of wealth creation since the end of World War II, coupled with increased life expectancy, will make American Baby Boomers the first generation to inherit wealth after they have already retired.

The demographic forces in play are unmistakable and immense. Researchers at Boston College have reaffirmed their 1999 forecast that in the first half of the twenty-first century over $41 trillion in wealth would be transferred from generation to generation, and that of that total, $6 trillion would flow to nonprofits.[3] While many Baby Boomers may be dependent on their inheritances to afford retirement, a substantial number have already achieved the financial security that will enable them to use these assets to fund causes that reflect their most deeply held values. Whether they actually make the desired social impact depends on whether they can make the practical leap from strategy to tactics.

Efficiency Increases Output

In philanthropy, as in engineering, efficiency increases output. Thanks to the mix of philanthropic vehicles now available to efficiently structure, administer, and streamline financial transactions, donors can maximize the impact of their giving by optimizing the amount of assets they are able to transfer to a given nonprofit. Using private foundations, donor advised funds, charitable trusts, supporting organizations, and charitable gift annuities as well as outright gifts, tactical donors can efficiently leverage their cash, and other types of assets, and restructure them in a way that increases their ability to give, without changing the after-tax cost of giving.

Technology also increases efficiency. One of the most important impacts of the Internet is its broad ability to distribute information in a cost-effective manner. Informing oneself about a relatively complex concept, such as a charitable remainder trust, has been democratized, making it accessible to anyone capable of typing the phrase into *Google*. In addition to disseminating valuable but esoteric knowledge to an enthusiastic audience, Internet technology has also dramatically reduced the expense and labor associated with creating and administering a philanthropic vehicle. Technology also enables simplicity. Today, making a grant from a donor advised fund can be as effortless as logging on to a secure Web site, selecting a nonprofit, and typing in a dollar amount. There are no longer any checks to write, compliance issues to monitor, or records to keep. Similarly, Internet administration allows charitable trust donors to monitor the amount of income they will receive, and to handle the complex tax accounting, without exertion.

Perhaps most impressive of all is the way that Internet technology has slashed the cost and complexity of running a private foundation. Until only a few years ago, it was generally regarded as gospel that starting up a private foundation required initial funding of at least $3 to $5 million to justify the overhead. Connecticut-based Foundation Source pioneered technology that brings private foundations to a broader cross-section of Americans, by centralizing administration and allowing families to make grants, run reports, and research charities online. Foundation Source has proven that you can operate a private foundation with as little as $100,000 in initial funding, and do so without an overwhelming amount of paperwork. By lowering the cost of entry into the philanthropic universe, this technology has opened a path to giving for thousands, if not millions, of potential philanthropists.

A New Species of Philanthropist

Today's Tactical Philanthropists realize the benefits of "institutionalizing" their giving process, taking advantage of the benefits of structuring their philanthropic capital. However, the Tactical Philanthropist also chooses not to imitate existing institutions the way America's first major philanthropists did. Many of today's donors feel that they can produce a more profound impact by focusing their grants on smaller, niche nonprofits that are being overlooked by traditional funding. While Tactical Philanthropists are often willing and able to invest in unproven nonprofits, and take on greater risks with their grant making, they also demand accountability in a way earlier generations of philanthropists did not. The contemporary concept of Venture Philanthropy is an obvious example of this desire for accountability. Just as publicly traded companies have discovered that modern investors demand clear, complete, and frequent communication regarding their results, more and more nonprofits are finding themselves under pressure to show the tangible outcomes of the grant money they receive.

REDEFINING THE PHILANTHROPIC DISCIPLINES

As awareness of philanthropic vehicles continues to rise, advisors from many different disciplines must prepare to serve the needs of the new breed of Tactical Philanthropists. Just as falling costs and increasing wealth attracted a flood of new investors into the financial markets during the 1990s, the falling costs and increase in philanthropic capital will spur on the rising tide of donors, who want to structure their giving in the most efficient way. New technology will allow some donors to achieve their goals without much professional guidance, but unprecedented demand will exist for advisors who can help clients navigate the complex world of charitable giving.

Donors now consult with a broad array of advisors such as lawyers, accountants, financial advisors, and nonprofit planned giving officers. Unfortunately, it is difficult to judge the quality of advice they receive because professional philanthropic credentials for such advisors are still being developed. Accountants must earn a CPA designation, lawyers must pass the bar, and doctors must get a medical degree, but there is no "must-have" credential for philanthropic advisors. In response, the American College, which administers the well-regarded Certified Financial Planning program for financial advisors, launched the Chartered Advisor in Philanthropy program in 2003. As of this writing, fewer than 200 individuals across the country have completed the program, but it is a substantial first step toward creating a new generation of advisors, to give tomorrow's Tactical Philanthropist the advice they need to make sense of the complex world of philanthropy.

THE NEXT GENERATION

In the next great wave of philanthropy, the mere awareness of funding vehicles will not suffice to meet the needs of the Tactical Philanthropist. Actively selecting, assembling, and structuring them into intelligent functional combinations—while simultaneously optimizing the base of assets that fund the individual vehicles—forms the core of the practice of Tactical Philanthropy. It is not simply an administrative process of implementation, but rather an intellectual process in its own right. The Tactical Philanthropist represents the next stage in the evolution of the American donor. Those engaged in advising or appealing to such donors should remember what Tactical Philanthropy means to this new generation of patrons: a new awareness of philanthropic vehicles, a flexible and astute application of structural entities, investment management, a streamlined approach to administrative processes, a willing-ness to explore less conventional recipients, and a focus on accountability.

■ NOTES

1. *Foundation News and Commentary,* May/June 2001.

2. Karen Richardson, "Gates Foundation to Use Warren Buffett's Donation for Disease Control, Education," *Wall Street Journal,* June 26, 2006. http://online.wsj.com/article/SB115134434118990935.html.

3. "Why the $41 Trillion Wealth Transfer Is Still Valid: A Review of Challenges and Questions," *Journal of Gift Planning.* Vol. 7, No. 1 (Committee on Planned Giving: 2003): 11–15, 47–50. http://www.bc.edu/research/swri/news/releases/tidings/.

It Really Is a Small World after All: Globalization and Philanthropy

SUSAN RAYMOND, PHD

One searches for a way to avoid being hackneyed. The term *globalization* seems at times to begin every third sentence of every article written and published today. Still, perspective does provide some appreciation of the pace and scope of change, not just for America as a nation, but for Americans as a people. As the Secretary General of the United Nations, Kofi Annan, has remarked, arguing against the impact of globalization is like arguing against the impact of gravity.

The economic dimensions are best understood, in part, because they are most discussed. By 2020, less than 15 years from now, the global economy will be 80 percent larger than it was in 2000. Average per capita incomes will be 50 percent higher. Trade now accounts for a quarter of the global economy, compared to just seven percent in 1965.[1] Nearly every element of the American economy is now intimately tied to global markets.

> Globalization is no longer elite. It is part of the experience of a vast majority of citizens of the United States. Americans today spend over $90 billion annually on international travel. That is approximately the size of the annual gross domestic product of Bolivia.

The ties that bind are not only found in the flow of goods like cars, refrigerators, shoes, and bobble heads. Services have also become global. Your hotel reservation in Dubuque, Iowa, is as likely to be processed in Calcutta,

India, or Accra, Ghana, as anywhere else. The code that underpins your online banking was as likely written in Bangalore as in Seattle. It is not just U.S. oil and mining companies whose workforces are abroad; 56 percent of Citigroup employees and 37.8 percent of Goldman Sachs' are overseas.

To some extent, economics underportrays the nature of the change. What is happening to ordinary Americans in their everyday lives drives the point home more forcefully.

Globalization is no longer elite. It is part of the experience of a vast majority of Americans. Of course, the titans of the America economy were always global. A century ago, they sailed the luxury liners to Europe and Asia. Their children toured the European continent during their "coming out" years. Their social circle was the wealth and glitterati of the world. Meanwhile, the average American toiled in a very narrow geographic and therefore experiential, world, mostly defined by neighborhood.

Those days are gone. In a single decade, between 1990 and 2000, the total number of passengers flying from American airports to foreign destinations increased by 70 percent (see Exhibit 1.12). Americans today spend over $90 billion annually on international travel. How big is $90 billion? It is ten times greater than the U.S. government's annual foreign assistance budget, and about equivalent to the gross domestic product of Bolivia. This is not just the elite of New York's boardrooms flying to Paris for paté; the highest rate of growth in international travel is from Chicago and Detroit.

EXHIBIT 1.12   AMERICANS TRAVELING OVERSEAS (1960–2000)

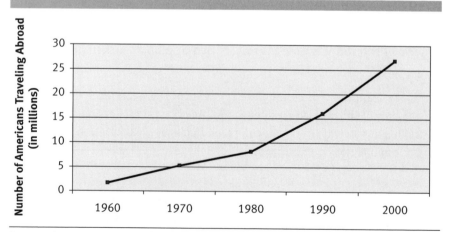

Source: Historical Statistics of the United States, Volume 4.

In 1988, only a third of the visitors to the United States came from out-side of Canada and Mexico. Today, nearly half do so. Even Americans who stay home are increasingly rubbing shoulders with visitors from afar. This is not just a matter of immigration, although the diversity of places of origin of immigrants has readily expanded. It is a matter of tourism and an expan-sion of foreign investment in U.S. markets.

Telecommunication tells much the same story. In 2003, the top five countries representing the most heavily used links for billed phone calls accounted for only 37 percent of all U.S. international billed minutes (see Exhibit 1.13). In 1950, international toll revenue represented just four per-cent of total telephone revenues for U.S. carriers. By 2003, they represented over 20 percent. The number of U.S. billed minutes of international calls has risen from 1.6 billion in 1980 to 42.7 billion in 2003, nearly a 30-fold increase in just two decades. The total flow of all international switchboard minutes, irrespective of billing sites, topped 100 billion in 2000.[2]

There are, of course, other measures. In just over one decade, from 1995 to 2006, the percentage of American adults online increased from 15 per-cent to nearly 75 percent.[3] The Internet has, in effect, made every user global.

If all this is true, have Americans themselves changed their spots? A series of public knowledge and opinion polls taken since World War II have traced the degree to which Americans know about foreign affairs or international events. In 1946, Hyman and Sheatsley published a landmark study of Amer-ican knowledge about foreign affairs. They found that 32 percent of the

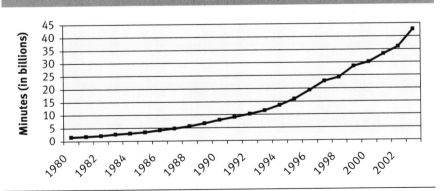

EXHIBIT 1.13   INTERNATIONAL TELEPHONE MINUTES BILLED FROM THE UNITED STATES (1980–2003)

Source: Federal Communications Commission: Trends in the International Telecommunications Industry.

public were what they termed "know nothings," people who had very low levels of information about international events (see Exhibit 1.14). Replication of the study in 1994 found that 32.9 percent of the public had very low or no knowledge of key international facts and events. In 2003, the Program on International Policy Attitudes, in Washington D.C., found that 58 percent of Americans followed foreign affairs "not very closely" or "not closely at all." Indeed, in 1997, the program found 15.7 percent of Americans followed foreign affairs closely, but in 2003 that figure was more than halved, dropping to seven percent.[4] Even after 9/11, even with the war on terror, few Americans judged themselves as following foreign affairs closely.

In April 2006, the Gallup Poll found that 70 percent of Americans agreed with the statement "We shouldn't think so much in international concerns but concentrate on our own national problems," compared to 54 percent, who agreed in 1964. The poll deemed only 24 percent to be "internationalist" in their views.[5]

So, the path from exposure and experience to knowledge and attitudes appears to be a long and complex one. The reality of economic globalization, as well as the reality of the increased personal exposure of Americans to the people and places of other nations, has not markedly made Americans more aware of international affairs, nor has it made them more internationalist in their worldview. This presents a challenge not simply for the political and policy processes which must guide American opinion about trade, economic,

EXHIBIT 1.14   HOW CLOSELY DO AMERICANS FOLLOW FOREIGN AFFAIRS?

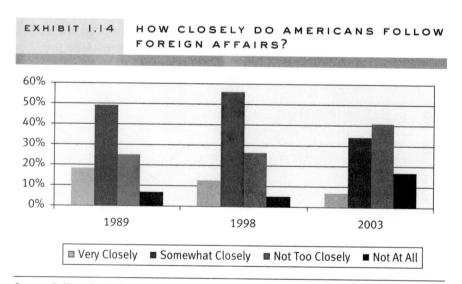

Source: Polling the Nations.

and foreign policy. It is a challenge for all leadership, public and private, to bring the realities of globalization, and the nation's self-interest in an integrated world, into both the boardrooms and living rooms of America.

And what of philanthropy? If the nation becomes more and more global, while citizen understanding lags, where are philanthropic institutions in the mix? There are two elements to that question: the engagement of American philanthropy with global issues that are, in effect, outside the United States; and the engagement of American philanthropy, with issues which are global, but whose effects are domestic. Let us examine these two separately.

Ruffin's estimate from Duke University[6] is that the top 10 international donors among foundations account for about 50 percent of all international giving by U.S. foundations. Even given such concentration, however, his estimate is that the number of foundations making international grants has risen steadily since 1990, and that the dominance of the 10 largest has fallen, from 71 percent in 1990 to 52 percent in 2001.

Is it true, then, that the propensity of U.S. philanthropy to fund international causes is rising?

Perfect comparability with Ruffin's data is not possible, but an approximate examination can be made. Assume that the pace of growth of foundation involvement in international giving continued through 2004. Examining the growth in interest, relative to the growth in the number of foundations in America, one finds that 0.7 percent of foundations made international grants in 1994, and 0.7 percent made such grants in 2004. The numbers have grown apace with foundation growth, but have not exceeded it. This is consistent with the pattern of total giving to international causes. While the absolute dollar amount has increased to $6.4 billion—an 88 percent increase in real terms, in the last decade—that now represents 2.5 percent of all giving, compared to 2.0 percent a decade ago.[7]

What about philanthropic engagement with issues inside the United States, whose roots lie in global change? Let us take a look at two examples: immigration and religion.

In 1959, immigration accounted for six percent of population growth. It now accounts for 40 percent. By 2030, non-Latin whites will be the minority of youth aged 10 to 19. The world of the young will belong to the "majority minorities." Even today, one in five New Yorkers is foreign born, up nearly 30 percent from the 1990s. Nearly half the population of the Bronx speaks a language other than English at home. From restaurants to healthcare clinics to every shopping district of every borough of New York, a linguistic potpourri swirls through the air.

There are problems of culture and comprehension associated with that change. The challenge may be less in a place like New York, which has been a melting pot almost since it has been at all. The challenge is perhaps greater in other areas of the nation. The fastest growth in immigrants, as a percentage of the population, will not occur in historically immigrant settings but in "new growth" rural states, a band that cuts across the heartland, and into the deep South (see Exhibit 1.15). These are states perhaps not as used to the complexity of a multicultural world, states where social safety nets may be less developed than in more urbanized settings. Immigration may test the resilience of social and economic policies. By 2015, the Bureau of the Census estimates that one in three low-income families will have immigrant parents. Indeed, all of the net increase in the absolute number of children with low-income parents is projected to occur in immigrant families.

As recently as 1970, fully 60 percent of immigrants to the United States were from Europe. Today, that portion is 10 percent. With diversity of origin comes diversity of religion. By 2025, adherents to Islam, Buddhism, and Hinduism will represent 42 percent of the world's population, compared to 33 percent in 1970.

These three religions have doubled their numbers in the United States in the last decade. Indeed, there are now 20 faith groups with more than 1 million adherents. By and large, we are a nation that respects religious diversity, but often does not work to understand its implications. For Islam in particular, the level of knowledge and understanding is extremely low,

EXHIBIT 1.15   ORIGINS OF IMMIGRATION TO THE UNITED STATES

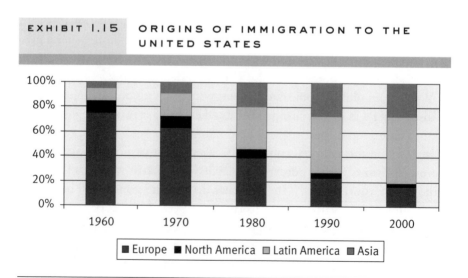

Source: U.S. Bureau of the Census.

among America's leaders as well as its people. Recent world events, combined with ignorance, have turned our valuing of faith that used to draw us together as a nation into a force pushing us apart.

The rise of electronic communication has only heightened the potential effect of global religious diversity in America. As the small nation of Denmark so painfully learned, the absolute size of a religious minority in a nation is no measure of the global reach of its believers. The publication of a cartoon, tasteless and insulting as it was, combined with the power of instant communication to result in local and global riots. Riots result in confrontation at the highest diplomatic levels, and all over a cartoon.

What happens in the world of religion matters on the streetcorners of America, and what happens on the streetcorners matters to the world.

What of philanthropy? There are on the order of 70,000 grant-making foundations in the nation, and no absolute way to know what each and every one of them actually thinks is important. There is only what they say they think is important. Turn, then, to the Foundation Center to try to gauge the scope of the interface between philanthropy and these two issues (immigration and non-Western religion).

The Foundation Center's prestructured issues categories will not allow a search solely for interests in immigration; one must combine immigrants with refugees, which are quite different. Hence, the results will overestimate immigration interests. That having been said, a search results in 81 foundations with explicit interests in immigrants/refugees. Only half have annual giving in excess of $1 million; nearly one-quarter have giving of $100,000 or less per year. Only five of the foundations are in the South (in Florida, Arkansas, Texas, and Virginia), with 15 in the Midwest, seven in Minnesota, three in Michigan, two in Illinois, and one each in Ohio, Nebraska, and Wisconsin. The interest is largely bicoastal, even though future immigrant flows will impact the South and Midwest.

The disengagement of the philanthropic community from faith communities that are non-Western is even more striking. The Foundation Center logs only 60 foundations interested in Islam, 38 explicitly interest in Buddhism, and 23 interested in Hinduism. Only seven of this total of 121 have annual giving of over $1 million; 73 (60 percent) give less than $100,000 per year.

Does this mean that American philanthropy will necessarily be disengaged from America's need to absorb, and adapt to, globalization in the future? Three trends would argue to the contrary.

First, the new generation of philanthropists emerging from corporate wealth is widely traveled. They have run businesses which are (and have had to be) overwhelmingly international, taking advantage of globalized markets. They are used to seeing themselves as global leaders. Their corporate headquarters might be in New York or Chicago, but they do not see their companies or their careers as place-specific. Their propensity to think globally with their philanthropic dollars will also likely increase.

Second, our understanding of the nature of many problems is also changing. It is increasingly difficult to draw geopolitical boundaries around environmental issues, for example. There is no particular geography to human rights, to women's health, to literacy, to civil society, or to good governance. These are all issues that are on the forefront of interest for emerging leaders of wealth. They will naturally draw philanthropy toward cross-border strategies. Indeed, Brill points out that among the 25 wealthiest young philanthropists, half specified their interest in global issues or organizations.

Finally, two decades of high immigration mean that the U.S. population is increasingly diverse. Indeed, nearly a third of the population of the state of New Jersey is immigrant or children of immigrants. Despite banner headlines, this is not a statement about poverty. Indeed, Asian and Hispanic small businesses are the most stable and successful small businesses in the country. Immigrants become economically successful Americans and philanthropic leaders. One need look no further than the Hot Pockets inventor, Iranian immigrant Paul Merange and his wife. After selling his company to Nestlé for $2.6 billion, they are now leading philanthropists, with a portion of that philanthropy focused on global needs.

American philanthropy, and American nonprofits, will probably never be dominantly or even largely given over to global issues or problems. But there is reason to hope that the new generation of philanthropic leaders will see both the horizons of possibility beyond American shores and the reflection of those horizons in our own communities.

■ OTHER SOURCES

Bureau of Labor Statistics.

International Transportation Administration, Department of Transportation.

Bureau of the Census.

■ NOTES

1. A. T. Kearney, "Measuring Globalization," *Foreign Policy* 122, January/February 2001: 55–65.

2. "Trends in the International Telecommunications Industry," Federal Communications Commission, International Bureau, September 2005.

3. M. Madden, "Internet Penetration and Impact," data memo, Pew Internet and American Life Project, April 2006.

4. S. E. Bennett, "'Know Nothings' Revisited Again," *Political Behavior* 18:3 (September 1996): 219–233.

5. J. M. Jones, "Little Change in Isolationist Sentiment Among Americans," Gallup Poll, April 21, 2006.

6. H. Ruffin, *The Globalization of American Philanthropy* (Civil Society International and Duke University, October 31, 2003).

7. *Giving USA 2006* (Glenview, IL: Giving USA Foundation, 2006).

The Effects: The New World Meets the Old Ways

OVERVIEW OF THE ISSUES

The pressures exerted by the social and economic tectonic plates giving rise to a new world of American philanthropy are not occurring in a vacuum. The nearly one million charitable institutions in America, and the 70,000 foundations that support them, already have modes of action, organizational structures, and "rules of the road" that have served them, for better or for worse, for generations. The nonprofit sector now represents nearly 10 percent of the U.S. economy, and philanthropy moves something on the order of one-third of a trillion dollars of economic wherewithal to nonprofits. These are significant resources in an economically significant sector. Size and longevity create assumptions about the future, which are not always consonant with the changes taking place in the world.

> Despite uncertainties about how big "massive" is likely to be, how the interplay between trends in innovation and change and the historical and current operations of nonprofit and philanthropic systems unfolds, will drive the nature of tomorrow's nonprofit sector.

The new world emerging may question those old ways. New approaches to family wealth and philanthropy, indeed, new ways of thinking about philanthropy itself, may result in funds flowing, not to old ways, but to entirely new categories of nonprofit institutions and needs, in entirely new ways. Venture philanthropy provides a case in point, where the philanthropist's role is denominated less in cash than in expertise and hands-on management.

Where the money comes from may also change old assumptions. The role of employees in determining the directions of corporate philanthropy, for example, may erode the influence of executives and community leaders in resource allocation. The rise of women as philanthropists may bring whole new perspectives to problem identification. New approaches to planned giving may increase the total philanthropic resources in the planned giving sector, but change the way in which nonprofits access them. The list of changes is long.

The essays in this section address a variety of aspects of the rising new world of philanthropy that may call into question old assumptions and old ways, ranging from the pathways through which philanthropy might flow to the management consequences of its sheer scale.

As that great Bronx philosopher, Yogi Berra, is noted for observing, however, "It's tough to make predictions, especially about the future." Indeed. Hence, this section begins with an ear turned to the critics who caution that the transfer of wealth may be illusory. Despite uncertainties about how big "massive" is likely to be, however, how this interplay between trends in innovation and change and the historical and current operations of nonprofit and philanthropic systems unfolds, will drive the nature of tomorrow's nonprofit sector.

Listening to the Critics: Who Is Actually Transferring What?

Susan Raymond, PhD, and
Mary Beth Martin, Esq.

W hen several tens of billions of dollars pass to philanthropy, the stars do indeed seem to be aligned in philanthropy's favor. Such is certainly the case with the creation of the Gates Foundation and its new partnership with Warren Buffet. As Senator Everett Dirksen once so famously observed, "A billion here and a billion there, and soon you're talking about real money." Amazingly, his observations about the federal budget now apply equally to American philanthropy. This is a stunning statement and comparison.

There is a temptation to conclude, therefore, that something fundamental has changed. With billions moving at the top of the nation's income structure, there is an assumption that there are, if not billions of dollars, at least millions now moving to philanthropy from an aging and increasingly affluent population. Is this all so simple? However compelling the arithmetic of the combination of increased affluence and rapid aging may be, is the result of increased philanthropy necessarily so straightforward? There are reasons to believe that the philanthropic path, no matter how much it leads forward, will not be so easily trod.

> However compelling the arithmetic of the combination of increased affluence and rapid aging may be, is the result of increased philanthropy necessarily so straightforward? There are reasons to believe that the philanthropic path, no matter how much it leads forward, will not be so easily trod.

There are three complicating dimensions that need to be acknowledged, and their implications understood far better than we do today: how people live, what people intend to do, and what wrench public policy may throw into the philanthropic gearbox.

First, will people actually accumulate large amounts of money? Casual observation suggests that what constitutes an acceptable lifestyle for many Americans is quite different from what previous generations of Americans expected. Let us look at several measures. In the two decades between 1980 and 2000, the U.S. Census Bureau estimated that the number of vacation homes owned by Americans has more than tripled (see Exhibit 2.1). Indeed, 16 percent of the homes in Florida, 15 percent of those in Vermont, and 10 percent of those in New Hampshire are vacation homes. In 1950, only seven percent of American families owned two or more automobiles. Today, over half of all households own two or more cars (see Exhibit 2.2).

In 1960, 1.6 million Americans traveled abroad. In 2000, that had increased more than 20-fold, to 26.9 million Americans. Nearly one in ten Americans travels abroad each year. Moreover, the highest rate of growth in passengers departing to foreign destinations came not from New York, but from Detroit, Chicago, and Orlando. America's heartland and its elderly have come down with the travel bug. Second homes, second cars, and vacations abroad all require resource expenditures.

EXHIBIT 2.1   NUMBER OF SEASONAL, RECREATIONAL, OR OCCASIONAL-USE HOMES IN THE UNITED STATES

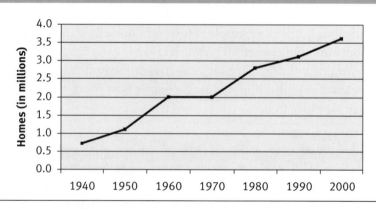

Source: U.S. Bureau of the Census and Historical Statistics of the United States.

EXHIBIT 2.2   HOUSEHOLD MOTOR VEHICLE OWNERSHIP

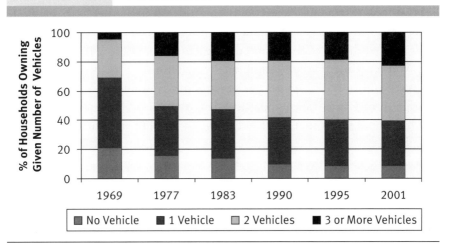

Source: U.S. Department of Transportation.

Moreover, what the *New York Times* has called the "Bank of Mom and Dad" is increasingly in demand.[1] On average, college students now leave school with $20,000 in loans. The combination of debt, rising housing costs, and stagnant entry-level employment compensation has led to extended parental financial commitments to adult offspring. Researchers estimate that parental outlays for support of adult offspring will be as much as one-third again the total cost of raising a child from birth to 18 years.[2] Overall, a study by the RAND Corporation estimates that the average American between the ages of 60 and 70 will spend 58 percent of their accumulated wealth before they die.[3]

Second, however much money they may have accumulated, do people actually leave it behind? A study by the Allianz Life Insurance Company of North America found that Americans aged 65 years and older were seven times more likely to believe they owe their children an inheritance than the "Boomers," aged 40 to 59.[4] Similarly, nearly 40 percent of the older group felt it was "very important" to transfer financial assets or real estate to their children, compared to just 10 percent of Boomers. In 2004, median inheritances were about $29,000. Adjusted for inflation, this was about $10,000 less than the median inheritance 30 years ago.

Third, how will public policy changes affect the tax incentives to transfer wealth to philanthropy? Predicting public policy is particularly fraught with risk. Nevertheless, there is considerable and consistent momentum toward change in some areas of public policy. The nation's estate tax structure is one of them. While the estate tax is scheduled to be eliminated by 2010, it is also slated to be reinstated in 2011. Attempts to make the elimination permanent have, so far, failed. Nevertheless, there is the expected congressional horse trading, aimed at reaching some type of compromise that would maintain at least some of the reductions. The most likely strategy is to remove the estate tax from estates of $10 million (for couples) and $5 million or less (for individuals), leaving the tax on larger estates.

This would mean that, in effect, only 0.5 percent of estates would face a tax burden.[5] If the tax advantages of wealth transfer to philanthropy are removed, the future philanthropic picture becomes more complex. Not only are expenditures going up while propensities to leave inheritances are going down, but the tax threat may be disappearing for all but America's wealthiest. The transfer of wealth to philanthropies and nonprofits, therefore, will need to be motivated by beliefs, desires, and values, not necessarily by the long shadow of the IRS.

Mapping the bumps in the road toward wealth transfer does not reveal much about direction, only about difficulty. All of these trends, of course, do not necessarily mean that wealth will not cascade toward philanthropy, even for those with fewer means than America's mega-rich. Examination of a few other indicators gives considerable comfort that the predicted directions of that transfer are likely to be correct.

While the expenditures of American households are growing, so is income. Total consumer expenditures, as a percentage of aggregate personal income, have declined since 1950. Incomes have kept pace with expenditures.

Moreover, more Americans hold financial assets than ever before in the nation's history. In 2005, over half of all households owned equities, compared to just 19 percent in 1983, and 18 percent of those aged 65 or older who hold equities do so with a primary goal of making them part of an inheritance. That reason, however, is a rationale for holding equities for only four percent of those aged 50 to 64.[6]

It is true that huge wealth is highly skewed. In America, 20 percent of households account for 50 percent of the wealth. It is tempting to conclude, therefore, that there are two tracks to the wealth transfer: one with the mega-wealthy giving, and one with everyone else increasingly using wealth to support other needs. That conclusion would have the transfer of wealth being only a matter that concerns the very, very rich. Indeed, one might conclude that only extremely wealthy households are building philanthropic momentum. That conclusion would be incorrect.

In fact, despite the vacation homes, cars, and subsidies of Billy and Buffy's apartments, the average American is still charitably inclined. Based on deductions taken on tax returns, the percentage of income given away by those with incomes of more than a million dollars fell, from 4.1 percent in 1995 to 3.6 percent in 2003, while the percentage given away by those with income less than a million rose, from 2.8 percent to 3.5 percent—nearly the same level as the very wealthy. Indeed, if there is philanthropic advocacy to be done, it is among the nation's richest, not its middle class. In 2004, 47.7 percent of the richest estates, worth $20 million or more, gave nothing to charity.[7]

The transfer of wealth works well arithmetically. When it comes to the wealthiest households in America, it would appear that what is needed is not arithmetic, but leadership.

■ OTHER DATA SOURCES

Bureau of Labor Statistics.

U.S. Department of Transportation.

Historical Statistics of the United States, Earliest Times to the Present, Millennial Edition (Cambridge University Press, 2006).

■ NOTES

1. A. Bahney, "The Bank of Mom and Dad," *New York Times,* April 20, 2006: G1–2.

2. R. Schoeni and K. Ross, "Family Support During Transition to Adulthood," *Network on Transitions to Adulthood: Policy Brief,* Issue 12, October 2004.

3. M. D. Hurd and J. P. Smith, "Anticipated and Actual Bequests," NBER: working paper No. W7380, October 1999.

4. *The Allianz American Legacies Study.*

5. E. L. Edwards, "Timber Becomes Tool in Effort to Cut Estate Taxes," *New York Times,* June 21, 2006: C1.

6. *Equity Ownership in America: 2005* (New York: Investment Company Institute and the Securities Industry Association, 2005).

7. D. C. Johnston, "The Ultra-Rich Give Differently from You and Me," *New York Times,* July 2, 2006: WK3.

Family Foundation Formation

STEVEN DISALVO, PHD

Family foundations have historically been set up by high-wealth individuals, with enough capital to create sustainable giving far beyond their lifetimes. These were primarily elderly men in the twilight of their careers, with a passion for a specific social issue. It was thought that if enough money could be dedicated to improving problems in healthcare or education, for example, these families would eventually effect change.

AN ERA OF GROWTH AND CHANGE

One hundred years ago there were few families both willing and able to start foundations. Today, the infusion of wealth has come at a much younger age. Women have taken a more active role in philanthropic initiatives within families, and next-generation education has surfaced as a critical area for families wishing to maintain quality control and sustainability. Also, families are not going about it alone. They seek professional advisement in their philanthropic efforts much like they do for their financial investments.

Public figures often turn to family and friends during the early stages of foundation development. While family and friends seem like logical choices at first, it does not take long to realize that expert guidance is necessary to take the organizations from the confines of the kitchen to the power of the boardroom.

Men such as Carnegie and Rockefeller amassed personal wealth early in the twentieth century and spent the latter part of their years figuring out how to give most of it away. The Carnegie and Rockefeller Foundations, established in 1905 and 1913, respectively, created a benchmark that was difficult for other families to achieve. Prior to 1940, approximately 20 percent of some 500 established foundations were classified as family foundations, according to a survey conducted by the Foundation Center. By 1998, that number had risen to 60 percent of 4,912 established foundations. While families in the Northeast controlled the largest share of family foundations, the highest growth of new family foundations in the 1990s occurred in the West. Overall, more than two-thirds of larger family foundations were formed in the last two decades of the twentieth century.

Today's philanthropists often start family foundations with nominal start-up costs and the objective of adding principal to the fund over time. Celebrities and athletes are among the growing number of foundations with the ability to raise money for their organizations, with the intent of passing through funds to grant recipients. Public figures often turn to family and friends during the early stages of foundation development. They turn to people they trust to help create the infrastructure for their family foundation, just as they rely on their publicist and agent for advice and counsel. While family and friends seem like logical choices at first, it does not take long to realize that expert guidance is necessary to take the organization from the confines of the kitchen to the power of the boardroom. Issues of governance and program development are overshadowed by the ability to raise enough money to support the growth rate of the organization.

There is a direct correlation of asset ranges for family foundations and the number of active board members with fiduciary responsibilities (see Exhibit 2.3). Family Foundations 2000 reported that foundations with assets under $5 million had an average of three board members, while those organizations with more than $100 million were represented by approximately eight individuals. Ironically, only 14 percent of family foundations reported paid staff responsible for day-to-day operations. The challenge is to keep operating expenses below the accepted 15 percent range, so that the majority of funds can be directed towards programs.

Family foundations have traditionally focused on four key areas: education, arts and culture, the environment, and science. Most of the programs and organizations had a mission focused on the health and education of children. While there may be strategic thought behind each decision, it is more often a case of a personal experience that prompts families to help improve the lives of young people.

EXHIBIT 2.3   NUMBER OF FAMILY FOUNDATION
BOARD MEMBERS IN RELATION TO
ASSET SIZE

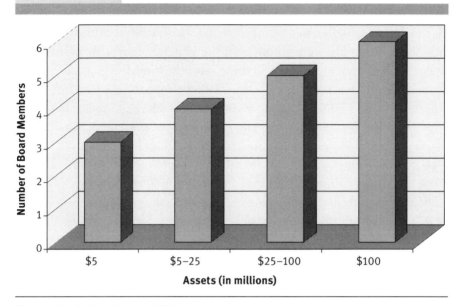

Source: Family Foundations 2000.

ILLUSTRATIONS OF TODAY'S PHILANTHROPY

It was Memorial Day weekend in 2003 that I found myself on a private jet en route to Chicago, hosted by Walter Hester, CEO of Maui Jim Sunglasses, and Ali Torre, wife of baseball legend Joe Torre. During the flight, Ali and I drafted the initial documents for a foundation that would bear her husband's name. The Joe Torre Safe at Home Foundation was born out of the deep passion held by Torre, then manager of the New York Yankees. Torre, who was raised in an abusive home in Brooklyn, had grown up fearful of his own father, who physically and verbally abused his mother. Joe rode his bicycle home after school and would not enter the house if his father's car was parked in front. The youngest of five children, Joe did not witness the abuse, but still suffered the emotional scars, which he discovered later in his life. As an adult, Torre had learned that his father had thrown his mother, Margaret, down a flight of stairs when he found out she was pregnant with Joe. Joe was labeled "the mistake," and grew up thinking that maybe the abuse his mothered suffered would not have occurred if he had not been born. The foundation was created to provide education to children about domestic violence, so that no child need ever grow up living in fear.

Joe and Ali Torre invested their own time and money to begin the foundation, but knew they had to raise substantial funds if their dream of rolling out programs was to become a reality. The initial board members included their accountant, agent, sisters, attorney, and each other. There was healthy debate about whether to develop their own curriculum or utilize aspects of existing programs. They pondered the benefits of in-school programs versus after-school programs, and there was little knowledge about research and evaluation. Finally, the group was faced with the daunting task of trying to raise at least a million dollars to publicly launch the foundation.

It became very clear that the Safe at Home Foundation could no longer operate out of their residence. It needed a home of its own, and a professional staff, to follow the lead of the board. Upon accepting the position of executive director, I immediately hired a program officer and a special events director, so that the foundation could capitalize on the celebrity of its founder. A gala dinner and golf outing generated close to two million dollars the first year. That, coupled with donated office space, kept the ratio of operating expenses to total revenue extremely low. More than 85 percent of funds raised went directly to programs, a ratio rivaled only by the Robin Hood Foundation, which is supported at 100 percent by its board of directors.

During the first three years since inception, the Safe at Home Foundation embarked on a regional advertising campaign. Two television commercials were developed by Chiat Day, one of which won a local Emmy award. A cause-marketing campaign, with Samsung and Circuit City, generated over half a million dollars in annual revenue, the highlight being a home run contest, which generated both awareness and money. For every home run hit by the home team at Yankee Stadium, $1,000 would be donated to the foundation. With fundraising on a fast pace, the organization focused its attention to the implementation of 10 educational program sites, called Margaret's Places, named after Joe's deceased mother. Margaret's Place sites were rolled out in schools throughout the New York tri-state area. Today, board members include executives from Fortune 100 firms, entrepreneurs, and educators. The foundation raises more than four million dollars annually, and has maintained the expense-to-revenue ratio they achieved in year one.

Most importantly, approximately 3,000 students each year are exposed to some type of domestic violence educational program to learn about warning signs and where to go for help in a desperate situation. While the foundation is no longer managed by family and friends, their presence on the board has kept the mission of the organization close to Torre's heart. The image of Joe Torre as a baseball player and manager is now rivaled by his identity as a philanthropist.

The Imperative for Leverage

Family foundations have evolved over the years, from stand-alone enterprises, combating a single cause, to leaders leveraging others with similar missions around an issue. Like Joe Torre, Michael Bolton found himself in a difficult situation early in life. Forced to raise three beautiful girls on his own, Bolton found solace in understanding the needs of women and children. As his songwriting and singing career took off, he never lost sight of the need to provide for those less fortunate. The Michael Bolton Charities began by underwriting the cost of shelters, so that women and their young families had a safe place to live. In the near future, Bolton plans to embark on an innovative program that will provide music education to inner city youth, as an outlet to express themselves and perhaps to tell their stories of hardship through their own songwriting and singing.

Other organizations, such as the Kanye West Foundation and VH1 Save the Music Foundation, find themselves working in a similar space. Kanye West's *Loop Dreams* program also aims to encourage music education through the use of technology, allowing young people to write and store their own musical loops. Like Michael Bolton, Kanye West hopes to provide an outlet for young people, while seeking to improve academic performance. Kanye's mother, Donda West, has a doctorate in English literature, and is intent on keeping the dream alive for all children.

VH1 Save the Music, another possible partner, already works with some of the schools in the same area, to provide music equipment to educators with limited or no budgets, in order to preserve the art of music education. Together, these organizations can have a greater impact, leveraging the value of music as a medium to improve the lives of children.

The Demand for Anonymity

Most philanthropists do not have household names, but have amassed their fortunes through hard work, dedication, and sometimes inheritance. Some want their names on buildings, while a select few give their money for altruistic reasons. I have been fortunate to have known one of America's ultimate philanthropists. He was a man you may have met crossing the street, or at a ballgame, or on the golf course. He lived the American Dream, starting a company with a few hundred dollars after graduating from college, and selling it for hundreds of millions 20 years later. He gave his money away anonymously, and for that reason, his identity will remain a secret. When he passed away last year, even his wife did not realize the magnitude of his simple generosity.

During the initial public offering for his company, I first realized the magnitude of his wealth. Here was a man who sat in our backyard, eating hamburgers with my family before driving himself to the local Marriott Hotel. He could have had a limousine, stayed in a presidential suite, and dined at a four-star restaurant. Instead, he was living the life he knew as a young man, and was determined to make life better for those who would come after him. His children were shielded from the magnitude of his giving but knew in a heartfelt way that he was genuine in his actions.

My role was simple—to help give away money to organizations that needed it most. I was the messenger, yet reaped the rewards of feeling thanked each time a grantee would learn of a gift. There was no name on the check, and we did not use stationery that would reveal the source. There were many attempts to personally thank him, but I could not allow it, for the ultimate philanthropist had a plan in life, and I know he succeeded. He wanted to encourage others to do good, and he wanted this because it was the right thing to do, not because there was a reward in store. He kept everyone guessing, so they had something to talk about. He protected his family while opening the eyes of those he touched. And he touched the lives of thousands of children, through schools, hospitals, religious organizations, and communities. When he died, he left a void for the handful who knew his secret, and for thousands whose lives he touched but who never knew him. His children will carry on his legacy in ways that only they can truly appreciate.

AT THE CORE: FAMILY VALUES

Family foundations have gone through several transformations in organizational structure, leadership, and motivation. At the hearts of these foundations are the families themselves. The people, the passion, and the vision are dictated by the desire to improve the lives of others. Whether it is through the work of an athlete or celebrity, new wealth or old money, business leaders or average citizens, family foundations are seeking to effect sustainable change. They lead by example, and do so for no other reason than because they care.

The Rise of Donor Advised Funds

EILEEN R. HEISMAN

Donor advised funds (DAFs) are separately managed charitable giving accounts that exist under the umbrella of a larger public charity. Donors who create DAFs do so with the intent to make grants to other operating charities, to support causes that are important to them. A DAF is often an alternative to creating one, or several, private family foundations.

Donors who elect to use this giving vehicle can create their DAF in a day, name the DAF after their family, a pet, or use a name that protects their anonymity, and fund the DAF with many different kinds of liquid or illiquid assets. The assets donors use to fund their DAF must be of a kind that the umbrella charity is willing and able to accept. For example, some umbrella charities will accept gifts of real estate into a DAF, while others will not.

> What is so attractive about these giving vehicles? The donor does little to no administrative work in the grant making process—but still gets to enjoy the pleasure of being a philanthropist.

Once the donor funds the DAF with a personal asset, the asset is usually liquidated quickly, if possible. From those liquidated funds inside the DAF, donors can recommend grants to other charities. The umbrella charity hosting the DAF will need to approve both the charitable recipient organization the donor recommends and the purpose of the grant inside that charity. This is important, as donors cannot have final control, and someone must ensure that DAF regulations are being followed.

While most donor-advised grants are approved, there are some prohibited uses. For example, the umbrella charity cannot pay tuition to private schools or universities for the donor's children (but can support a carefully managed scholarship program). It also cannot pay for auction goods the donor recently won, or for any purpose for which the donor has received goods or services, in exchange for their grant. Donors cannot support political campaigns with DAF grants. Some umbrella charities prohibit grants based on the beliefs of the umbrella charity's mission.

For nearly all recommendations, donors' DAF grant requests are approved, and they do support a wide variety of charitable uses, including but not limited to capital campaigns, annual campaigns, specific projects, or for unrestricted use. Donors can be anonymous or identify themselves for each grant. At some charities, donors can make grants internationally.

Donors who start DAFs at umbrella charities are subject to the rules and practices of the umbrella charity that manages their DAF. That is one reason why donors need to find an umbrella charity that is a good match for their interests. Some host charities are regional in focus; some are religious, while others wish to limit the donor's support for their charitable mission, such as a university or hospital. Some are national and neutral to the donor's grant-making recommendations, while others have strong religious convictions and might deny a grant based on a specific point of view.

Some umbrella charities have spending rules for their DAFs—that is, they only allow donors to give a certain percentage of their DAF's *corpus* away, while other umbrella charities allow donors to spend the "income and principal" of their DAF. Donors who are looking for an umbrella charity should consider this possible limitation.

One of the most appealing aspects of organized philanthropy is using it to teach values and community involvement to the next generation or others. To this end, some umbrella charities will allow DAF donors to pass the DAF's advising powers along to an unlimited number of generations, while other host charities limit the number of people, or generations, that can have the chance to advise their family's DAF. This can be an important difference among the charities that house DAFs.

In most umbrella charities, donors can recommend an asset allocation for their DAF's investments. Investment options that are offered inside DAFs are usually unique to the umbrella charity selected by the board or staff of the host charity. Typically, investments are a conservative mix of equities and fixed income products. Some umbrella charities offer more flexible investments, and this can be an attraction for some donors or their advisors.

What is so attractive about these giving vehicles? The donor does little to no administrative work in the grant making process—but still gets to enjoy the pleasure of being a philanthropist. Once the donor makes a grant recommendation, now often online, the charity liquidates funds, sends the grant checks, checks to see if the grant check has cleared, records the grant for the donor's statement, watches investment performance, and maintains necessary documentation for the grant.

The umbrella charity maintains all the donor's records and transaction history, and sends the donor quarterly statements. Additionally, the umbrella charity prepares the 990 tax filing to the IRS and manages an annual audit.

HISTORY

DAFs as we know them today were born in the aftermath of the Tax Reform Act (TRA) of 1969. The precursor vehicles to DAFs were being established at a handful of community foundations since early in the twentieth century—most notably in Cleveland. However, it was not until the early 1970s that DAFs began to spread more widely and took on the form generally utilized today.

The catalyst was the TRA, which imposed significant new constraints, reporting requirements, taxes, and other "penalties" designed to curb the perceived abuses of many private foundations. Many believe that the severity of the remedy in 1969 far outweighed whatever abuses might have existed.

However inappropriate or justified, the TRA significantly changed the competitive landscape between public charities and private foundations. It was in this context that a little noticed section of the 507 Regulations was added to provide safe-harbor guidelines for those donors who wanted to terminate their private foundations and create a similar vehicle within an existing public charity.

Key volunteer leaders, including the late Norman A. Sugarman, Esq., in the community foundation world and the Jewish Federation system, recognized the great opportunity that had been created. In the early 1970s, fortified by a series of letter rulings, the first broadly adopted "model guidelines" for the operation of DAFs were published, and DAFs spread widely among community and Jewish Federation foundations. Through the late 1980s, community and Jewish Federation foundations held a virtual monopoly on these vehicles, which were generally structured to comply with the safe harbor provisions of the 507 Regulations.

In 1991, Fidelity created the Charitable Gift Fund, now by far the largest single DAF program in the country. Fidelity, and the other trust/financial services companies that followed suit, changed the DAF landscape forever. There were, and still are, many in the charitable community who resent the proliferation of "commercial" DAF programs or national donor-advised programs. Many in the charitable arena have come to understand that the nature of DAFs is forever changed, and that no one type of charity can lay ownership to this giving vehicle.

In the 15 years since Fidelity's Charitable Gift Fund opened its doors, the spotlight has been on DAF regulations in Washington, D.C. This is partially in response to criticism from the traditional sponsors of DAFs; both an aborted attempt by the Clinton administration to create DAF legislation, and the recent Senator Grassley efforts to address DAFs in the Senate; and increased scrutiny from the IRS. In the early 2000s, a consortium of national DAFs (NDAFs) has worked together to create common guidelines. Interestingly, while these guidelines are quite similar in most aspects to those utilized by community and Jewish Federation foundations, they make no reference to the 507 Regulations.

In parallel, the community foundation world, fostered by the Council on Foundations, has worked at self-monitoring its DAF practices among its many members who offer them. There are now in excess of 1,000 community foundations, with different governing boards and CEOs. Each one can offer different DAF policies and practices and oversee all such elements inside its own organizations.

DAF Growth

DAF growth is difficult to fully document. For years, charities housing DAFs did not separate out, or document, their DAF gifts from other types of contributions to their charities. Since there are many different kinds of charities that can be an umbrella charity, and there are no common DAF reporting requirements to the federal government, there were no common statistics that existed among those charities.

However, starting in 1999, as DAF popularity soared, aggregate DAF data started to become more available. The data captured in the charts shown includes DAF data from the national programs, community foundations, and Jewish Federation foundations, where a majority of the DAFs are housed.

As Exhibits 2.4 and 2.5 illustrate, in the seven years represented in National Philanthropic Trust data, the number of DAFs grew by 150 percent, and

EXHIBIT 2.4   GROWTH IN DONOR ADVISED FUNDS:
ASSETS UNDER MANAGEMENT

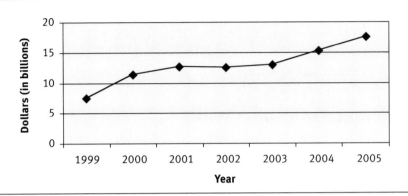

Source: National Philanthropic Trust.

assets have tripled. The *Chronicle of Philanthropy* has noted that DAFs are the fastest growing form of philanthropy, outpacing both CRTs and private foundations.

Awareness of DAFs continues to increase among donors and their advisors, as the umbrella charities who manage the DAFs often advertise or market in more traditional financial services magazines and newspapers. In addition to community-based organizations like community foundations and Jewish

EXHIBIT 2.5   GROWTH IN DONOR ADVISED FUNDS:
ACCOUNTS

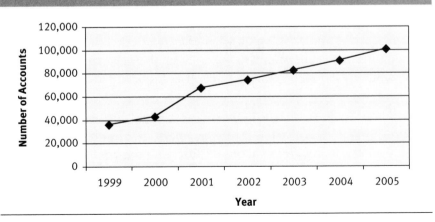

Source: National Philanthropic Trust.

Federations, DAFs have attracted the attention of large financial service companies, many of whom view DAF programs as essential offerings, or else they might lose those assets to other outside competitors who do offer DAF services.

In short, it has become a competitive and crowded marketplace for DAFs. As a result, technology, fees, and flexibility are important, and donors have many choices to make regarding where to place their charitable funds.

WHO USES DAFS AND WHY?

DAFs are used by the extremely wealthy and moderately wealthy, to help them make grants and support causes important to them.

The Very Wealthy

Very high net worth donors will often use a DAF to complement their family's private foundation, to give their children their own philanthropic vehicles apart from a private foundation or even to hide their identity to grantees. For some, the DAF might be their main and only philanthropic vehicle.

However, it appears to be more common among very high net worth individuals to have multiple grant-making vehicles within and among the adult generations of their family. Families house their multiple DAFs in a variety of umbrella charities to serve different purposes. Some umbrella charities might be religious in focus, others regional, and perhaps some may serve as teaching vehicles to future generations. They can match their DAF to their grant-making goals, or to the umbrella charity's flexibility in certain policies, like a spending rule.

Some families argue too much when they try to do joint philanthropy among or between generations, so they split up their charitable giving into smaller chunks, and each family member uses his or her own DAF for that purpose.

In contrast to 20 years ago, donors of great wealth are diversifying their philanthropy vehicles, just as they do their personal wealth. This gives the donor more flexibility, greater access to different program information and investments, and can provide anonymity, if desired.

The Moderately Wealthy

Moderately wealthy individuals use DAFs because they are easy to use, provide Web service for grant making, and do all the paperwork and tax filings.

Perhaps most importantly, DAFs give those donors the very accurate notion that they have a formal, named philanthropic vehicle—akin to a private foundation—from which they give back to their communities.

Donors who can part with $10,000, $25,000, or $100,000 are capable of making, and do make, significant gifts to charities; and they are using DAFs to formalize their giving. Private foundations would not be available to them, but DAFs are. DAFs give those donors a strong sense of empowerment that only used to be accessible to the very wealthy and their private foundations.

Giving Circles

Some donors use DAFs for giving circles, where many donors give to a single DAF in support of a cause that collectively interests them as a group. Those giving circles can be enlightening for donors who are only marginally involved in giving but excited that their dollars can be joined with others. In many communities, women or groups of younger professionals have been highly effective in pooling their funds in a single DAF for a common cause. Often, they spend time educating the group with nonprofit presentations and engaging in formal discussions before voting to decide which specific charities might get their collective funds.

In Conclusion

One of the most dramatic changes affecting DAFs in the last 15 years is the Internet and computers. By automating much of the work, technology has played a huge role in making DAFs available beyond the very wealthy, to the upper middle class. It is possible that with even more sophisticated technology—a very likely prospect, given what we know about our ever changing world—DAFs will reach even more citizens who wish to embrace the ease of this kind of organized philanthropy.

Also among the longer-term issues with DAFs are regulatory matters. The charities that sponsor DAFs, and the rules they employ on donor control and benefit, are coming under increasing scrutiny. In early August 2006, Congress passed new legislation on a number of charitable issues, one of which were new and long-awaited DAF regulations. Congress demonstrated its concern that donors or their families should not get personal benefit of any kind from their DAFs. The parent charities who manage the DAFs will have to make explicit that the donor does not have control, nor can benefit in any manner. Much more detail on the new legislation can be viewed on a variety of Web sites, including the Independent Sector (www.indepedentsector.org).

DAFs are so commonly used by such a variety of charities that new regulations make it clearer to the parent charities what is and is not allowed. Further, more clarifying legislation might follow beyond the August 2006 bill.

For donors, this is good news. Clarity on rules and regulations should translate into clear policies. For that reason, and for the ease of administration, DAF assets will continue to grow at a rapid pace. Charities will both self-police and look to the government to help guide what a donor can and cannot do within a DAF.

DAFs provide donors with an extremely flexible and easy giving vehicle. Donors can have as little as $10,000, or as much as $100 million, in their DAFs. They can house them in one or many charities and use them alone or with children or even friends. They are popular because they can be many things to many people and are likely to be around for a very, very long time.

New Philanthropy Has Arrived—Now What?

Maureen Baehr

What should big foundations do to be best positioned to address the societal issues on the horizon for the twenty-first century?

Providing definitive answers to this question is difficult, since every month brings another frame-shifting event. Bill Gates will quit Microsoft to lead his foundation full-time. Warren Buffett is investing much of his $40 billion fortune with the Bill and Melinda Gates Foundation. Google has decided to have a for-profit foundation. The Clinton Global Initiative just raised over $7 billion in pledges to change the world for the better. This includes at least $3 billion from Richard Branson over the next 10 years, to research and develop renewable energy initiatives.

Analysts[1] and pundits[2] are writing about the blurring of the lines between philanthropy, social entrepreneurship, cause-related marketing, and "doing well by doing good" corporate investment.

> To maintain relevance and value in this "new" philanthropy environment, foundations, big and small, old and new, will need to rethink their missions, core competencies, structures, and financial situations.

And there's no reason to believe it will settle down. The wealth transfer of trillions; the "giving while living" trend; the for-profit/nonprofit continuum, with all its permutations; and the Baby Boomer residual dream of changing the world for the better will continue to evolve new species of organizations.

The "flattening" of the world will open new possibilities for solving social problems. And every solution will bring an abundance of new problems to solve.

To maintain relevance and value in this "new" philanthropy environment, foundations, big and small, old and new, will need to rethink their missions, core competencies, structures, and financial situations. This essay presents six principles to help guide the process.

THE GATES PLUS BUFFETT EQUATION REALLY DOES CHANGE EVERYTHING

If the $1.5 billion that the Buffett investment is likely to yield per year[3] is added to the $1.3 billion in grants paid by the Bill and Melinda Gates Foundation, the *pro forma* Buffett plus Gates payout for 2005 would be more than the payouts of the next nine largest foundations (by 2005 assets) combined (see Exhibit 2.6).

Bill and Melinda Gates created the biggest foundation in the world, yet it was Warren Buffett's decision to invest in it that changed everything. By structuring his gift so Gates must spend all Buffett gives each year, he is

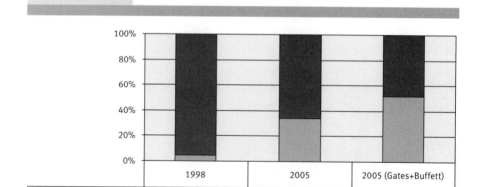

EXHIBIT 2.6	THE CHANGING MIX: GATES AND TOP 10 FOUNDATIONS		
	1998	2005	2005 (Gates+Buffett)
■ Next Nine Largest Foundations by Assets	$2,229,101,507	$2,659,100,301	$2,659,100,301
◻ Bill and Melinda Gates Foundation	$113,409,103	$1,355,279,478	$2,855,279,478

Source: Chronicle of Philanthropy Facts and Figures, March 2006, http://philanthropy-.com/stats.

hyperpowering Gates's grant making, forcing the solutions to a higher level and deeper impact.

PRINCIPLE #1: FIND INVESTORS

Example: Rockefeller Foundation Establishes New Philanthropy Partnership with Gates

In April 2006, Judith Rodin, president of the Rockefeller Foundation, wrote a letter outlining how she sees the need to transform the organization she leads.

> The mission of the Rockefeller Foundation, set out by John D. Rockefeller, Sr., to "promote the well-being" of humanity, has guided the work of the Foundation since it was formed in 1913. This mission has not changed, nor has our steadfast commitment to achieving it by addressing the root causes of some of the world's largest problems. Our values, likewise, endure. But the world in which the Foundation operates has changed considerably, and the ways in which the Foundation must operate have been transformed.[4]

On September 12, 2006, Rodin, and Bill and Melinda Gates, announced:

> Today, we are announcing that the Bill and Melinda Gates Foundation and the Rockefeller Foundation will form an alliance to spur a "Green Revolution" in Africa. We expect it to dramatically increase the productivity of small farms, moving tens of millions of people out of extreme poverty and significantly reducing hunger. We are committing an initial total of $150 million to this effort over five years.

The Alliance for a Green Revolution is a strategic act of philanthropy. It brings together the experience and expertise of the Rockefeller Foundation with the commitment and vision of the Gates Foundation.[5]

Rockefeller will contribute $50 million and Gates will contribute $100 million over a five year period.[6] The Alliance for a Green Revolution in Africa (AGRA) will be a public charity. There is a supporting organization, which will administer several programs, not all of which will be funded by the $150 million.[7] AGRA's board members are from Gates and Rockefeller; the senior staff officers, at least for the start, will be Rockefeller staff with agricultural expertise.[8]

This is much more than a joint grant to an existing nonprofit; it is a complex and creative deal that forms a framework for additional investors and investments, both for profit and nonprofit. Ten thousand agro-dealers will receive training and credit, to allow them to start businesses to distribute seeds. Sixty African seed companies will receive business management training and investment. Two hundred new crop varieties are expected to be developed and commercialized within the next five years.[9]

PRINCIPLE #2: DON'T PRETEND THAT NOTHING HAS CHANGED

Example: Pew Foundation Switches from Private Foundation to Public Charity

The Pew Foundations of Philadelphia began transformation work in 2001. President Rebecca Rimel was charged by the board to leave no stone unturned in determining if the foundations were organized effectively to deliver its mission. Pew decided to switch from a private foundation to a public charity because:

> It provides us more administrative flexibility and efficiency—important as we improve our ability to fulfill our programmatic and institutional objectives. It also enables us to raise funds from new sources for charitable initiatives, just as universities, think tanks, and other nonprofits do. And we will be able to partner with a wide range of donors to create joint ventures and pooled funds that can magnify the impact of what individuals or organizations might accomplish on their own.[10]

Pew consolidated several foundations, got a new IRS ruling, reorganized to take advantage of economies of scale, and now leverages its endowment income with grants from other foundations and contributions from the public.

PRINCIPLE #3: RE-FORM YOUR STRUCTURE TO BEST ACCOMPLISH YOUR MISSION IN THE NEW PHILANTHROPY ENVIRONMENT

Example: Atlantic Philanthropies Will Spend down Its Entire *Corpus* and Go Out of Existence by 2020

In 2002, Chuck Feeney, the founder of Atlantic Philanthropies (assets over $4 billion), decided to put his foundation out of business. He believes that new wealth is being generated all the time, and upcoming billionaires will create new foundations to work at solving the societal problems of the future. Knowing that its legacy is not open-ended invigorates the foundation; it will have its final evaluation in less than 15 years.

> The other big foundations, they have an unlimited life. They're perpetual organisations. If you decide to limit your life, it concentrates the mind wonderfully. Somebody will be able to make a judgment on this organization within our lifetime as individuals. That really causes you to ask very tough questions. What will we do? How will we do it? How will be sure that it will have an impact? It's a very different approach to philanthropy.[11]

There are certainly many societal issues that require decades of concerted attention, some that are likely to be with us forever. But working on an issue over decades is not the same as being too focused on self-perpetuation. If protecting the *corpus* becomes more important than funding the mission, a foundation can become stagnant.

In the world of new philanthropy, foundations that are good at demonstrating results and adopting an investor-friendly structure are likely to attract enough funds, not only to stay in business, but to achieve more significant and lasting mission outcomes.

PRINCIPLE #4: DON'T PROTECT "IN PERPETUITY" AT THE EXPENSE OF WORLD-CHANGING ACTION NOW

Example: David and Lucile Packard Foundation Tops 2005 Program-Related Investment Spending

In 2005, the David and Lucile Packard Foundation made over $26 million in program-related investments (PRIs), the largest amount by a foundation. PRIs are generally loans and are made in addition to grant funds. They can be used to leverage grants, to fund start-up costs for social ventures that are expected to return profit on the investment, or to provide the grantee with a credit history, for future commercial purposes.[12] Whereas grants can be given only to nonprofits, PRIs can also go to for-profit organizations, if they advance an exempt purpose, like building affordable housing.[13]

More foundations are shifting their asset allocation mix toward more risky alternative investments—hedge funds, venture capital, and private equity—in order to maximize return to the *corpus*.[14] But these asset categories rarely have any connection to the foundation's mission. As foundation risk tolerance increases, it follows that more of the assets can be put to work on mission-related investment.

PRINCIPLE #5: PUT YOUR ENDOWMENT TO WORK TO SERVE YOUR MISSION

Bill Shore, the founder of Share Our Strength, a nonprofit dedicated to ending child hunger in America, compares pursuing a great and difficult goal to building a cathedral, in the following five ways:

1. Cathedral builders *worked backward,* from a grand vision and a detailed blueprint that, if followed, would produce the desired outcome.
2. Cathedral building requires the *sharing of strength.*
3. The great cathedrals are built, literally, upon the *foundations of earlier efforts.*
4. Cathedrals were sustained and maintained because they actually *generated their own wealth and support.*
5. Cathedrals, through their stained-glass panels, statues, and paintings, were intentionally designed to convey *stories and values to people.*[15]

There are (at least) two categories of problems that require new cathedral building for the twenty-first century. Though not intractable, these problem categories will not yield to short-term solution funding alone. And, if not addressed and managed, they will thwart and ultimately undo many of the grand initiatives already under way.

The first problem category is about lowering barriers to *solution scale-up.* At the Clinton Global Initiative Conference in September 2006, Julie Gerberding, head of the Centers for Disease Control, explained one aspect of the issue, saying:

> We need a knowledge distribution system. We need to somehow be able to take the kinds of technology that made the world flat, or the connectivity that made the world flat, and use them in innovative ways in the areas that aren't flat yet. That may be people. That may be a cell phone in the hands of a health aide in the rural area that can reach back to the county and get information, or reach back to the tertiary care center and get a consult. We have such extraordinary innovation, but we aren't innovative about using it the poorest areas of the world, or the poorest countries. So if we could figure out how to redistribute our knowledge, and it is more than

one direction, we learn as much as we contribute. I really think we could accelerate the solution to the problems, but fundamentally we're all saying the same thing. We know what to do, but we can't develop the systems to deliver on that in the places that need it the most.[16]

If we don't solve the problem of scale-up in global health, education, and poverty eradication, the work that foundations are doing today will not sustain. There are too many successful proof-of-concept projects that do not translate into large scale. The cathedral needed here will span the world. It will figure out how to respect the wisdom of the community while sharing and teaching global best practice.

The second problem category is *emerging problems,* identified and inevitable, that we recognize today from the demographics of the globe, but have not yet addressed adequately because other problems are more visible and urgent. An example is the issue of aging and chronic disease in the less developed world.

By 2020, there will be more people over 65 in the developing world than children under five. Chronic conditions such as heart disease and diabetes, which are already more prevalent causes of disability and death than are communicable diseases in all regions except Africa, will become even more widespread. As this trend unfolds, the lifetime costs of treating these ailments will far outpace the costs of managing communicable diseases.[17]

The cathedral needed here will span both geography and time. It is a multi-generational problem, and requires interventions on prevention as well as treatment.

PRINCIPLE #6: BUILD NEW CATHEDRALS

■ NOTES

1. http://www.onphilanthropy.com/site/News2?page=NewsArticle&id=6731.
2. Ibid., 6735.
3. http://www.berkshirehathaway.com/donate/bmgfltr.pdf.
4. Judith Rodin, "Responding to the Challenges of the 21st Century," http://-philanthropy.com/premium/articles/v18/i23/21st_century_short_version.pdf.
5. Remarks of Judith Rodin, September 12, 2006. http://www.rockfound.-org/Library/rodin_agra_points.pdf.
6. http://www.rockfound.org/Library/agra1.pdf.

7. http://www.rockfound.org/library/agra_glossary1.pdf.

8. http://www.rockfound.org/library/agra_officers1.pdf.

9. http://www.rockfound.org/library/agra_glossary1.pdf.

10. Rebecca W. Rimmel, "President's Message 2004: Transformation," February 2004. http://pewtrust.com/pubs/pubs_item.cfm?content_item_id=2102&-content_type_id=17&page=p2.

11. http://www.atlanticphilanthropies.org/news/news/john_healy_profile.

12. http://www.packard.org/assets/files/capacity%20building%20and%20-phil/program%20related%20investments/pri_history_and_successes.pdf.

13. http://www.nhi.org/online/issues/116/fundraising.html.

14. http://philanthropy.com/premium/articles/v18/i16/16b00101.htm.

15. Bill Shore, *The Cathedral Within* (Random House: 1999), 36.

16. http://www.clintonglobalinitiative.org/NETCOMMUNITY/Document.-Doc?&id=74 p. 27.

17. Susan Raymond, "Foreign Assistance in an Aging World," *Foreign Affairs,* March/April 2003. http://www.foreignaffairs.org/20030301faessay-10341/susan-raymond/foreign-assistance-in-an-aging-world.html.

Work for a Giving: Anticipating the Future of Corporate Employee Involvement Programs

TAMARA BACKER

> While profits are required for business just as eating is required for living, profit is not the purpose of business any more than eating is the purpose of life. . . . Who, with a palpable heartbeat and minimal sensibilities, will go to the mat for the right of somebody to earn a profit for its own sake? If no greater purpose can be discerned or justified, business cannot morally justify its existence.
>
> —Theodore Levitt

While everyone may not agree that there is a purpose beyond profit in business, profit is becoming, and will continue to be, dependent upon business strategies that reflect a greater good. As a projected shortage of skilled labor grows closer, and corporations place greater emphasis on employee recruitment and retention, the expectations of an incoming workforce will drive companies to change the focus and structure of their employee-community involvement programs. Initiatives such as volunteerism, matching gifts, and employee giving campaigns—which are typically a function of community relations within a corporation—will migrate to the human resources domain. Consequently, nonprofits will be forced to adjust the way they market themselves to the corporate world.

> Employee involvement programs have been shown to increase employee morale, improve recruitment and retention, build employee skills, and enhance corporate reputation.

RESPONDING TO A CHANGING WORKFORCE

Recruitment and retention of a skilled workforce will become a significant priority for companies in the near future. While a projected dip in the workforce, occurring in the next few years, is disputed by many for a variety of reasons, other factors, such as a decline in foreign-born talent and the prevalence of schools that don't meet global standards, point to a significant skills gap. In addition, it is important to note that 80 percent of employment is now in industries subject to structural change, which means that once an individual moves out of a job, that job is lost permanently (this is in contrast to cyclical change industries, where lost jobs are eventually replaced).[1] Under such conditions, companies increase reliance on part-time and contract workers, a population which is often difficult to reach and motivate.

As companies prepare for a competitive climate, to attract the most qualified employees—both full-time and part-time—an emphasis on staff development, training, and providing appealing benefits packages will be necessary. More than ever, companies will be required to respond to the needs, preferences, and priorities of the population they seek to recruit and retain.

One relevant priority of today's workforce is its involvement in the community (see Exhibit 2.7). The employed are more apt to get involved in their communities than their unemployed counterparts, and in particular, part-time workers have the highest rate of volunteerism.[2]

In addition, the educational system has set the precedent for community involvement for the young people now entering the workforce. This population is the first to grow up with mandatory community service in school. Beginning in the 1970s, educators began embracing the concept of "service learning," and by the 1990s, a variety of initiatives helped promote the practice within schools.

In 1999 the National Center for Education Statistics conducted the first, national-level study of service learning in America's K–12 public schools.

EXHIBIT 2.7   VOLUNTEERS BY EMPLOYMENT STATUS

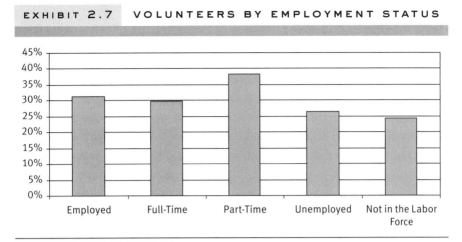

Source: U.S. Bureau of Labor Statistics.

The study found that roughly one-third of schools had incorporated service learning to some extent, generally as an integrated component of the curriculum.[3] Institutions of higher education are also increasingly emphasizing the importance of community commitment in the business world. A growing number of business schools require one or more courses in ethics, corporate responsibility, or business and society, with the higher-ranked schools offering more variety and opportunities to their students.[4]

The prevalence of community involvement within primary and secondary schooling and higher education is leading to a growing expectation that the workplace will be the next institution to cultivate young adults' positive role in the community. In fact, studies are already showing that a company's commitment to society can play a key role in attracting employees. A study conducted by the Stanford Graduate School of Business found that more than 97 percent of MBA graduates were willing to sacrifice an average 14 percent of their expected income to work for a company reputed to be socially responsible and ethical.[5]

As companies seek to be more competitive in their recruitment and retention efforts, employee involvement programs that support employees' desires to play an active role in the community will become increasingly important. This is particularly true for part-time workers. This in-demand population, which has a propensity to be involved in the community, cannot be offered competitive benefits packages, and thus must be reached through alternative incentives.

BENEFITS OF EMPLOYEE INVOLVEMENT PROGRAMS

Employee involvement programs typically include organized volunteerism, matching gifts, and employee giving campaigns, and can vary widely from company to company. Employee involvement programs have been shown to increase employee morale, improve recruitment and retention, build employee skills, and enhance corporate reputation. Aware of these benefits, 77 percent of U.S. companies recently surveyed said employee involvement is a high priority or a growing concern and/or interest for their company.[6]

There are, in fact, indications that investing in employee involvement programs pays off for companies. For example, AngelPoints, a volunteer management software provider, analyzed the financial performance of its clients against the Dow Jones Industrial Average and the S&P 500. Using the average adjusted share price for its publicly traded clients, from 1994 through 2006, the AngelPoints Index (APIX) typically outperformed both the Dow Jones and the S&P 500 (see Exhibit 2.8).

Causality of such results is unknown. Does community commitment lead to profitability, or do profitable companies merely have more to invest in

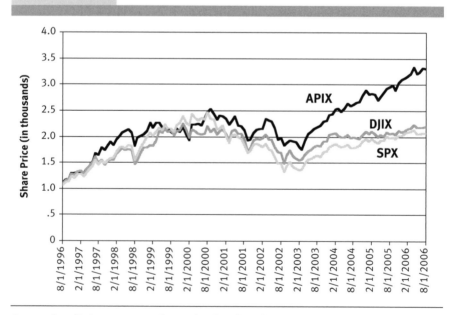

EXHIBIT 2.8   ALTERNATIVE STOCK INDICES PERFORMANCE 8/96–7/06

Source: AngelPoints company share price data from finance.yahoo.com.

such programs? Or, are there other variables altogether that impact both profitability and community involvement? This study suggests that a correlation between employee community involvement, and business success, does indeed exist. According to AngelPoints Chief Executive Officer Andrew Mercy, improvements to brand, corporate culture, and the employee skills base are clear benefits of community involvement. However, maximum gains are not realized and returns on social investments are not as clearly understood today as they will be in the future, when an effective social investment management infrastructure exists. AngelPoints and other companies like it are seeking to build that infrastructure.[7] With the growing realization that there is a return on investment from employee involvement programs, and the development of systems that track and evaluate such gains, come fundamental changes to the way such programs are focused and structured.

TRENDS IN EMPLOYEE INVOLVEMENT PROGRAMS

Program Focus

Given that many companies utilize employee involvement programs as a means of securing a satisfied current and prospective workforce, supporting employees' priorities and preferences is critical. In an effort to do this, both the focus and geographic scope of such programs will expand.

Studies have shown that one of the greatest success factors for employee giving campaigns is allowing donors to choose where their money goes.[8] The programs, which seek to raise individual donations from employees to create cumulative size and leverage when granted back to the community, have seen declines in participation rates, as well as in the amounts raised over the last several years. As a result, companies that traditionally managed their programs through the United Way have expanded their campaigns to include additional charities. Alternative funds that generally allow for more donor choice, transparency, and responsiveness to local needs have increased in popularity.[9]

Supporting individual choice is also an important factor in matching gifts programs, where companies demonstrate their commitment to employees by supplementing donations made to individuals' charities of choice. While these programs often match company funds to a limited selection of groups, such as arts and cultural organizations, or employees' *alma maters,* a growing number of programs are expanding, and will continue to expand, to include eligibility to a wider range of nonprofits.

Increased connectivity, spurred by technology, is also creating changes in employee giving. People are more connected to the world around them than ever before and are more aware of issues and problems, both at home and abroad. With a rising awareness of global issues comes the desire to help those in need. Employee involvement programs will require the flexibility to respond to employees' desires to address such needs.

In addition to broadening the focus of employee involvement programs, to support employees in the areas that matter to them most, technology will cause companies to redefine their geographic focus, in order to address the needs of an increasingly mobile workforce. Recently, while training an employee committee as part of a large company's workplace giving campaign, there was a heated debate on the geographic eligibility of certain nonprofits. While some committee members argued that the program should stay within the confines of the community in which the company's offices are head-quartered, others noted that technology now allows employees to work from home, often far from the headquarters, and so the definition of "community" should likewise be more broadly interpreted. As a result of emerging technologies, companies will need to rethink the boundaries of "community."

Program Implementation

Just as the focus and geographic scope of employee involvement programs will change, so too will the way in which they are delivered. Companies will increasingly involve employees, not just in defining their programs' focus, but also in their core operations and decision making.

Consider that one of the key objectives companies hope to achieve, through their employee involvement programs, is the development of business skills; the workday is limited, and building key skills through community involve-ment activities is an effective way to maximize time and resources. Volun-teerism, in particular, is an area in which the promotion of skill-building activities is on the rise. More and more companies are promoting activities that build core competencies, such as deploying accountants to help non-profits with their finances, as opposed to having the accountants plant trees.

If companies narrow their programs too heavily, they may find that employees will resist; perhaps accountants would prefer to take a break from accounting, and instead roll up their sleeves and plant trees.

Companies will need to carefully balance their desire to satisfy employees with the desire to build skills. One way in which this can be accomplished is to use activities such as tree planting as a training ground, for instilling professional and management skills such as leadership, decision making, problem solving, and team building. For example, instead of simply sending employees into a park to pick up litter, an organized structure—in which employee leaders are assigned to teams, comprised of members from a variety of functions within the company—will ensure that individuals are gaining valuable planning skills and a sense of responsibility while cross-functional relationships are being forged.

Employee giving campaigns will also involve employees in a more sophisticated way, to ensure that they are helping to produce a more skilled workforce. Such campaigns will increasingly utilize employee committees that are trained in proposal review and grant making. In the process, committee chairs will learn important leadership and presentation skills as they seek to motivate and lead the team. Committee members will share a sense of responsibility, and accountability, as they struggle to assess nonprofit grant proposals, and make funding recommendations. The entire committee will learn important team-building and decision-making skills, as they make difficult funding decisions as a group.

Program Awareness

One significant trend that cuts across all types of employee community involvement programs is the trend toward increased communication, both internal and external. In order to achieve the business objectives set forth—whether they are improved retention and recruitment, or building skills among employees—effective communication is increasingly critical.

First, information must be readily accessible across a company's employee base, in order to maintain and ideally raise participation rates. This entails setting up systems to reach all eligible employees with details regarding various programs, and allowing sign-up for potential participants to be as painless as possible. Software that alerts employees of relevant community involvement activities, tracks their participation, and reports back on company-wide results already exists, and will grow in popularity among companies. Utilizing these software programs will also make it easier to offer community involvement opportunities to employees overseas, thus expanding the definition of community even further.

As employers provide employees with the tools to access myriad involvement opportunities at the click of a button, nonprofit organizations will be forced to invest in their online presence, to differentiate themselves from their competition in an increasingly crowded, nonprofit landscape.

Interactivity and the ability to make personal connections will be critical for these organizations.

Corporate communication related to employee involvement, to external parties via Web sites, advertisements, and press releases—as well as the number of CEOs who report on their philanthropic, community, and volunteer activities in letters to shareholders—is becoming more prevalent. An increasing number of companies are also reporting about community involvement in their annual reports, and/or producing completely separate community or citizenship reports. Such communication is not only important for the enhancement of a company's reputation with the general public, it promotes a sense of pride among current and retired employees and sends a positive message to prospective employees as well.

Program Ownership

As companies increasingly view employee involvement programs as a mechanism to increase employee morale, aid in recruitment and retention, and build skills within the workforce, the governance structure of these programs, and specifically the corporate departments in which they are housed, will shift.

Currently, employee involvement programs typically fall within the domain of community relations, and are aligned with the company's corporate contributions and/or foundation; both functions are often closely tied to a company's communication efforts. While philanthropy and community involvement programs share many of the same goals, the primary objectives of each are beginning to diverge.

Whereas the primary business objectives of employee involvement programs are increasingly human resources centered, corporate philanthropy is increasingly used as a tool to enhance a company's reputation, and promote brand awareness within the general public. To protect their reputations in a climate of heightened corporate scrutiny, companies are developing clearer giving policies and guidelines, and shying away from merely writing checks to the CEO's pet cause. To achieve greater visibility in the community, companies are narrowing their philanthropic focus to causes that align with their brand and business platform (e.g., a food company focusing on obesity issues). This leads to a trend of companies partnering with a smaller number of larger, strategically aligned organizations, allowing for clearly defined, high-profile, multifaceted campaigns that integrate cause marketing and other tools for promoting widespread awareness.

While collaboration between corporate philanthropy and employee involvement will be maintained, as corporate philanthropy programs become more strategically aligned with marketing objectives, they will increasingly become the responsibility of the marketing departments. At the same time, as employee involvement programs focus more on objectives such as retention, recruitment, and skill building, they will become a function of the human resources department.

This shift will cause nonprofits to change the way they must appeal to companies for funding. Based on size, there will be a bifurcation in the type of skills nonprofits need to develop to effectively compete for corporate support. As corporate philanthropy programs are more apt to be aligned with fewer high-profile organizations, the large, national nonprofits will need to hone their ability to garner widespread visibility through cause marketing and signature corporate initiatives. As employee involvement programs seek to support the talent and interests of the workforce, smaller organizations will cater their corporate outreach strategies toward the human resources domain, developing and highlighting their unique capabilities to engage and build skills among employees.

■ NOTES

1. E. L. Groshen and S. Potter, "Has Structured Change Contributed to a Jobless Recovery?" *Current Issues in Economics and Finance,* Federal Reserve Bank of New York, August 2003: 9:8, 1–8.

2. Bureau of Labor Statistics, "Volunteering in the United States," December 2005.

3. National Center for Education Statistics, "Service Learning and Community Service in K–12 Public Schools," September 1999.

4. Aspen Institute, "Beyond Grey Pinstripes 2005: Preparing MBAs for Social and Environmental Stewardship."

5. Stanford Graduate School of Business, "MBA Graduates Want to Work for Caring and Ethical Employers," January 2004.

6. The Consulting Network, "Practices in Corporate Employee Involvement Programs," a survey of 100 U.S. companies representing more than five million employees, December 2002.

7. Personal communication, August 2006.

8. National Committee for Responsive Philanthropy, "Giving at Work," 2003.

9. The Consulting Network, "Practices in Corporate Employee Involvement Programs," December 2002. The percentage of companies that have broadened their campaigns to include nonprofit organizations, in addition to United Way–affiliated charities, increased from 30 to 40 percent between 1997 and 2002.

Planned Giving: Risks and Rewards in a Competitive Marketplace

MARY BETH MARTIN, ESQ.

The world of planned giving has changed dramatically in recent years, due to the explosive growth of nonprofits, the heightened awareness of donors of the various gifting opportunities available to them, and the maturation of the planned giving officer into a highly specialized and technically proficient professional. The National Committee on Planned Giving reports that in the year 2000 there were more than 110 planned giving councils, comprised of 12,000 individuals, located throughout the country (see Exhibit 2.9). Two-thirds of council members were employees of nonprofits. This tremendous increase in councils—up from only 13 in 1986— illustrates the fact that more nonprofits are entering the planned giving marketplace, and hiring staff with the express task of seeking and securing bequests and life income gifts. Heavily influencing this investment in planned giving is the specter of the much-anticipated "transfer of wealth," which is predicted to deliver $6 trillion, by way of bequests, into the coffers of nonprofits by the year 2052.[1]

The rising interest among nonprofits in obtaining planned gifts, combined with the increase in oversight and regulation, has placed many in a precarious position. In their eagerness to please their donors and ensure a future stream of revenue, it is not uncommon to find organizations offering planned gift arrangements, without a full understanding of the consequences of the gifts to the donors and to the organization.

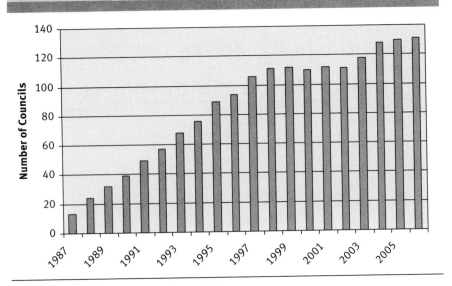

Source: National Committee on Planned Giving.

The expansion of the planned giving marketplace, and the corresponding increase in competitive marketing, has led to an increase in oversight and regulation by state and federal authorities. The Philanthropy Protection Act of 1996 is merely one in a series of protective measures, implemented by governing authorities, to ensure that individuals are fully aware of the consequences of making certain forms of irrevocable life income gifts.

The proliferation of state regulations, relating to the issuance of charitable gift annuities in particular, has had a tremendous impact on the "business" of planned giving. Specifically, the need to understand and comply with state requirements that apply to gift annuities has increased the work of planned giving officers and increased the burden on smaller nonprofits seeking to compete for this very popular form of gift. This comes at a time when educated donors and board members are calling on their favorite nonprofits to offer more planned giving options.

The rising interest among nonprofits in obtaining planned gifts, combined with the increase in oversight and regulation, has placed many in a precarious position. In their eagerness to please their donors and ensure a future stream of revenue, it is not uncommon to find organizations offering planned gift arrangements, without a full understanding of the consequences of the gifts to the donors and to the organization.

This great interest in planned giving is understandable. With charitable organizations receiving nearly $20 billion from bequest income in 2004, even the potential repeal of the estate tax does little to deter nonprofits from investigating the potential benefits that may be obtained from marketing bequests or life income gifts.[2] A July 2004 Congressional Budget Office report predicted that a repeal of the estate tax would decrease charitable bequests by as much as 28 percent. Given the nearly $20 billion passing to nonprofits by way of bequests in 2004, that still leaves a significant pool of bequest income available, to those organizations willing to make the investment in planned-giving marketing and outreach.

THE DRIVING FORCES

With a multitude of factors driving nonprofits into the planned giving marketplace, there are three common situations that push an organization to enter into an irrevocable planned giving arrangement, without laying the proper foundation.

1. *Donor Direction.* Bequests and life income gifts, such as charitable gift annuities and charitable remainder trusts, offer many donors the opportunity to make a larger, more significant gift than would be possible utilizing current, disposable income. The combination of life income and a charitable income tax deduction provides additional benefits that make a major gift feasible, which otherwise may have been out of reach. Given the attractiveness of this form of giving, donors who have established a life income gift (often a charitable gift annuity) at one nonprofit may seek to replicate the experience at another favorite charity. The second nonprofit may not yet offer this form of giving, but may be encouraged to do so by the donor.

2. *Board Pressure.* Board members who have personal experience in establishing a planned gift at one of their own favorite charities, fearful of losing a potential revenue stream, may encourage the nonprofit they oversee to begin offering planned gifts as well.

3. *Lack of Awareness.* Nonprofit staff, unaware of the complexities surrounding planned giving vehicles, may launch a program focused on life income gifts just to be competitive with other nonprofits.

In addition to the obvious concerns of entering into life income arrangements without a true understanding of the consequences, a nonprofit can also be trading current, major gift support for deferred income. This is true when the organization launches a planned giving program prior to developing a solid major gift effort. While planned gifts may offer security, and a guaranteed future stream of income, organizations that solicit prospects for the planned gift, without first exploring the possibility of a current major gift, may be the losers. In considering when to invest staff time and resources into planned giving, nonprofits should take into account the breadth and scope of their fundraising programs, the resources available to them, and their current financial needs.

While this may be particularly true for small organizations with limited staffing and resources, it is also true of larger nonprofits that have historically relied upon current, annual donations to support ongoing programs and operations. Cultivating and soliciting a major gift donor requires a significantly different set of activities than those supporting an annual fund. Only when an organization is prepared to make the investment in obtaining the staff and training necessary to launch a major gift program is a full, planned giving program on the horizon.

THE MAJOR GIFT/PLANNED GIFT CONNECTION

Planned giving programs are most successful when offered in combination with a solid major gift program. Planned gifts offer donors the opportunity to maximize their giving potential. While 97 percent of bequest donors and 91 percent of charitable remainder trust donors cite "a desire to support the charity" as an important factor in making their gift,[3] the benefits of life income and a charitable income tax deduction can be quite attractive. However, it may not benefit an organization to encourage a planned gift without first exploring the potential for an outright gift. Planned gift vehicles are valuable tools for a major gift officer. Too often, however, the pressure of offering planned gifts can lead a small organization to focus on them, at the expense of annual or major gift fundraising.

When considering a planned giving program, organizations should balance the need for current income, and the staff and resources available to obtain that current income, with the staff and resources needed to effectively market, close, and steward planned gifts. Included in this analysis should be the costs of retaining knowledgeable counsel and the possibility of utilizing an outside planned giving manager. Many smaller organizations do not have the luxury of specialized development staff. In some cases, the executive director may also serve as the chief fundraiser. It is unlikely that a cost/benefit analysis in these situations will result in the creation of a full planned giving program. The organization may, however, consider phasing in planned gifts while building a major gift program, and the most logical way to begin the planned giving program is by focusing on bequests.

A Phased-in Approach

Bequests remain the cornerstone of planned giving. Statistics show that 80 percent of planned gifts come in the form of bequests and revocable trusts.[4] Bequests are simple to market and generally do not require an extensive use of counsel. Organizations can use existing publications to promote the benefits of a charitable bequest. This marketing adds no additional cost, yet begins the cultivation process. As the organization grows in size and sophistication, the program can be expanded. Known bequest donors now become strong prospects for other forms of planned gifts, including charitable remainder trusts and charitable gift annuities.

The importance of marketing bequests cannot be overstated. With the vast array of nonprofits competing for the charitable dollar, the organization that does not actively promote bequests will be losing a potentially significant future revenue stream. Thirty-four percent of bequest donors cite marketing materials from the nonprofit organization as the first source of the idea; 11 percent cite a visit from the organization.[5] Organizations that are proactive in their outreach will reap the benefits for years to come.

A Cautionary Word

The benefits of bequests and life income gifts to nonprofits cannot be disputed. The ability to market and manage bequests and planned gifts can maximize a donor's giving potential and bring significantly greater revenue to the nonprofit. There is, however, a time and place to offer planned gifts. Understanding the financial needs of the organization, the state of the fundraising program, and the true costs and obligations of offering planned giving vehicles are vital considerations for every nonprofit.

▨ NOTES

1. John J. Havens and Paul G. Schervish, "Why the $41 Trillion Wealth Transfer is Still Valid: A Review of Challenges and Questions," *Journal of Gift Planning* (2003), 7(1):11–50.

2. The National Committee on Planned Giving, *Planned Giving in the United States 2000: A Survey of Donors* (Indianapolis, IN: NCPG, 2001).

3. Ibid.

4. Vince Fraumeni, "10 Reasons to Promote Bequests," *Planned Giving Mentor,* March 2004. https://www.pgtoday.com/pgmentor/articles/10_reasons_beqeusts.htm.

5. The National Committee on Planned Giving, *Planned Giving in the United States 2000: A Survey of Donors* (Indianapolis, IN: NCPG, 2001).

The Influence of Women Philanthropists

NORA CAMPBELL WOOD

There is a commonly held belief that women and men have different approaches to philanthropy. In this case, the "men are from Mars, women are from Venus" mentality may merely be a convenient assumption. Further examination reveals complexity behind the generalization. The existing literature on the subject must be taken with a grain of salt, as the little research that does exist contains opinions and statistics drawn from surveys, polls, and studies that have limited scope and reliability. Current research can be contradictory, and is dependent on whom you are asking and how they choose to respond at that moment. Because women are beginning to play a more substantial role in the philanthropic sector, however, an effort must be made to clarify and expand the existing research. As women play a larger and larger role, understanding the female perspective on giving will become critical to successful fundraising.

> It stretches credulity, however, to say that Melinda Gates wants to make a difference but Bill Gates does not. Generalizations about womens' motivations may, indeed, apply to women. But that does not mean that they do not apply to men.

What's Out There

GuideStar.org

In honor of Women's History Month, GuideStar.org looked at women's approach to philanthropy. They cited Trish Jackson, Education Vice President of the Council for the Advancement and Support of Education, who said, "Men like to be involved in the institutions they support, women demand it. . . . Men and women approach philanthropic decisions differently." On the other hand, GuideStar also cited Robert Sweeney, who believes that age, not gender, affects philanthropic behavior. He sees it as more of a generational issue.

> As corporate and entrepreneurial women come into prominence they tend to respond much more like men in their giving. People between the ages of 20 and 40 see themselves as much more empowered. They don't look at the artificial segmentation we [fundraisers] try to place on them—law benefactors or business benefactors. They're much more issue-oriented and integrated in their thinking. They tend to be interested in specific things: peace and justice issues, quality of life issues, technology.

GuideStar.org's work suggests that perhaps something other than gender affects a person's philanthropy.

Hard Statistics

An introductory caveat is important. *Hard* is a relative term. As noted above, most statistical analysis is on the basis of opinion surveys. Furthermore, in almost no case has this survey data been subjected to statistical tests of significance. As a result, we know what people think (or at least what they say they think), but not necessarily what they do, and there is no indication of the actual significance of differences between men and women.

That having been said, statistics on the subject support the idea that men and women may be more alike than the widespread attitude research suggests. In a 1996–1997 study, by the National Survey of Giving, Volunteering, and Participating (NSGVP), of Canadians aged 15 and older, it was found that 68 percent of women were more likely to donate to health organizations, compared with 63 percent of men (see Exhibit 2.10). Men were 21 percent more likely to give to philanthropic and voluntary organizations, compared with only 16 percent of women. Interestingly enough, a gap of

EXHIBIT 2.10   PERCENTAGE OF DONORS
SUPPORTING SELECTED TYPES
OF ORGANIZATIONS, BY GENDER

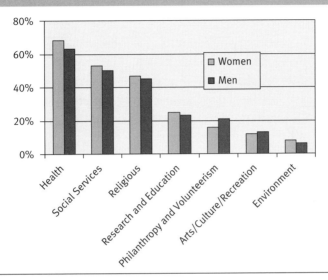

Source: National Survey of Giving, Volunteering, and Participating.

only five percentage points was the most significant difference between the types of organizations that men and women support. These are hardly compelling margins.

To confuse the issue, the University of Tennessee's Alliance of Women Philanthropists found that women give to education, science, and health-care, while men give to the arts and humanities. Further muddying the waters, a 2001 study by Elizabeth Greene found that women were more likely to help groups concerned with health, the homeless, and the elderly. Men were more likely to support the arts and political organizations. However, the National Foundation for Women Business Owners identified education as one of the top three causes supported by women business owners, followed by women-related groups and the arts. Yet in the previous surveys, men not women, supported the arts. Other causes include: health, religion, youth services, social and human services, local community services, politics, and the environment. Clearly, the answer to this question depends on whom you ask and who is doing the asking. The NSGVP also looked at the differences in the motivations for giving, between men and women. The top motivator for both men and women was "compassion towards people in need," with 95 percent of women and 92 percent of men saying it was their greatest motivator. Once again, these differences are not very significant. Women and men look more alike than different (see Exhibit 2.11).

... And Soft Observations

Frequently cited as explaining the purported differences in womens' philanthropy are "The Six Cs of Women's Giving." These "Six Cs" were originally conceived by Sondra C. Shaw-Hardy and Martha A. Taylor, in their book *Reinventing Fundraising: Realizing the Potential of Women's Philanthropy*. The "Six Cs" are an attempt to explain womens' motivations for giving. Shaw-Hardy and Taylor assert, based on conversations with women philanthropists, that these motivations are different from those of men. These motivations are to:

- *Change:* Women have a desire to make a difference rather than preserve status quo.

- *Create:* Women place value on their involvement in the creative process, for developing charitable solutions.

- *Connect:* Women want to establish a relationship with the organization that goes beyond the request and receipt of a donation.

- *Commit:* Women are committed to giving, traditionally expressed through volunteer work, and increasingly through financial support.

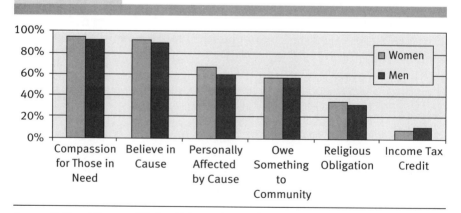

| EXHIBIT 2.11 | PERCENTAGE OF DONORS ENDORSING SPECIFIC MOTIVATIONS FOR GIVING, BY GENDER |

Source: National Survey of Giving, Volunteering, and Participating.

- *Collaborate:* Women understand the necessity and enjoy the process of working with others to solve problems.

- *Celebrate:* When women enjoy the process of giving and asking for charitable contributions, the process becomes more than an obligation or a responsibility.

The "Six Cs" beg the question, "are these motivations solely attributable to today's female donor, or are they more universal?"

In a similar example, a 2002 donor development brief, produced by the Council of Michigan Foundations, outlined some of the differences they saw between men's and women's approaches to philanthropy.

1. Women contribute to twice as many organizations as men do, but make smaller donations to each.

2. Women, unlike men, do not tend to base philanthropy on business connections or a desire for public recognition.

3. Women want to make a difference.

4. Women want to be involved with organizations to which they contribute money, while men cherish recognition and status.

5. Women do not have as many role models for philanthropy as do men.

6. Women donors ask more questions than men do.

7. Women, in contrast to men, may give less than they can because they do not want to appear wealthier than their friends.

8. Women value a sense of connection with the solicitor, while men stress that "who asks" is important.

9. Women seem to be more concerned about a solicitor's commitment to the cause and relationship to the prospective donor than are men (although more study needs to be done in this area).

We need to take a look at women as fundraisers and how we can capitalize on the immense human talent we have in our constituencies.[1] Once again, these differences could also be attributed to other factors. Much of the material on the subject of women and philanthropy has the potential to be explained in a different manner. Kay Sprinkel-Grace outlines 10 things you should know about the impact of women on philanthropy, in a 2000 article in *Contributions Magazine*. These 10 things were based on a UCLA study on women and philanthropy, conducted in the early 1990s. Grace states the following:

1. Women seek relationships.

2. Women have very personal motives and an ethic of personal commitment in their giving.

3. Women give from a greater sense of tradition.

4. Women want to see the continuation of philanthropy and are committed to an intergenerational continuum.

5. Women get involved before giving.

6. Women want to make a difference.

7. Women want recognition in their own right.

8. Women feel a responsibility to give.

9. There is a need to create a climate for women's giving.

10. We need to take a look at women as fundraisers and how we can capitalize on the immense human talent we have in our constituencies.

The implication, of course, is that men seek other things. It stretches credulity, however, to say that Melinda Gates wants to make a difference but Bill Gates does not, or that men do not seek tradition. Men, after all, also give to traditional charities, like Harvard's endowment! Generalizations about women's motivations may, indeed, apply to women. But that does not mean that they do not apply to men.

What Is Happening?

What is happening here? Many of the reasons listed in these studies and ways women differ from men in their philanthropy, may be explained by looking at the overarching, changing trends in philanthropic giving itself. For example, the often repeated notion that women seek relationships proves to be true of today's average donor. Recently, a large percentage of donors have become interested in forging stronger relationships with the organizations they support. People are interested in seeing what their investment is doing. Secondly, the idea that women want to make a difference is also true of the average donor today. Regardless of gender, more and more donors want to make an impact with their philanthropy, however small it may be. It is also plainly true that not just women are committed to an intergenerational continuum of giving. This has become an overall theme in philanthropy, resulting from the realization that at least $41 trillion will be passing from one generation to the next by 2044.

The Donor Education Initiative identified a similar trend over the past decade. The Donor Education Initiative is a project of New Visions PRD, a nonprofit formed to encourage effective philanthropy. The Initiative, co-sponsored by the Ford Foundation, William and Flora Hewlett Foundation, W.K. Kellogg Foundation, and David and Lucile Packard Foundation, is a research, convening, and brokering project to better understand and improve donor philanthropy. The Initiative found that donors want to be better informed, and more engaged in their giving, than ever before. The Initiative suggests that this trend will most likely continue. Donors will understand that, among other things, they can use philanthropy to make an impact in their communities, connect more deeply with the world, be more intentional, and have a plan for how they give. Once again, this seems to echo some of the ways that have been given for how women view philanthropy differently than men.

What Are the Implications?

There remains great ambiguity in the evidence available, to answer the question of the differences between how women and men view their philanthropy. However, I believe that in the coming years this question will be of increasing importance because women are playing an ever-expanding role in philanthropy. Women control more wealth than ever before. In 2000, women held 60 percent of the wealth in the United States, and that number is only expected to increase. Women make up more than half the population in America, women's wealth is increasing, and women's participation as philanthropists has expanded exponentially, even in the last 10 years. An analysis released by the Employment Policy Foundation, in 2004, found that the proportion of women working full time and earning more than $100,000 tripled between 1991 and 2001. In fact, every income bracket above $40,000 saw increases in the proportion of women working, and at rates of increase that were significantly higher than the corresponding growth rates for men.[2] According to the U.S. Small Business Administration, women-owned businesses in the United States employ 27.5 million, and contribute $3.6 trillion to the economy. They also found that women business owners are philanthropically active—7 in 10 volunteer at least once per month, 31 percent contribute $5,000 or more to charity annually, and 15 percent give $10,000 or more, annually. In a 2000 speech to the Rhode Island Foundation, Janet P. Atkins noted that women have the power to influence over $50 billion per year in foundation and corporate gifts. This is because 51.4 percent of the CEOs of U.S. foundations were women; 71 percent of corporate giving programs were run by women; 56.3 percent of community foundations are led and run by women; and 49.5 percent of all family foundations are run by women. Research has revealed that men and women may have more comparable views regarding philanthropy than common wisdom previously suggested. In order for the nonprofit sector to respond to the ever-increasing role that women are playing in philanthropy, more research is needed regarding their expectations and interests. It is vital that nonprofits recognize this and include women in their fundraising efforts.

■ NOTES

1. Council of Michigan Foundations.
2. *Philanthropy News Digest,* April 17, 2001.

The author acknowledges, with gratitude, the comments of Tim Wood and Will Schneider.

The Nonprofit as a Business Enterprise: Adapting to the Expanding Philanthropic Market

ANTOINETTE M. MALVEAUX

Philanthropy in America is evolving, rates of giving are increasing, large gifts are being noted, and the sources of the growth are increasingly from new wealth, created by the dot-com era. According to Giving USA,[1] Americans contributed an estimated $260.3 billion, a 6.1 percent increase over 2004. While the bulk of this giving comes from individuals (76.5 percent), the balance comes from bequests, corporations, and foundations. This growth, coupled with large gifts such as that of Warren Buffet to the Gates Foundation, and the expected growth from new wealth is being referred to as a "golden age" for philanthropy.

While the outlook for the growth of philanthropy is extremely positive, it creates tremendous challenges for the nonprofit service delivery segment to absorb this capital and deliver effective, innovative, and sustainable solutions. There are greater requirements for accountability of nonprofit organizations. These requirements come from the philanthropic community and government, along with the pressure government brings for philanthropy to do more as government does less, while lax management, and sometimes unethical behavior, have led to a number of recent scandals.

Capacity of the nonprofit organization is critical. The consequences of investing in organizations that are capacity constrained will often result in squandered resources. The pressure for nonprofits to absorb this increase in capital presents management challenges that must be tackled effectively, in order to ensure that the potential of philanthropic resources is maximized.

From the perspective of the board of directors and the executive director charged with running the nonprofit, the challenges of managing an enterprise are obviously increasing, but appropriately so. However, for the philanthropic organization the challenge is great for finding the nonprofit with the clearly articulated vision and mission, with the adequate level of resources aligned to deliver, in a well-run, cost-efficient, cost-effective manner, and with good solutions and new ideas. Capacity of the nonprofit organization is critical. The consequences of investing in organizations that are capacity constrained will often result in squandered resources. The pressure for nonprofits to absorb this increase in capital presents management challenges that must be tackled effectively, in order to ensure that the potential of philanthropic resources is maximized.

In meeting the needs of a community, whether the community is local, national, or global, the nonprofit organization is faced with the management challenge of building a sound and effective social enterprise. Irrespective of size, this enterprise is no less complex than any other business of comparable size. The challenges involve attracting, developing, and retaining the right leadership; securing the appropriate level of resources; developing and implementing an effective delivery model; and creating a strong position in the community. As the nonprofit sector has become more crowded and the reliance of the American public on the nonprofit community to help solve community issues has grown, the outreach required of nonprofits has also grown. This growth necessitates establishing adequate external relationships and collaboration with community stakeholders and communicating the organization's value to them.

MISSION AND VISION

The nonprofit organization should be relevant to the community that it seeks to serve, and therefore its mission and vision should be reflective of the particular needs of that community. The challenge of many nonprofits is not as much in articulating a mission as it is staying focused on it, by keeping sight of the big picture in the midst of day-to-day operational management priorities, and safeguarding against "mission creep."

The capacity of the organization to be a proper steward of the mission and vision rests in the quality and capacity of the board and executive director to maintain this focus, by implementing a quality strategic planning process that includes input from community partners, collaborators, and other stakeholders. Strategic planning all too often does not occur regularly in nonprofit organizations. Either the understanding of the value of this process does not exist, the skill set to conduct it is not present in the nonprofit, or the nonprofit has not reached out to secure external resources in achieving this task. Many nonprofits fall into the trap of only addressing the annual business plan and budget, which more than likely will keep leadership trapped in an operational perspective, while not allowing that outlook to be balanced with a strategic one.

Management must be disciplined about pursuing funding that is aligned with its vision and mission, and must exercise caution in "chasing the dollars" where certain funding sources might push the organization in a direction that takes it off mission. Funding sources should be helpful in implementing the mission, enabling the nonprofit to transform as it gains success in meeting the prescribed needs of the community.

It is essential that the board clearly understands its role in developing and shaping the mission and vision of the organization, and then ensuring that the organization stays on point. Far too often, boards of nonprofits tend to be far more operational and less strategic than they are required to be. The capacity of the board and of the executive director, and the quality of their relationship, is probably the most important management area to be addressed to ensure a solid management capacity for the organization.

LEADERSHIP

The business principle being brought into philanthropy during this new golden era has been referred to by *The Economist* as "philanthrocapitalism," which is described as "an approach that draws on modern business practices, and an entrepreneurial spirit, to get more from its money." Most venture capitalists will affirm that once the business model is determined to be sound, the investment decision is made based on the leadership, talent, and skill of the management team. Assessing management's capacity and character is as crucial an element of the due diligence process as examining the potential of the business idea itself. For this reason, the venture capitalist is often challenged with generating a substantial "deal flow." Finding the deal flow means not only finding the right business model for a new opportunity, but finding the right management leadership and talent to implement this business model, which is key to achieving success.

Investing in nonprofits is no different, and oftentimes the investment decision in philanthropy is more difficult than one in venture capital, because philanthropic organizations are required by IRS guidelines to spend a certain percentage of their asset value annually. While there is some flexibility in the guidelines, to provide adequate time to reach the requisite level of investment, real pressure exists for the foundation to create this "deal flow."

Too many times, boards put too little thought into the talent, skill, and values required of the leader. More often, decisions seem to be personality driven, rather than talent and values driven. Finding a leader who can not only articulate and effectively communicate the vision and mission, but can also develop, manage, and grow a sound operation, is the most important responsibility of the board. Additionally, boards often do not focus on their own development and effectiveness. They need to be as sound and effective as they expect the operation to be. If the board is successful in addressing these two areas—creating a sound governance structure and process and attracting sound leadership and management talent—chances are the organization will be successful in delivering on its vision and mission, in a sustainable manner.

Two aspects of leadership often overlooked by boards are development and succession of leadership. *Daring to Lead 2006,* an important study authored by Jeanne Bell, Richard Myers, and Timothy Wolfred (for a joint project of Compass Point Nonprofit Services and The Meyer Foundation) provides interesting findings, based on input from almost 2,000 nonprofit executive directors in eight cities.[2]

The objective of this study was to raise important questions about future executive leadership of nonprofit organizations and to provide insight for boards, grant makers, and other nonprofit stakeholders seeking to support their current executives and develop new ones for the pipeline. Unfortunately, the results don't provide a positive outlook.

- Over 75 percent of the executives planned to leave their posts within five years, and less than a third had discussed succession planning with their boards.

- Boards and funders contribute to executive burnout. Many executives don't appear to have strong strategic partnerships with their boards, and fundraising is overwhelmingly identified (73 percent) as the key area for board improvement (see Exhibit 2.12).

- Compensation is sorely lacking, and executives believe that they make significant financial sacrifices to lead nonprofits. This issue was exacerbated for the female executive.

- Executives are concerned with organizational sustainability and are seeking new skills and strategies.

- Bench strength, diversity, and competitive compensation are critical factors in finding future leaders.

Many small and mid-sized nonprofits lack the bench strength to develop leaders outside of their organizations, and while an increasing number of people of color represent a rapidly growing segment of the nonprofit population, 82 percent of executive directors are white. Furthermore, it is believed that the successors of existing nonprofits will require higher salaries, which will challenge the small and mid-sized nonprofits.

Clearly, the board's charge in getting this area of management correct is a strategic imperative. The grant makers' assessment of the capacity of the organization cannot take the area of leadership lightly. Key findings of the study suggest the need for a better understanding of the needs of nonprofit management *and* those of their boards. Understanding the capacity constraints of the organization will lead donors to more effective grant making.

EXHIBIT 2.12   WHERE EXECUTIVES MOST DESIRE IMPROVED BOARD PERFORMANCE

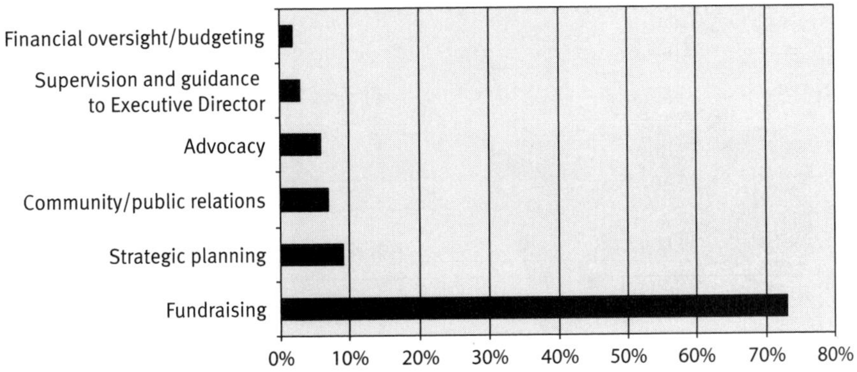

Source: Daring to Lead.

EFFECTIVE RESOURCE MANAGEMENT

Financial management, while crucial to the survival and growth of any organization, must not be the beginning and end of management's focus. Risk management is a growing aspect of resource management, as is the consistent need to focus on human and physical resources.

Financial management must be sound. Securing the appropriate talent, systems and processes is paramount to any successful organization. Ensuring compliance with state and IRS regulation is as central as expense management and revenue generation, and is a growing necessity. Instituting not only financial audits but operational audits as well is critical, particularly as Sarbanes-Oxley increases expectations about nonprofit accounting at all regulatory levels.

Although most nonprofits focus on securing financial resources, many fall short in this area. Fundraising is as much a skill and talent as is financial management (see Exhibit 2.13). There is a plethora of individuals serving in the area of fund development who lack the skill and talent to be successful. The sector is littered with grantwriters who, while their skills are necessary, only provide one of the technical aspects of the fundraising process. Yet nonprofit management often functions as if a grantwriter covers the human resources requirement for fundraising; or, they believe that if they have someone with strong networks, then they have addressed the requirement. They could not be more wrong.

EXHIBIT 2.13   DONORS' AND FUNDERS' UNDERSTANDING OF THE EXECUTIVE JOB

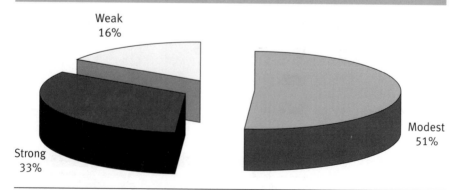

Source: Daring to Lead.

There is a growing professionalism in the fundraising segment of the nonprofit sector, and an executive director would do well to seek individuals who have professional training and/or a proven track record of delivering in this crucial area. At a minimum, the executive director should be willing to invest in the development of selected talent to help build the skill in this area. One key mistake that executive directors make is that they believe this to be a skill learned on the job. With the sophistication of philanthropy evolving, however, and the expectations of grant makers growing, a nonprofit is well served when strong talent and skills are represented in the organization in this area (see Exhibit 2.14).

Many nonprofits must be creative, flexible, and resourceful in getting their work done. They tend to operate on shoestring budgets, often overlooking the areas that require their attention the most. While ensuring that fiscal management is sound, the growing need for risk management, including complying with certain new Sarbanes-Oxley guidelines, puts increasing pressure on the nonprofit to secure strong talent with appropriate expertise.

Talent acquisition and retention is critical. Many individuals are interested in giving back and want to work in the nonprofit sector. Often, their passion for the cause must be equally balanced with their talent to deliver services. Human resource management is an important area that does not

EXHIBIT 2.14   EXECUTIVES' SELF-PERCEIVED SKILL-ENHANCEMENT NEEDS

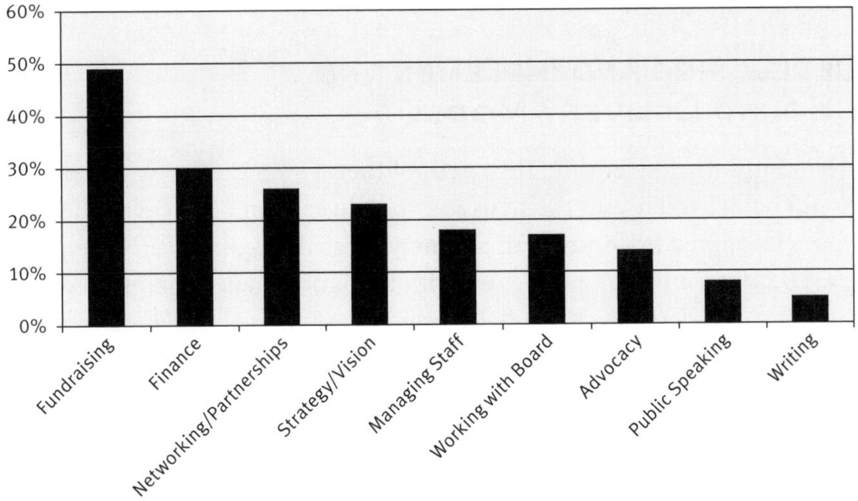

Source: Daring to Lead.

get the appropriate time and attention. Most executives say their people are their greatest asset. Acquiring that asset, then investing in, developing, and leveraging it has to be one of the most important roles an executive performs.

Small and mid-sized nonprofits often do not have the proper human resources infrastructure — including adequate staff, policies, recruitment, retention, and compensation strategies. All too often, the organization will publish an employee manual and believe that their human resource requirements have been satisfied. If executive management and its board do not attend to these issues with an appropriate level of priority, the organization will waste considerable time dealing with "people issues" and putting out fires, rather than moving toward the mission. Having a board member with considerable human resource expertise can prove to be invaluable to a nonprofit organization.

A resource area that requires increasing attention is the area of physical resources, and most significantly technology and telecommunications. This is probably one area in which many small nonprofits struggle. Having an adequate technological infrastructure can make a difference in the survival and growth potential of an organization, so technology is a crucial investment area. Many executive directors have sunk money into a technology that fails to provide the core of what is needed, only to have to invest more resources to get the correct business solution. This is an extremely risky area for the organization and requires strong and prudent talent, knowledge and skill, to safeguard the financial assets of the organization while finding the best means to meet the need.

DEVELOPING AND IMPLEMENTING A SOUND DELIVERY MODEL

Most nonprofits understand the needs of their communities, what services should be delivered, and the best way to deliver them. However, they are often challenged by innovation and new ideas. Being innovative requires a certain degree of risk taking, which often goes against the grain of the nonprofit. Funders can certainly be helpful in this area, by seeking to invest in new and different solutions, while committing to sustaining those that are working well.

Determining what works well is another area where nonprofit management is challenged. Most nonprofits tend to measure output, knowing that impact on societal outcomes is much more important today, from the funders' perspective. The growing sophistication of philanthropy focuses more keenly on the return on investment, as it should. The challenge to nonprofit management is to understand and secure the resources necessary to reasonably measure this return.

Outcomes measurement requires more, albeit necessary, expense, along with the knowledge of different methods of measurement. Often, funders do not accompany their measurement expectation with financial support, and this is an area where foundations need to work more closely with non-profit management. Foundations should be careful in setting their expectations regarding measurement, and should also be clear in articulating them to the nonprofit.

Nonprofit management needs to accept this growing trend toward measurables as a part of doing business and must acquire the necessary resources to put forth a credible case showing the impact of their nonprofit on the social cause it addresses. Additionally, the effective measurement of outcomes will also inform management of areas that require refinement, or strengthening, to develop and implement a strong delivery model.

Marketing and Public Relations

With nonprofits operating in such a crowded sector, the marketing and public relations needs of the organization present growing challenges for management. For most nonprofits, particularly small and mid-sized ones, the focus on delivering programs and services with tight budgets consumes most of their time. If a dollar is raised, the thought is to put the dollar into programs, not into a public relations event or a marketing activity. However, nonprofit management must distinctively position its organization vis-à-vis others that are delivering similar programs and services in the community. It is imperative that nonprofit management cultivate and maintain supportive networks of funders, volunteers, and community collaborators, and that the outreach required to do so not be overlooked. Fierce competition for funding dollars dictates that a strong outreach strategy be developed and implemented.

Conclusion

The nonprofit organization is a business enterprise and should be managed as one. Obviously, the pressures are great, as are the challenges. The growing expectations of the philanthropic community, and of government, put more pressure on nonprofit boards and executives to increase the professionalism and performance of their operations. Boards need to understand this and structure themselves in a manner that allows them to provide the necessary oversight; they must choose wisely in their executive director and then focus on the director's development to ensure success.

In concert, the director should be an individual who possesses the skill and talent to manage and grow the nonprofit, soundly and successfully, and put the proper infrastructure and business systems in place, to deliver to the community the positive impact it seeks in its mission. Finally, funders need to ensure that their understanding, and that of the board, is adequate regarding the needs and constraints of nonprofit management. Opportunities in this era of American philanthropy are great, including the opportunity to squander resources if the nonprofit community does not develop talent and capacity in management.

◼ NOTES

1. *Giving USA 2006* (Glenview, IL: Giving USA Foundation, 2006).
2. J. Bell, R. Myers, and T. Wolfred, *Daring to Lead* (San Francisco: Compass Point and the Meyer Foundation, 2006).

Philanthropic Solutions: Better Capacity for More Complex Times

JANICE SCHOOS

In the past, individuals and families often created private foundations or other charitable giving vehicles at the suggestion of their financial advisors. These funds helped the donors organize their giving, minimize taxes, address societal needs, as well as create personal or family legacies. Many donors passively managed their foundations, making grant decisions once a year, commonly at Thanksgiving, when gathered with family members. Some may have collected a year's worth of solicitations from a variety of worthy charities, and stored them in a manila envelope to be considered for funding from the foundation. This reactive giving may have served the earlier generation very well. A modestly funded foundation with $1 million in assets could easily have supported several charities, with its IRS-required minimum payout amount of $50,000. A sincere letter of thanks for the charity's executive director would follow the grant check, and that would be the last the donor would hear from the organization until it was time to solicit the next year's support.

> Measuring impact is often the real challenge. It's not enough to assume that the charity will be effective. Newly minted philanthropists, who are not trained giving professionals, require access to resources to help them gain the skills to evaluate the success of the organizations and programs they support.

Today, philanthropists find this type of unengaged giving not only emo-
tionally unsatisfying but fiscally irresponsible. Average independent foundation assets have increased from approximately $98.6 billion in 1987, to
$246.4 billion (inflation-adjusted) in 2003 (see Exhibit 2.15).[1] Furthermore,
that figure does not include the increased popularity of other charitable
giving vehicles, such as donor advised funds, which are the fastest growing
charitable giving vehicle, with approximately $16 billion in assets.[2] All this
growth requires individual donors to think and act more like professional
philanthropists. Foundation trustees and directors must exercise their fiduciary responsibility, to ensure that grants are made to financially stable organizations that will make a philanthropic impact. Measuring that impact is
often the real challenge. It's not enough to assume that the charity will
be effective. The senior team may have every intention of carrying out a
project as it was described but unforeseen circumstances frequently prevent
that project from being effective. These newly minted philanthropists, who
are not trained giving professionals, require access to resources to help them
gain the skills to evaluate the success of the organizations and programs they
support.

**EXHIBIT 2.15   CHANGE IN INDEPENDENT
FOUNDATION ASSETS (1987–2003)**

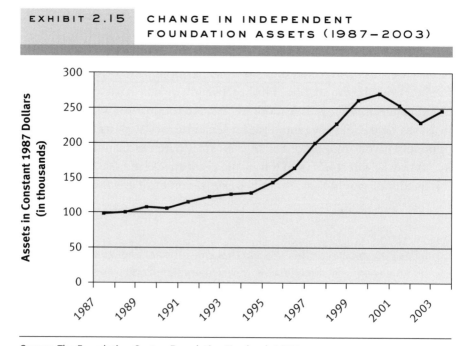

Source: The Foundation Center, Foundation Yearbook 2005.

Like everything else, information on charitable activities has never been as plentiful as it is now. However, with more information comes more confusion. Even the leading charity watchdog groups cannot agree on what information should be used to evaluate charities. How are donors expected to sift through pages of IRS Form 990 tax returns and make sense of this data? Only 40 percent of nonprofit organizations are required to complete a tax return, and an estimated half of the total returns submitted are incomplete.

The most important thing donors need to understand is that grant making is part art and part science. Even the best measurement tools will only get donors so far in determining whether an organization is the right one for their particular foundation. It is necessary to trust personal instincts and also to trust the organization. After completing a level of due diligence, where a relative level of comfort with the charity is attained, a certain amount of uncertainty will still remain. Many great nonprofit institutions were started by pioneering philanthropists who believed in an idea and the leadership of the organizations. When John D. Rockefeller created Rockefeller University (originally known as Rockefeller Institute for Medical Research), there were no guarantees that the biomedical research that scientists conducted would lead to breakthroughs, including discovering that genes are made of DNA. Corporations and governments considered such investments too risky, but philanthropy's role is to take on those kinds of risks that will, hopefully, yield great rewards.

MEASURING FINANCIAL SUSTAINABILITY

To get the complete financial picture of a nonprofit organization, it is best to review its financial statements over a five-year period. Organizations with operating budgets of greater than $50,000 (excluding religious entities) are required to file a tax return with the IRS. These tax returns, known as Form 990s, are available on the Internet through the nonprofit organization GuideStar (www.guidestar.org). GuideStar provides comprehensive data on more than 1.5 million nonprofit organizations. While the tax return and the organization's annual report provide a great deal of financial data, it is still often difficult to analyze its financial stability.

Here are a few guidelines for evaluating a nonprofit organization. By reviewing five years of data, the donor can determine whether the organization's finances have changed dramatically over time. Measuring change is important since shifts can indicate potential problems with the financial stability of the organization.

Four elements of financial performance provide important parameters for donor decision making. I offer a grading system for each that can contribute to measured assessments about performance that will differentiate the capacities of alternative nonprofit recipients.

Financial Variability

The operating performance of the nonprofit over a period of time can be measured by tracking total revenue and expenses on its income statement. Has the organization experienced dramatic decreases in revenue? If so, the decreases should be easily explained by management. For example, government funding of a specific project was eliminated; however, in following years, the organization made up the shortfall by increasing the amount of private foundation grants. Look for any other inconsistencies or red flags that should be raised with the senior management team of the nonprofit.

Financial Variability	Level of Change	Rating
0 to 1 out of 5 years	5%	Good
2 out of 5 years	6%–10%	Fair
3 out of 5 years	11%–20%	Poor

Cash Reserves/Savings

Another indicator of a nonprofit's financial stability is the amount of cash reserves it has on hand to sustain its operations if it did not have access to additional revenue. When examining the balance sheet of a nonprofit, look to see if the organization's total assets have changed significantly over the five-year period. Current assets should be greater than current liabilities, by a comfortable margin, to decrease the likelihood that the organization may suffer a cash shortage during the next year. When reviewing the amount of cash reserves, provided current outflows remain constant, consider how long the organization would stay in business if there were decreases in revenue. Based on that length of time, a grade of good, fair, or poor might be assigned as follows:

Length of Operation	Rating
1 to 2 years	Good
6 months to 1 Year	Fair
Zero to 6 months	Poor

Fundraising Expenses

Most donors desire efficiency in funds acquisition. That is, exactly how much does an organization spend to raise $1? The first thing to understand about fundraising expenses relates to where a nonprofit organization is in its fundraising cycle. If a nonprofit has just launched a major five-year capital campaign, its fundraising expenses are expected to be higher than one that is not in a campaign. The other major challenge in evaluating this data is that organizations report fundraising expenses differently. Some include the salary of fundraising staff within its external affairs budget, so that expense is not captured as fundraising expense. Judgment in this element can be contentious at best, and donors should probe the topic further with the executive director, if there are concerns about the overall fundraising efficiency. In general, some industry standards are as follows:

Amount Spent	Rating
15 cents or less	Good
16 cents to 30 cents	Fair
31 cents or more	Poor

Management of Investments

Donors expect the nonprofits they support to invest their assets wisely, whether the assets are operating funds or endowments. Over time, if investment performance consistently falls below average market return, this may be a sign that senior management, the board of directors, and its investment committee may not be exercising appropriate fiscal responsibility. Again, it is important to use these indicators as tools for discussions with senior management.

Investment Return	Rating
2%–10% greater than market rate	Good
1%–1.99% greater than market rate	Fair
Below market rate	Poor

Measuring Potential Philanthropic Impact

To properly assess whether a philanthropic investment will result in a positive philanthropic impact, it is essential for a potential donor to ask the nonprofit to provide specific information early on in the grant review process. The donor will use that information during the decision-making process and, if a grant is approved, as a means of evaluating the program's success. Nonprofits will welcome the opportunity to participate as partners in the grant review process.

The first step, when asking a nonprofit to submit a request for support, is to inform them of the potential size of your support (e.g., $30,000 to $50,000 range). The organization should then be asked to describe its area of greatest need and how it believes a grant in that range could be used to make the greatest impact. The organization needs to include in the proposal how it intends to measure the success of the project for which funding is being requested.

It is important to remember that outputs do not equal outcomes. There are plenty of things an organization can measure, but the key is to determine what things should be measured to determine overall success. Statistics and data are important, but personal success stories of clients the organization has served also provide powerful insights into the real work of the nonprofit. Nothing is more convincing than learning about a single mother who attended employment-training classes, came off welfare, and is now supporting her family as a result of the comprehensive services provided by the nonprofit community center.

Measuring Capacity

The following are types of information that may be useful when evaluating a specific organization.

Staffing

- What is the capacity of the current staff? Can they manage new or expanded programming?
- Is the current staff qualified to address the needs of the population it serves?
- What is the staff-to-client ratio? How many volunteers work on this project?

Delivery of Services

- How will this funding help expand the current services?

- What is the unit cost of the services? How does this compare to other similar organizations?
- If the costs are different, is the reason justified? (For example, the cost of a Meals on Wheels program is significantly higher than one in another county; however, the lower-priced group has access to donated food from Second Harvest, and the other does not, resulting in higher operating costs.)
- Does the organization collaborate with other nonprofits serving the same population to provide complementary services?
- Does the project budget make a case for your support?

Funding Sources

- What would happen if the organization did not receive the funds being requested?
- If less than the requested amount was given, would the project still be successful?
- Where else is the organization seeking funds? Do they get funding from other private foundations, corporations, government, individuals, or fundraising events?
- Would the grant be eligible for matching funds from another funder?
- How important is it that the amount of funding being requested is greater than 50 percent of the total project?

Governance

- What is the professional experience of the board members?
- Does the makeup of the board reflect the population the organization serves?
- What is the overall financial commitment of the board members?

MAKING GRANT PROPOSAL DECISIONS

The most critical thing philanthropists should consider when asked for support is how the organization, project, or issue fits with their overall philanthropic goals. In order to be good stewards of their giving programs and to obtain the greatest satisfaction from their giving, donors need to be thoughtful in considering all aspects of their philanthropic investments. The greatest return will come from investing in areas in which a donor is most passionate and by supporting groups that can make the most of those investments.

EVALUATING FOUNDATION PERFORMANCE

In addition to measuring the performance of specific grants, foundations aim to assess their overall philanthropic impact. According to a recent report of the Center for Effective Philanthropy,[3] evaluations are the most common tool for assessing overall foundation performance. Over 70 percent of CEOs surveyed used project or program evaluations for performance assessment compared, for example, to one-third using administrative costs, or 10 percent using changes in targeted public policies. Yet, there is irony here. Although evaluation is by far the most important tool, CEOs surveyed reported evaluating less than half of their grants. While the tool is clearly important, it appears to be applied quite judiciously (see Exhibit 2.16).

Increasingly, foundation leaders are relying on additional indirect measures to help improve their own performance and to drive management decisions. These indirect measures fall into categories related to achieving impact, setting the strategy/agenda, managing operations, and optimizing governance.

| EXHIBIT 2.16 | CEO PROPENSITY TO EVALUATE GRANTS |

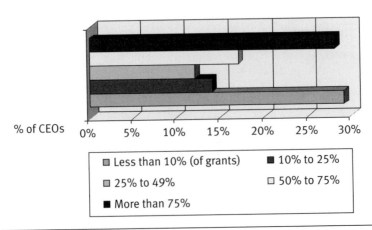

"For What Approximate Percentage of Grants Does Your Foundation Conduct an Evaluation?"

% of CEOs   0%   5%   10%   15%   20%   25%   30%

- ▦ Less than 10% (of grants)   ■ 10% to 25%
- ▦ 25% to 49%   ☐ 50% to 75%
- ■ More than 75%

Source: Center for Effective Philanthropy.

The report points out that, even with the best indicators in place, such measures of overall foundation performance should be viewed on a relative basis. Measuring the success of individual foundations takes time and requires a clear understanding of the foundation's overall objectives.

OTHER RESOURCES

The measurement tools suggested here are only guides. There is no substitute for sharing experiences with other philanthropists. Giving circles provide an opportunity for grant makers to come together, to learn about philanthropy and potentially pool their funds for greater impact. Giving circle members often review grant proposals as a group, and learn from each other by asking questions, and sharing best practices. Regional associations of grant makers, affinity groups, the Council on Foundations, and the Association of Small Foundations are just a few associations that convene donors to share best practices.

The take-away is that donors do not need to become philanthropists on their own. So many people are passionate about their philanthropy and are eager to share what they have learned. Donors should seek out and attend meetings of these professional organizations or attend other networking events. People who are involved with any charitable organization are likely to want to share what it is that they like best about their giving. Watch how they come to life describing their experiences.

We are privileged in the United States to be encouraged by our government to be philanthropic. With that privilege comes responsibility. Great care must be taken when making philanthropic decisions, and with the right information, donors can partner with nonprofit organizations to accomplish great things.

Addendum: Nonprofit Resources

Organization	Web Address	Measurement
American Institute of Philanthropy's Charity Rating Guide	http://www.charitywatch.org/	A nonprofit charity watchdog and information service maximizes the the effectiveness of every dollar contributed to charity by providing donors with the information they need to make more informed giving decisions.

(continues)

Addendum: Nonprofit Resources *(Continued)*

Organization	Web Address	Measurement
Association of Small Foundations	http://www.smallfoundations.org/	Membership organization of foundations with few or no staff, providing the donors, trustees, and staff with peer learning opportunities, targeted tools and resources, and a collective voice in and beyond the philanthropic community.
Better Business Bureau's Wise Giving Alliance	http://www.give.org/	Financial accountability, governance; willingness to disclose information; honesty of solicitations; donor privacy; organizational effectiveness
Charity Navigator	http://www.charitynavigator.org/	Helps charitable givers make intelligent giving decisions, by providing information on over 5,000 charities, and by evaluating their financial health.
Community Foundations	http://www.cof.org/locator/	Tax-exempt public charities serving thousands of people, who share a common concern for improving the quality of life in their area.
Council on Foundations	http://www.cof.org	A membership organization of more than 2,000 grant-making foundations and giving programs worldwide; provides leadership expertise, legal services, and networking opportunities
GuideStar	http://www.guidestar.org/	Provides comprehensive data on more than 1.5 million nonprofit organizations.
Regional Associations of Grantmakers	http://www.givingforum.org/	Helps bolster the philanthropic community and improve the quality of life in their regions.

Organization	Web Address	Measurement
The Foundation Center	http://www.fdncenter.org/	Collects, organizes, and communicates information on U.S. philanthropy.
Wealth & Giving Forum	http://www.wealthandgiving.org/	A gathering that provides an opportunity for an exchange of ideas among families who are dedicated to making intelligent decisions about their philanthropy.

■ NOTES

1. The Foundation Center, Foundation Yearbook, 2005.

2. The National Philanthropic Trust (http://www.nptrust.org/philanthropy/-philanthropy_stats.asp).

3. *Indicators of Effectiveness: Understanding and Improving Foundation Performance* (Boston, MA: The Center for Effective Philanthropy, 2002).

Technology Ascendant: Connecting the Philanthropist with Philanthropy

JENN THOMPSON

GROWTH OF RELATIONSHIPS THROUGH TECHNOLOGY

Undeniably, technology has transformed nearly all aspects of the personal and professional lives of Americans, indeed of many people, in most countries. Governments have replaced long lines and monotonous paperwork, with online tools, to renew a driver's license or pay taxes. Businesses have empowered consumers with personalized, online shopping experiences. The Internet and social networks have removed the time and space separating like-minded individuals, making knowledge sharing an instant reality. Technology has taken relationships and communications to more convenient and deeper levels.

Through the last few decades, our ability to communicate has grown exponentially. A brief look at how communications have changed over time (see Exhibit 2.17) shows the emergence and adoption of new networks and devices. With each new technology, relationships moved beyond a 1:1 ratio. With telephones, the communication was between two individuals. Television and fax enable a single entity to push out communications to multiple parties.

> What we have yet to see is whether technology can make the leap beyond basic business, and really put the philanthropist, the nonprofit, and the beneficiaries in control—creating something of a social network between those needing help and those providing the means for change.

EXHIBIT 2.17   EMERGENCE OF COMMUNICATION
TECHNOLOGIES

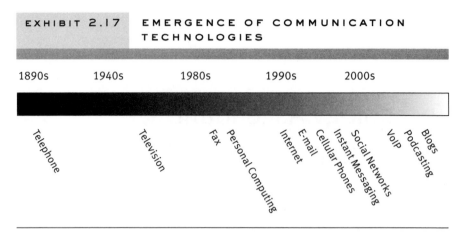

Source: Author's creation based on information from Changing Our World, Inc.

Today, the Internet enables thousands of people to collectively share information, exchange ideas, and communicate across multiple media. These new communication and relationship multiplicities are just beginning to trickle into the philanthropic sector.

Adoption of Technology by Nonprofits

Let's step back and look at how technology first impacted the nonprofit sector. Just as it changed business processes, technology brought the automation of routine office tasks to charitable organizations. The dot-com boom, complemented by social responsibility programs, brought an influx of programs, providing free or discounted hardware and software to the public and nonprofit sectors. E-commerce applications quickly followed, though they have not been as quickly adopted as other online consumer activities.

In 2005, it is estimated that 63 million Americans performed some banking online,[1] yet only 8 million Americans made a donation using the Internet.[2] This fledgling adoption of the Internet for fundraising was stirred more by recent events than nonprofit marketing—the terrorist attacks in America on September 11, 2001; the Indonesian tsunami on December 26, 2004; and Hurricane Katrina in 2005. With each disaster, new donors were introduced to the online giving process. But these individual gifts, made in support of disaster relief efforts, are just a single step toward realizing the full scope of how technology can initiate and foster the relationship-building process.

Following their day-to-day business needs and fundraising components, nonprofits began to realize the awareness and marketing opportunities made possible by the immediate and "viral" marketing nature of the Internet. Viral approaches rely on one-to-one strategies and relationships where word spreads quickly from one use to the next. Using technology to promote a campaign or appeal was quickly adopted and, for some, accelerated results beyond any other medium. Advocacy efforts can be heard around the world, from the smallest to the largest voices, and they are heard—not in weeks or days, but overnight. The Human Rights Campaign raised $550,000 in 48 hours, after launching a campaign to defeat an anti-marriage amendment.[3] The Dean for America campaign raised $7.4 million online in a single quarter, by engaging individuals to promote the campaign to friends and family.[4]

What we have yet to see is whether technology can make the leap beyond basic business and really put the philanthropist, the nonprofit, and the beneficiaries in control—creating something of a social network, between those needing help and those providing the means for change.

Technology Challenge

How can technology transform the nonprofit's role in fulfilling a mission? An illustration will cast light on the possibilities. A retired business owner makes a major gift that will generate microcredit loans to multiple third-world entrepreneurs. The donor has taken a trip to visit communities and individuals who are likely to benefit from the funds, and now he would like to develop relationships with those who will receive loans made possible by the gift. Technology can bridge the communications between donors and loan recipients, even in developing nations.[5]

With direct access, the donor can offer his own advice on starting a business, guidance on how to handle challenging regulations, and insight into navigating vendor relations. In essence, the donor has the opportunity to become a partner in the new start-up business. In fact, the technological uses can enable multiple, interconnected partnerships to develop. The loan recipient can disseminate updates, and a collection of donors can share their own personal business experiences across a network.

Role of the Donor   To be successful, these social networks may entirely depend not on the technology, but on the training and passion of those who can make use of it. The younger generation, of MySpace, Flickr, Face-Book, and Classmates.com users, will quickly take advantage of a network to connect with others. But an older generation of philanthropists has yet to fully *rely* on twenty-first-century technology to handle all communications.

According to some studies, the Baby Boomer generation has taken the lead in American giving. This age group now contributes to "more charities, causes, and campaigns than their elders."[6] But the study shows these givers have not fully adapted their philanthropic interests to the opportunities made available online. The survey data (see Exhibit 2.18) indicated that the percentage of people in younger, post-Boomer generations had used online giving more frequently than Boomers and pre-Boomers.

Sites like MySpace.com cater to the 13–25 crowd, while LinkedIn.com touts a community of 6 million professionals, with an average of 15 years' experience. Depending on the donor's experiences and interests, the nonprofit may spend the time building a relationship between the donor and the technologies that will enable the real-time connections.

Role of the Beneficiary   The role of beneficiaries, those either directly or indirectly receiving funds, may need the most support from the sector. For any relationship to have a chance, this group must play an active role. Whether it be the microcredit recipients or an environmental project, those most affected, and most supported, by the philanthropic efforts need to be at the table—or in this case, at the keyboard.

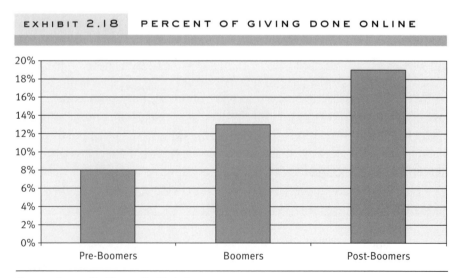

EXHIBIT 2.18   PERCENT OF GIVING DONE ONLINE

Source: Craver, Matthews, Smith & Company.

It is highly likely that the true beneficiaries may not be able to speak for themselves. The polluted waterway cannot write about the effects of off-shore oil drilling, so the voices that represent it are often the nonprofits. We can already see the emergence of social networks being built around such issues. Oceana, a nonprofit in Washington, D.C., working to protect the world's oceans, produces a successful blog, attracting activists and volunteers to the organization.

Role of the Nonprofit   The future holds the potential for nonprofits, through technology, to facilitate this connection between donor and recipient in a responsible and meaningful manner. Nonprofits are already moving in this direction by bringing human-interest stories to life through technology and blogs. But beyond the direct relationship between donor and recipient, there is also a relationship to be built between the nonprofit and the donors themselves.

Throughout the relationship-building process, charities must still prove that they are fulfilling their missions. With technology building more connections and automating the day-to-day work, the nonprofit may evolve into the role of overseer.

Today, an instant report can be sent, through phone, fax, e-mail, text messaging, podcast, and more. But it is the report *creation* that technology cannot fully replicate, at least not without a human touch. Yes, a database can crunch the complex numbers, to show whether the microcredit business is turning a profit, but it is often the human-to-human impact, the softer statistics, which cannot be as easily counted. The observations by field workers, who notice local children with a burgeoning interest in business, and thus improve their studies on secondary benefits to the community spurred by increased start-up spending—these are the outcomes that an automated report will never capture. It is this insight, by the nonprofit's own staff that will determine the real, overall value and impact of the loan program.

It is possible that technology can help facilitate some of the softer reporting that will be needed. Just as you purchase a product online and supply your own user reviews, or evaluate the technology as you use it, a donor can use the technology to facilitate relationships, measure progress, and evaluate the technology throughout the process. The nonprofit's ability to observe what to evaluate and who should provide the evaluation will be pivotal in allowing social networks to develop among philanthropists and the causes they care about.

Future Challenges

Relationships accentuated or made possible by technology will bring new challenges to the fore. A philanthropist with direct access to the loan or grant recipient sounds like a manageable option. However, it will require program staff to ensure that the donor does not demand too much control over those who receive the funds, how funds are used, or what specific goals are to be achieved. Coverage of the nonprofit sector has its share of stories about demanding donors who seek control over a program or demand too much in return for their gift. Even without an exigent donor, the cost for managing the relationship, and the technology behind it, may be too high.

Nonprofits need to clearly define expectations and approaches before technology can be funded and applied, especially as social networking technologies continue to emerge. Donors less likely to use technology in their day-to-day lives may not desire the same level of contact needed by the beneficiary or made possible through technology, while other donors, conditioned to free networks, may need an education on the funding required to bring blogs, podcasts, and really simple syndication (RSS) feeds into their philanthropic efforts.

These challenges are not new. Throughout time, nonprofits and donors have successfully adapted and adopted new technologies—in this case, phone, fax, e-mail, and Internet—to further their efforts. But now, as technology is poised to build profound connections between the philanthropist and their philanthropy, we wait to see how it takes hold to generate the social networks to share ideas, establish deeper relationships, and ultimately change lives.

■ NOTES

1. Susannah Fox and Jean Beier, "Online Banking 2006: Surfing to the Bank," Pew Internet and American Life Project, accessed June 2006. <http://www.-pewinternet.org/pdfs/PIP_Online_Banking_2006.pdf>.

2. Kintera and Luth, "Study: U.S. Online Giving Surpasses $3 Billion in 2004," accessed June 16, 2005. <http://www.kinterainc.com/site/apps/nl/content-2.asp?c=owL8JoO7KzE&b=1510553&ct=2099953>.

3. GetActive, "Human Rights Campaign grew its email list by 464 percent, sent over 1,500,000 letters to decision makers in 13 months, and raised over $550,000 in 48 hours—all using GetActive," accessed March 24 2005. <http://www.getactive.com/pdf/HRC_CS_032405.pdf>.

4. Convio, "Howard Dean Uses Convio to Raise $7.4 Million Online in Third Quarter, $11 Million Via Internet Since April 2003," accessed October 16, 2003. <http://www.convio.com/site/News2?page=NewsArticle&id=2600-703>.

5. Larry Landweber, "Internet Connectivity," accessed 1997. <http://www.-cybergeography.org/atlas/census.html> and <http://www.cybergeography-.org/atlas/landweber_version_2.gif>.

6. Craver, Mathews, Smith & Company and PrimeGroup, "Boomer Giving Now Tops That of the Older Generation," accessed August 17, 2005. <http://-www.cms.convio.net/site/PageServer?pagename=boomer>.

The Impacts: Shifts, Adjustments, and Realignments

OVERVIEW OF THE ISSUES

As the tectonic plates beneath philanthropy and the nation's nonprofits shift, adjustments and realignments are likely to occur. These changes will occur in several arenas and will pose both opportunities and challenges for all institutions.

Nonprofits themselves, by virtue of the pace of their proliferation, will face an increasingly competitive marketplace for funding. There are just over 1.4 million nonprofit organizations registered with the IRS, about 850,000 of which are public charities. In the last 20 years, the number of public charities has increased by 66 percent. Given that growth, there will likely be a shaking-out from within the sector, with the strongest taking advantage of change and the weakest growing ever weaker. How nonprofits and philanthropies adjust their mission and their management to cope with, and indeed take advantage of, increasing resource flows and increasing competition will provide a telling window into the future.

> How nonprofits and philanthropies adjust their mission and their management to cope with, and indeed take advantage of, increasing resource flows and increasing competition will provide a telling window into the future.

Philanthropy is also adjusting. Indeed, the very definition of philanthropy is changing, with greater emphasis on impact and effectiveness and less emphasis on check writing. Whole new approaches, which emphasize donor interests and benefits, as well as those of recipients, are leading to a blurring of the line between the mission of those who give and the mission of those who receive. Indeed, some who observe the philanthropic landscape are beginning to argue that philanthropy itself, if defined as a gifting process, can at least be supplemented by (if not replaced by) a more "capital markets" approach to nonprofit funding. As nonprofits grow and become more central to the economy, there may be an opportunity to move whole parts of the sector away from traditional definitions of philanthropy, into classic market finance.

Adjustments in the relationship between nonprofits, commercial markets, and the government can also be expected. Indeed, even now, medium to large nonprofits do not rely on philanthropy for their income. They rely on revenue from the provision of goods and services. The second largest source of revenue is government. Only then is giving important, at least in quantitative terms. As the large grow larger, one can expect that markets, and government, will become even more important in determining nonprofit financial viability.

The essays in this section examine the impacts of growth and explore how nonprofits and philanthropies have embarked to reengineer their revenue streams and their relationships to both public and commercial institutions.

Expansion of the Nonprofit Sector: Bigger, for Sure. But Is That Better?

SUSAN RAYMOND, PHD, AND
MARY BETH MARTIN, ESQ.

There is no denying that, taken as a whole, the nonprofit sector—however it is measured—has experienced significant growth over the last decade. It is a phenomenon whose dimensions are inescapable.

The number of registered 501(c)3 public charities has increased by two-thirds, now totaling about 850,000. Currently, about 44 percent actually file complete tax returns with the IRS, the remainder being too small (less than $25,000 in annual revenue) or registering as religious organizations.

> Growth itself may be a greater discipline on the sector than purposeful philanthropic decision making. The more there is competition for resources, the more crowded the field gets, the more demonstrated innovation, efficiency, and discipline will become the standard within the nonprofit sector.

Taking that 44 percent alone, gross reported revenue totaled $1.8 trillion, an 89 percent increase since 1995. The assets of this group now total over $2.2 trillion, nearly double the assets held by reporting nonprofits in 1995. Any time numbers get into the trillions, perspective is required because the imagination begins to fail. How big is $2.2 trillion in assets? It is, for example, larger than all of the assets managed by all of the hedge funds in America in 2005.

How long the growth of the last decade will continue is difficult to predict. To some extent it has been fueled by the growth of philanthropy itself. Private foundation assets more than doubled in the decade between 1996 and 2006. Taking a conservative view, if the number of nonprofits grows at only the annual median rate (about five percent) of the last decade (i.e., no year higher than the rate at which half the years saw higher growth and half saw lower growth), then one can expect to see well over 1.4 million nonprofits on the landscape by 2015. (See Exhibit 3.1.) The rate of growth could be higher, of course, particularly if current patterns of exit and entry continue.

An Urban Institute Study from a sample of human service nonprofits indicated that nearly three human service nonprofit providers were formed for every one that failed. Moreover, the rate of growth in the number of human service nonprofits in metropolitan areas was as much as 10 times the rate of growth of the population.[1]

As in all matters, of course, the overall viewpoint masks important differences. In the case of the nonprofit sector, the three most important elements of differentiation are sector, size, and location.

EXHIBIT 3.1   NUMBER OF REGISTERED 501(c)3 ORGANIZATIONS

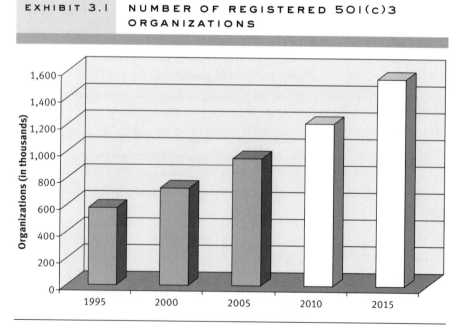

Source: 1995–2005: National Center for Charitable Statistics; 2010–2015: Changing Our World Projections.

Five states (California, New York, Texas, Florida, and Pennsylvania, in that order) account for over a third of all public charities, and also account for over a third of all public charity revenue. The 10 states with the largest number of nonprofits (the next five being Ohio, Illinois, Michigan, North Carolina, and New Jersey) account for half of all public charities and 51 percent of revenue. Public charities in these 10 states hold 67 percent of all the assets of public charities filing tax returns.

The rankings and distributions of these numbers have not changed markedly over time, which masks the growing capacity in the remaining 40 states. Albeit from a smaller base, and hence lost in the shadow of the sheer size of the sector in the top 10 states, the rates of growth of nonprofits and their assets in smaller states have often outstripped the top 10. For example, while the number of nonprofits in California—the sector leader on all measures—has grown by a third in the last decade; in places like Alabama, Alaska, and Louisiana the number of nonprofits has grown between 40 and 50 percent, with total assets often more than doubling. So, even given concentration, nonprofit growth is a real phenomenon in all markets across the nation.

Size, however, certainly qualifies the picture of growth. Of reporting public charities, 68 percent have under a million in assets, while their revenue represents five percent of total public charity revenue. At the other end of the spectrum, less than five percent of reporting public charities have over $50 million in assets, but their revenue represents 66 percent of total sector revenue. In the last five years, the number of returns of the smaller charities has increased by 44 percent, while the number of returns of the largest has only increased by 15 percent. Yet, the fair market asset value of the largest is up 30 percent, compared to just 20 percent for the smallest category. One is tempted to conclude that, as the sector grows, the big are getting bigger faster than the small.

Perhaps that is driven in part by realities of the nonprofit world and the sectors that comprise it. Health and education are the 800-pound gorillas on the nonprofit landscape. Overall, health and education represent only 10 percent of registered public charities (16 percent of those reporting). Together, however, these two groups represent 42 percent of revenue and an equivalent portion of public charity assets. While the portion of nonprofits accounted for by these two sectors has been stable over the last decade, their financial dominance has grown. A decade ago they accounted for 38 percent of all revenue and 39 percent of all assets.

In a place like Boston—home not only to the Red Sox but also (and perhaps less importantly) to the likes of Harvard, MIT, and Massachusetts General Hospital—the education and health subsectors represent nearly three-quarters of all nonprofit revenue. Within healthcare, hospitals account for nearly half of all revenue.

The explosion in the number of nonprofit organizations, concentrated in organizations of smaller size, raises a series of concerns as wealth changes generational hands.[2] The first set of concerns, of course, is efficiency. In a city of any size there are hundreds of educational or social service non-profits. On its face, this is not necessarily bad. Innovation and flexibility tend to be inversely related to size. Small is not necessarily bad, nor is the competition that large numbers create necessarily bad. The best ideas and the most effective programs are more likely where there is robust competition among organizations and leaders than where there are monopolies. Still, the proliferation does imply duplication of administration and organizational support services, drawing resources from actual service provisions to support functions. Proliferation also raises concerns about quality. A hodge-podge of small organizations can impede the adoption of best managerial practices in today's world of information and inventory management. There is strength in size on these dimensions.

In the end, as with most markets, it is the flow of funds that will adjust the organizational chessboard. The capital base of the nation's philanthropic foundations has more than doubled in the last decade alone (see Exhibit 3.2). This extraordinary growth has been fueled both by asset appreciation that has far outpaced grant making, and by the well-publicized entry of new capital into the sector, from several of the nation's extraordinarily wealthy families. Andrew Carnegie, who famously remarked, "There is no class so pitiably wretched as that which possesses money and nothing else," must be gazing upon the current sector expansion with something approaching glee.

If those new to the philanthropic scene exercise due diligence in sorting through sectoral confusion, they may either demand consolidation as a price for support, or by *de facto* favoring of those nonprofits with the best combination of management efficiency and innovation, gradually starve the nonprofits whose size or sclerosis impedes their efficiency or effectiveness.

Of course, that assumes a great deal on the part of philanthropy. It assumes that a significant amount of the dollar value of philanthropic flows will be governed by giving criteria that emphasize such organizational aspects as efficiency, quality, and managerial sophistication. It is not clear if this is an

EXHIBIT 3.2   ASSETS OF PRIVATE FOUNDATIONS

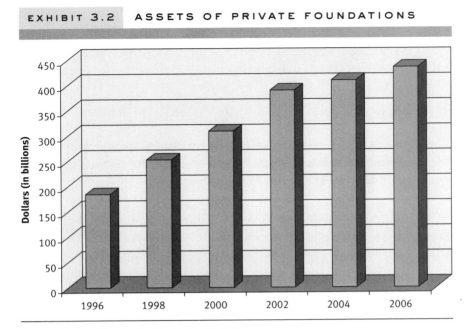

Source: National Center for Charitable Statistics.

accurate assumption. While it is true that there has been much talk about, and some movement toward, more business-like decision making on the part of philanthropies, such changes are far from universal. Personal relationships between nonprofit and philanthropic leaders are probably as important now as they ever were. Moreover, as in all human endeavor, the comfort of the familiar tends to crowd out innovation. It is much easier and less trying to stick to one's programmatic and funding knitting than it is to take up whole new endeavors or risk new organizational strategies.

Hence, even greater due diligence is not likely to fundamentally change the personal nature of many philanthropic decisions. Though funders may be able to alter the efficiency impacts of growth and duplication at the margins of the nonprofit sector, it is unlikely that the core directions and trends will be altered, at least in any foreseeable future.

Growth itself may be a greater discipline than purposeful philanthropic decision making. The more there is competition for resources, the more crowded the field gets and the more demonstrated innovation, efficiency, and discipline will become the standard within the nonprofit sector. So, far from being a bane, multiplication may be a superior arithmetic function than subtraction.

■ SOURCES

National Center for Charitable Statistics.
Internal Revenue Service.

■ NOTES

1. E. C. Twombly, "Human Service Nonprofits in Metropolitan Areas during Devolution and Welfare Reform," The Urban Institute *Charting Civil Society* Series, No. 10 (The Urban Institute: 2001).
2. J. Hall, "Too Many Ways to Divide Donations?," *Christian Science Monitor,* June 20, 2005. W. Seldon, "In Praise of Fewer Nonprofits," *Perspectives,* The Independent Sector: July 2004.

Flexing Economic Muscles: The Nonprofit Sector and Economic Growth

Given the nonprofit sector's extraordinary diversity—in size, substance, location, and mission—generalizations about its economic impact often underestimate the role this sector plays in the economy. The facts startle nonetheless. The charitable nonprofit sector represents over nine percent of the U.S. economy. It has expenditures of over $1.2 trillion a year, a level that has doubled in the last decade. The sector has assets in excess of $2 trillion.[1]

When things begin to be denominated in trillions of dollars, perspective becomes important. This is not loose change out of the sock drawer. In terms of a flow of resources, how big is $1.2 trillion? Using World Bank measures, it's about the size of the entire gross domestic income of the country of Italy, or just over the entire gross domestic income of all of the world's low-income nations combined.[2] In terms of a stock of capital, how

> The nonprofit sector is not merely an expression of charitable culture, as important as that is to American values. In particular states at particular points in time, the nonprofit sector can be the economic platform that provides a basis for growth and impedes economic deterioration. The nonprofit sector can provide stability through economic cycles.

big is $2 trillion? It is bigger than the entire asset base of all hedge funds in America, which is not projected to reach $2 trillion until 2008.[3]

It is important to note that this does not represent the size of the entire nonprofit sector. Foundations (both grantmaking and operating) represent another half billion dollars in assets, and pour about $30 billion into the economy each year.

Revenue in the nonprofit sector has nearly doubled in the last decade. How fast will it grow in the future? Projections are not certainties, of course. Decca Records, for example, learned this lesson in 1962 when it declined to pursue a demo tape by the Beatles, with the assessment that "guitar music is on its way out." Some failed predictions have significant consequences.

Taking a conservative approach, therefore, one could use as a growth rate the median of the last decade. That is, if the sector's revenue grows each year only at the median, year-over-year rate of the last decade (half the years saw faster growth), where will the sector be in 2015? The last decade's median is about eight percent, yielding a 2015 projected revenue of $2.6 trillion—more than doubling in 10 years. Even if growth sags, it is likely that the sector will far surpass the $2 billion revenue mark by 2015 (see Exhibit 3.3). It is

EXHIBIT 3.3   EXPENDITURES OF IRS-REPORTING NONPROFITS

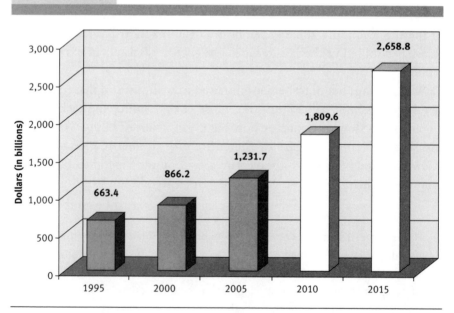

Source: 1995–2005: National Center for Charitable Statistics; 2010–2015: Changing Our World, Inc.

interesting to note that, as nonprofits take on a greater role in service provision in America, the structure of their revenue base is changing.

Long thought of as organizations dependent on bake sales and glittering galas, the nonprofit sector, in fact, gets only 14 percent of its revenue from private, voluntary contributions, a level that is actually less than the 20 percent five years ago (see Exhibit 3.4). Nearly three-quarters of charitable revenue is traceable to charges for program services. In turn, this reflects the fact that nearly two-thirds of charitable nonprofits are in the healthcare, education, and human services sectors, where fee-for-service or government reimbursement provides the scaffolding for financial structure.[4]

Such depictions of the sector must, however, be qualified for the impact of size. Only 34 percent of charities and 70 percent of foundations file annual IRS reports (see Exhibit 3.5). The remainder are either too small to be required to do so (less than $25,000 in income) or are religious organizations. Among public charities, moreover, size can skew economic generalizations, even among those large enough to file with the IRS. In terms of assets, for example, 68 percent of filing nonprofits have less than half a million in assets. Indeed, those nonprofits with more than $10 million in assets actually hold 88 percent of all nonprofit assets.[5] Hospitals and institutions of higher education hold nearly half of all the sector's assets. While it is huge, the asset base of the sector is highly concentrated. Overall size does not at all reflect the financial structure within the sector.

Size also affects revenue structure. While it is true that, in general, program service fees are the most important line item in nonprofit revenue

EXHIBIT 3.4   SOURCES OF INCOME FOR CHARITABLE NONPROFITS (2003)

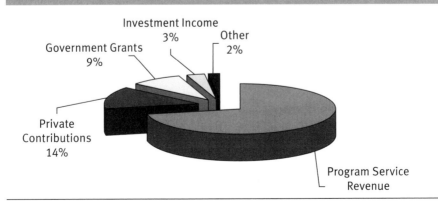

Source: National Center for Charitable Statistics.

EXHIBIT 3.5   IRS PROJECTED GROWTH IN PRIVATE
                FOUNDATIONS FILING FORM 990

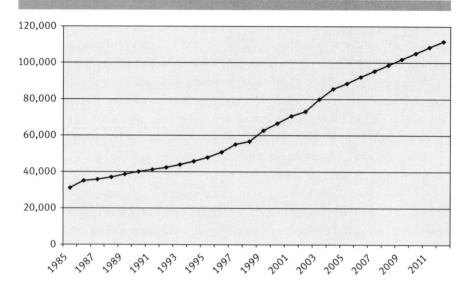

Source: T. Hussain, Internal Revenue Service.

reports, this is not true for smaller organizations. The smaller the organization, the more dependent it is on private, voluntary contributions. Nonprofits with less than $1 million in revenue rely on private contributions for
40 percent or more of revenue, compared to the 14 percent sector average.[6]

Employment is another important measure of economic significance.
Nearly 13 million Americans work in the nonprofit sector, representing
about nine percent of the U.S. workforce.[7] Over the past 15 years, nonprofit
employment has grown at about 2.4 percent per year, well above the 1.3 percent growth rate for total employment.[8]

Again, concentration characterizes the pattern. Healthcare and education
account for two-thirds of nonprofit employees. Geography also matters. In
2004, six states (California, Florida, New York, Pennsylvania, Texas, and Virginia) accounted for half of all nonprofit employment.

In particular states at particular points in time, the nonprofit sector can
either be the economic platform that provides a basis for growth and/or
one that impedes economic deterioration. Pennsylvania provides a recent
apt example. The nonprofit sector represents 13 percent of Pennsylvania's

employment. In the last decade nonprofits created 25 percent of the new jobs in the state, even as Pennsylvania lost 180,000 manufacturing jobs. Nearly half of Pennsylvania's 50 largest employers are nonprofits, again dominated by education and medical institutions. Indeed, between 2002 and 2003, nonprofit employment actually increased by 2.1 percent while private sector commercial employment decreased by 1.5 percent. As a result, nonprofit employment produced $21.1 billion in wages in Pennsylvania, more than three times the payroll of the state government.[9]

What goes on in the nonprofit sector, of course, does not stay in the nonprofit sector. Every nonprofit job creates other jobs. Florida estimates that spending by nonprofits and their employees creates three jobs for every four nonprofit jobs. In Florida, that means that over 750,000 jobs are attributable to the nonprofit sector.[10]

Such a robust role in the economy, and the likelihood that it will only increase in the future, may hold both good and bad news.

On the one hand, employment and economic growth are good things. Any growth is better than no growth and nonprofit spending does feed for-profit growth. Hospitals buy supplies, hire lawyers, and pay accountants. Universities are probably excellent clients for paper manufacturers.

On the other hand, because the nonprofit sector is so concentrated, relying on growth in that sector for overall economic health can result in a dangerously undiversified economy. Aggressive cost containment in healthcare at the national policy level, for example, can squeeze employment out of the healthcare sector. Without somewhere for that employment to flow, the result is higher overall unemployment, and the attendant social costs. The final result risks reductions in wealth creation and increases in social payments, a combination that is an economic death spiral.

◼ NOTES

1. *The United States Nonprofit Sector* (Washington, D.C.: National Council of Nonprofit Associations, 2004).

2. *World Development Report 2005* (Washington, D.C.: The World Bank, 2005): 257.

3. www.fimdstreet.org/2005/10/hedge_fund_asse.html.

4. P. Arnsberger, "Charities and other tax-exempt organizations, 1998," *Publication 1136 Statistics of Income Bulletin,* Special Studies Special Projects Section, Internal Revenue Service (Fall 2002).

5. T. Hussain, "Projections of Federal Tax Return Filings: Calendar Years 2005–2012," Internal Revenue Service, Projections and Forecasting Group, Office of Research.

6. Ibid.

7. C. J. Moore, "Nonprofit Organizations Are Hiring Workers at a Faster Pace Than Government, Businesses," *Chronicle of Philanthropy,* June 10, 2004.

8. J. S. Irons and G. Bass, "Recent Trends in Nonprofit Employment and Earnings: 1990–2004," OMB Watch Tax and Budget Staff Reports, August 2004.

9. L. M. Salamon and S. L. Geller, "Pennsylvania Nonprofit Employment," Johns Hopkins Center for Civil Society Studies, Nonprofit Employment Bulletin Number 18, January 2005.

10. "Economic Contribution of Florida Nonprofit Organizations: A Resource for the Public Good," Philanthropy and Nonprofit Leadership Center, Rollins College: April 2002.

Committees of Discernment: A Strategy for a Shared Vision for Philanthropy

The Very Reverend Dr. James A. Kowalski

> Never doubt that a small group of thoughtful, committed citizens can change the world; indeed, it's the only thing that ever has.
>
> —Margaret Mead, American anthropologist (1901–1978)

What informs the process by which people make philanthropic choices? The transfer of wealth projected to take place from 1998 to 2052 is estimated to range somewhere between $10–$41 trillion. The magnitude of money expected to be given to charities has people asking lots of questions about how donors will decide what to give.

Whether in terms of individual faith systems or as community-spirited, value-based citizens, philanthropists who seek new and broadly based insights create sounder opportunities to serve and results that last. In effect, they expect knowledge and appropriate responses to continue to be revealed. They seek to listen to voices different from their own, appreciating that serving the common good involves including people and issues that go beyond the partial worldview of any given individual or group.

Background

Paul G. Schervish, the Director of Boston College's Center on Wealth and Philanthropy, has studied wealth and wealth transfer for decades. He believes that the leading cultural and spiritual question of our time will be how those decisions are made in this age of affluence and he has explored the process by which religion actually induces charitable outcomes. Many would agree that process is still not well understood.

About a decade and a half ago, when Schervish wrote his essay "Wealth and the Spiritual Secret of Money,"[1] he stated that

> . . . religion or spirituality encourages philanthropy by explicitly linking givers to the concerns and needs of others . . . [and] wealth affords individuals the ability to have what they want . . . [and] philanthropy can be understood as the transformation of time and money from a pool of wealth into a disposable gift to others . . . [as] religion . . . as it takes its form in what I call the spirituality of money . . . motivates or spurs philanthropy . . . by shaping the quality of wants or desires among the wealthy.

At that time, Schervish was responding to his own "Study on Wealth and Philanthropy,"[2] in which he had examined the strategies of living and giving among 130 millionaires. He reported that for many wealthy people, philanthropy often was a way to expand their moral worldview, and also expand the power and control with which they experienced everyday activities. The wealthy, who could by definition have whatever they wanted, were able to master social construction just as readily as they had controlled their more personal worlds.

Schervish observed "a bond of care for others," by which the wealthy would do good works for others and give back to society as they redirected their personal wants. But there exists a danger that the wealthy could actually, in the process of philanthropy, seek to make society over in their own image. Schervish found, across various religious traditions, what he called a fundamental core of "vertical and horizontal connection" through which donors expressed empathetic bonds to others, because they believed that "a tie to the transcendent is a tie to the earth."[3] As they made that connection, upon what basis, beyond their personal worldview, would they decide what to invest in as benefactors?

Allow me to state the rather obvious: As Dean of The Cathedral Church of Saint John the Divine, I am beholden to a legacy of philanthropy. My purpose is not to critique the various ideologies, faith traditions, and worldviews that undergird some philanthropy. Just as the Cathedral I serve has a rich history of architectural images and icons, which represent the concepts of public good, divine revelation, and the mission shaped by its founders and patrons, I respect the rich variety of customs and beliefs involved in what has motivated people seeking the good society. Further, I sincerely want to encourage and nurture how people connect their personal happiness with care for others as part of a divine mandate. As someone who also endeavors to be philanthropic, I want to raise the question about *how we decide to what we give* and use, as a framework, the age-old theological context of idolatry.

THE DANGERS OF IDOLATROUS PHILANTHROPY

The Bible warns that anyone who has the power to create anything has the power to create something that could become a *graven image*. Any image created by people and then worshiped is an affront to God, because paying divine honor to anything other than the *wholly other* is idolatrous.

How is it possible that philanthropy, especially if it moves from self-absorption to other-relatedness, could become idolatrous? Peter Frumkin,[4] Professor of Public Affairs at the Lyndon B. Johnson School of Public Affairs, University of Texas, Austin, and Director of the Center for Philanthropy and Community Service, explains the trend toward what he calls "philanthropic disintermediation" among younger donors who "cut out all . . . middlemen, and instead look to themselves as the principal agents of their own philanthrophy . . . as the simplest solution to the agency question in philanthrophy, one that removes the threat of deviation from the donor's intent that delegating can create."

A donor's desire to assure that a gift is used as directed can backfire, however, if the stipulations and preconceptions redirect an already overstretched agency or program, or entice the grantee to go in less effective program directions out of fear of losing the gift. Underutilized bequests have been common tragedies when too-tightly restricted wills, over the years, held funds that could not be applied to emerging, related problems. No matter how brilliant our strategies, responses to social challenges are never time-less. All donors might better protect their gifts by assuming that an ongoing flow of more information and some long-term adaptability would ensure desired outcomes for generations.

Over the years, as Schervish has examined the wealthy, he has noted that they have social and political connections, with which they also have the power and capacity to be what he calls "world builders." Their "hyperagency" includes the way their lives are knit together, through social capital and political connections, as self-determined agents who set agenda and become agents of change. They are not interested only in meeting their own needs but are also genuinely concerned about the common good and public policies. Schervish observed that within their powerful frame of reference, the wealthy tended to "reinforce rather than . . . transform what the wealthy view as the nature of their responsibilities.[5] At its best," Schervish argued, "religious consciousness . . . rather than destroying such agency makes it a participative agency linked and responsive to the agency of God and other people."[6] Schervish continued to conduct "archeological interviews" with the wealthy, helping them to construct moral biographies of their wealth by which they are led to discover how they want to direct a gift.

Determining one's interests and the focus of one's philanthropy has not been difficult for many philanthropists. Nor has it been difficult for them to identify financial advisors who assist their selection of the specific financial tools that are most appropriate to their goals. A concern not often raised is whether or not such decisions, even if thoughtful and clear, may take place in the vacuum of one's own experience, without the insights and balance made available by reaching out to diverse points of view that broaden the donor's worldview. When people have already set ideas about what they want to give to, and what they hope to achieve, I believe they may short-circuit some important outcomes that ultimately build community. I have worked closely with donors who were part of the allocation process, for example, with the United Way. Agencies funded learned from donors, in addition to getting money, and some donors said their lives were changed by site visits and direct encounters with program staff, and clients served. Working as colleagues, donors and grantees on both sides of the evaluations and allocations tables broaden their worldviews and competencies.

Take the example of very bright and successful businesspeople who decide to fund and manage charitable enterprises. Mark Kramer, who founded the Center for Effective Philanthropy, was an especially irate voice when the great buzz arose around the emergence of "venture philanthropy." In 2002, he noted that "young entrepreneurs became our heroes, and we hailed a new breed of 'social entrepreneurs' to bring the magic of this success to charities and foundations."[7] Kramer cautioned that specialized genius did not always transfer, and that even the sound decision making of smart and successful businesspeople did not eliminate the need for a long-term plan for investing in the community, and a longitudinal review of results. Those new venture philanthropists were more effective when they included in their decision making various scholars and practitioners, who had already been on the ground for some time, immersed in the challenges the philanthropists wanted to address.

Journalist Jessica Guynn, reacting to the Gates/Buffet collaboration, took an arguably cheap shot at Bill Gates by comparing him to Andrew Carnegie, writing that he "wants to be remembered not just for how ruthlessly he made his fortune, but for how he gave it away." Guynn further lumped Gates into her category of "tech-boom benefactors" who are "reinventing philanthropy the way they reinvented business," asserting that "[t]hese nouveau philanthropists are getting involved in the public sector for the same reason they got involved in the private sector: They want to change the world. And they run their philanthropic endeavors the same hands-on way they run their businesses, creating models to raise money and awareness and finding ways to measure returns and increase efficiency."[8]

THE ADVANTAGES OF COMMITTEES OF DISCERNMENT

Alternatively, take for example, Steve Kirsch, who at an early age became a wealthy and disciplined philanthropist. Kirsch is the founder and chair of Propel Software, a Silicon Valley start-up, and is probably best known as the founder and chairman of Infoseek, acquired by Disney. In response to Gates's immersion in philanthropy, Kirsch told Guynn that, "The incremental contributions [Gates] could make to Microsoft are small compared to the potential contributions he can make to more serious problems that the world faces."

"Going public," in this sense, means an increased number of donor investors would fund an already public charitable enterprise. Kirsch has said that his vision of the future would be that rich Internet entrepreneurs, who have figured out that they have more money than they need, would start "bragging about the size of their charitable partnerships and how many people they helped last year . . . competing with each other to see who can build the charitable fund with the most assets the fastest . . . always out knocking on doors of nonprofit agencies asking people if they need money for an idea they have . . . [and making] a long term commitment to the success of the company. They sit on the board and help build the management team . . . Soon, the charity goes public. This allows the charity to accept donations from the public at large."[9]

Kirsch, like many other philanthropists, has created an advisory board and draws from various experts in the fields he funds. The remedy to what can otherwise be idolatrous philanthropy (making things over in your own image) may be found in the way some donors reach beyond their own interests and goals, and use a group-centered model of decision making to serve the common good. Committees of discernment create the checks and balances that can prevent the narrowness or preconceptions inevitable when individuals with enormous wealth unilaterally set the agenda for public policy and debates, by the power of their gifts.

Smart philanthropists have shown us how to invest in the social fabric without simply reinforcing one's own perceptions and assumptions. They work alongside others and discover new ideas to solve problems. The emerging, shared wisdom and experience can ensure dialogue that prevents public policies that are made over in a donor's image. Bill and Melinda Gates and Bill Clinton are examples of philanthropists who are putting together world-class discernment teams, representing many areas of expertise and experience. In doing so, they may ensure that their personal power and considerable genius do not overwhelm the social agenda which they will shape for decades.

Faith communities not only impart already received or agreed upon beliefs. Another function they serve is to test ongoing interpretations, applied as situations change, or when an individual or group believes a new revelation has been received. Whether or not a community has a mechanism of discernment can have enormous impact on the vitality and adaptability of the community and its members. Although an individual may be a prophet, the group may also have elders or wise ones. Otherwise, a trusted leader may be thought of as virtually infallible. Seeking out feedback from others as a process can be embedded as a safeguard to the members, and to the safety of the group. What some traditions have called "the community test" prevents a highly energized and powerful person, or subgroup—even if inspired—from becoming unilateralist. I believe that the stakes do not have to look that high for discernment to be important. If we seek out insights and new information from others, we invite imagination and strategic thinking that would otherwise not be captured for the benefit of the philanthropic venture.

In that model of exploring what is true and good, the assumption is that no existing dogma or experience is able to address fully the complex challenges of a particular time, nor is it able to endure wisely for generations without modification. Tradition literally means "being passed hand to hand." Such a community-based discernment process acknowledges that all traditions and worldviews are interpreted and culturally defined. By redacting and reinterpreting needs and circumstances, those involved in the discernment process acknowledge that they have blind spots, no matter how genuine and sincere their intentions, and that responses will at least need updating.

Whether in terms of individual faith systems or as community-spirited, value-based citizens, philanthropists who seek new and broadly based insights create sounder opportunities to serve and results that last. In effect, they expect knowledge and appropriate responses to continue to be revealed. They seek to listen to voices different from their own, appreciating that serving the common good involves including people and issues that go beyond the partial worldview of any given individual or group. How different history would have been if decision makers had asked, "Who is not at the table as we assess this situation and make this decision?"

We are part of a time in human history during which cycles of dispute, violence, and divisiveness seem to be driven by people on the extremes of issues. When things appear to be black and white, it becomes easier to embrace the temptation to reduce complicated challenges to simplistic causes and remedies. It can be difficult to know what the underlying problem is, let alone whether or not a response actually will address the root cause or make an enduring difference. People are sick and tired of band-aids being put on serious problems, and of getting seduced into the argument that we have to do something.

It is often impossible to sort through what the undercurrents of the debates really are — who is grinding what axe, and what the real agendas are. Oliver Wendell Holmes, the late justice of the U.S. Supreme Court who was often called "the Great Dissenter," is reputed to have said, "I wouldn't give a fig for the simplicity on this side of complexity; I would give my right arm for the simplicity on the far side of complexity."

Whether we have extraordinary resources or relatively few to invest philanthropically in building the Good Society, we are more likely to make the kind of difference every citizen should hope to make by examining the root issues collaboratively, and responding collegially. Even when a favorite charity or trusted leader within an organization that has served us zeroes in on clearly worthwhile projects, we and they will be well served by asking, "Is there a discernment process in place to be certain that we know what the problem really is, what the best strategy to address it is, and how we will measure the results?"

I suspect that in the next few years, such committees of discernment, with diverse representation, will function in the oversight of wise, community-responsive philanthropic agenda setting, much as ethics committees inform those in hospitals who struggle with the complex life-and-death issues, faced in the light of the technological resources we are blessed to enjoy.

Ambassador James A. Joseph,[10] who heads the U.S.-Southern Africa Center for Leadership and Public Values—which he founded, at both Duke University and the University of Cape Town—has served four U.S. presidents, most recently as United States Ambassador to South Africa. He was the first and only American ambassador to present his credentials to President Nelson Mandela, and was honored by the Republic of South Africa with the Order of Good Hope, the highest award presented to a citizen of another country. Joseph has said that "philanthropy in its most ideal state does not seek reciprocity or mutuality. It is self-giving without being self-serving, and it goes beyond tribal limits to embrace all of the created order."

Exciting models of philanthropic discernment are emerging as strategic philanthropic entrepreneurs enlarge the length and breadth of those decision making tables, and gather around them voices that can inform public policy choices that make their gifts even wiser investments in the common good.

▉ NOTES

1. Paul Schervish, "Wealth and the Spiritual Secret of Money," *Faith and Philanthropy in America: Exploring the Role of Religion in America's Voluntary Sector,* Robert Wuthnow, Virginia A. Hodgkinson, and associates (San Francisco: Jossey-Bass, 1990): 64.

2. Paul Schervish and Andrew Herman, "The Study on Wealth and Philanthropy," (final report, sponsored by T. B. Murphy Foundation, January 1985–August 1988); see also Paul Schervish, "The Sound of One Hand Clapping: The Case for and against Anonymous Giving," in *Voluntas: International Journal of Voluntary and Nonprofit Organizations* 5(1) (Springer, Netherlands: February 1994): 1–26.

3. Schervish, op. cit., 75-75.

4. P. Frumkin, *Strategic Giving: The Art and Science of Philanthropy* (Chicago, IL: University of Chicago Press, 2006).

5. Schervish, op. cit., 78.

6. Schervish, op. cit., 76.

7. Mark Kramer, "Opinion: On the Legacy of "Venture Philanthropy," *Chronicle on Philanthropy,* May 2, 2002.

COMMITTEES OF DISCERNMENT 165

8. Jessica Guynn, "Gates: The Carnegie of Our Time? His Decision to Move Full Time into Philanthropy May Influence Others," *San Francisco Chronicle,* June 20, 2006.

9. Stephen and Michelle Kirsch Foundation Web site, http://www.kirschfoundation.org.

10. James A. Joseph, "Building a Foundation for Faith and Family Philanthropy," *Faith and Philanthropy in America: Exploring the Role of Religion in America's Voluntary Sector,* Robert Wuthnow, Virginia A. Hodgkinson, and associates (San Francisco: Jossey-Bass, 1990).

Markets for International Development

DENNIS WHITTLE

IT'S THE FIRST TIME ANYONE EVER LISTENED TO MY IDEA

> It's okay. I'm just a little choked up because I have been working here 15 years, and today was the first time anyone listened to my idea.

The scene was the atrium of the World Bank, May 1998. The person speaking was a senior World Bank economist. I had approached him because he appeared to be crying, and I asked him if something was wrong. The first-ever Innovation Marketplace had just ended, and the Bank's president, Jim Wolfensohn, had just announced 11 winners, out of a total of 110 Bank teams participating. The teams were awarded a total of about $5 million in "angel funding" for their innovative ideas, for catalyzing economic growth, enhancing social development, and/or improving the environment.

Almost $2 trillion has been spent on foreign aid over the past 50 years. While some progress has been made in improving living standards, there is a general consensus that the money has had far less impact than hoped. One reason for this has been the lack of a market mechanism for allocating resources to the projects with the highest impact.

The senior economist had not been among those selected for funding. But he was overcome with emotion nonetheless—just because the bureaucracy had finally listened to his idea. And he had met another Bank staffer at the event who had a related idea, along with a small pot of money, and the two of them agreed to work together.

The Innovation Marketplace was a breakthrough in many ways. From the Bank's point of view, it was successful because it elicited key innovations from the front lines that otherwise would have gotten stuck in the bureaucracy. Over the next 18 months, about half of the 11 funded projects proved to be of strategic importance for the Bank's ability to respond to world events, like disasters, or trends, such as a special fund to encourage research into an AIDS vaccine.

Just Shut Up and Report to the Tenth Floor

In the winter of 1997, I was on a ski trip, recovering from a grueling five years spent working on the Bank's Russia Program. The last operation I led was one of the largest in World Bank history—a joint program with the IMF that ultimately provided billions of dollars to the government of the Russian Federation. In the previous six months, my colleagues and I had been to Russia seven times to conclude the deal. We were all exhausted, and given the often surreal situation in Russia, we were not sure exactly what results our efforts and funding would have.

After a morning of skiing, I returned to the condo to have some lunch and relax when the phone rang. On the other end was a friend and former boss, Mark Baird, who was now working with Jim Wolfensohn to lead a process of sweeping change there. Mark asked, "Do you know anything about new products?"

I said, "New products? What's that?" He said, "That's the whole problem. Jim [the bank president] says we haven't had many new products here over the last 50 years, and that's why people are protesting in the streets. So he wants to have a New Products team, and you are the new leader of that team."

"But I don't know anything about creating new products," I protested.

"Just shut up and report to the tenth floor when you get back," Mark commanded.

When I got back to Washington, Mark gave me a budget of $5 million, a suite of empty offices, and a young but dynamic consultant, Marcus Williams. I hadn't the slightest idea what to do. I was an economist, not an innovator.

Marcus and I set about implementing the recommendations provided, by a top-five consulting firm. They basically said, "Put an ideas box out in the hallway and collect ideas. Then establish two management committees. The first committee should eliminate 85 percent of the ideas, and the second committee should rule on whether the rest of them should be funded."

We proceeded to do this, and got a few hundred ideas, ranging from one-liners to full business plans. But in one year, we were able to get only one committee to meet one time, and they were reluctant to make any decisions whatsoever. "How should we decide?" and "Aren't we already doing too many things?" were the common refrains.

These questions irritated me when they were originally posed. They irritated me even more when it became clear that the whole new products initiative was failing. After nine months, we had failed to allocate any money to any really new ideas, and my boss was telling me that the program might be stopped altogether.

So Marcus and I finally did what we should have done long before. We decided to throw away the recommendations made by the consulting firm and ask our colleagues for help. We called about seven friends and begged them to help. We offered free pizza and beer in exchange for a few hours of brainstorming together.

After some arm twisting, we all got into a room and started with a blank white board. We got nowhere fast. Then someone said, "You know, what if we made the process of developing new products as innovative as the new products themselves?" And so we divided the board into two sections, and on the left we wrote "Existing process," and on the right we wrote "What is the opposite?"

And then we started filling the columns in. On the left we wrote things like "top-down loans," "$100 million," "two-year processing time," "200 pages of documentation," and so forth. On the right, we wrote "bottom-up grants," "$100,000," "two-day processing," "two pages of documentation," and so forth.

When we finished this exercise, we all laughed and said, "Sure, right, ha! There is no way any of that is feasible." And then we had a beer and talked about other things. Finally, my former colleague from the Russia department, Mari Kuraishi, said, "Well, why not?"

That meeting was the seed of the Innovation Marketplace, which later evolved into the very successful and ongoing Development Marketplace. The Development Marketplace, in turn, helped spawn a sibling—Global-Giving.com, which is an independent, eBay-like marketplace, for international development projects.

When the beer and pizza meeting was over, Mari, Marcus, and I were excited and terrified. How exactly would we bring this concept into being? Fortunately, we met another, less conventional outside consultant named Chris McGoff, and together we began designing a process that would culminate in a public event called the Innovation Marketplace, where everyone would be allowed to showcase their ideas in public. A "roving jury panel" made up of not only World Bank managers, but also NGO leaders and private sector representatives, would visit each team and grill them on their idea. The teams would be limited to four pages of written documentation and 15 minutes of presentation time.

Jim Wolfensohn, the Bank's president, probably thought we were crazy when we presented the idea to him. He was silent for a long time. Finally, he said, "Can you pull it off?" We said, "Sure!" with a great but undoubtedly unconvincing show of bravado. The next few months were an extraordinary experience in navigating bureaucratic minefields as we enlisted the help of many Bank staff in a strange initiative that in many ways flew in the face of the Bank's entire business model.

WHAT ABOUT EVERYONE ELSE IN THE WORLD?

The Innovation Marketplace was, as described at the beginning of this chapter, a great success. It elicited good ideas from everyone at the World Bank, including the secretaries, who got funding for a project to improve services to the Bank's clients. Many, if not most, of these ideas would never have made it through the bureaucracy otherwise.

What really struck me was the remark made by the senior economist— "No one ever listened to my idea before." Despite this guy's sense of exclusion, he actually had more access to the system than 99.99 percent of people in the world. When I heard what he said that day, I began discussing an even more radical idea with my colleagues. Shortly thereafter, the Bank's president called us in to congratulate us and confess he had been very doubtful about whether it would work.

"Will you consider doing this type of event again?" Wolfensohn asked.

"Sure," we replied, "except this time we are going to invite everyone in the world to participate."

Once again, he swallowed his doubts, asked us if we could pull it off, and watched our backs as we spent the next 18 months preparing for the next event, which took place in May 2000. We called this one "The Development Marketplace." The obstacles we faced along the way wore us down, and often left us wondering if we had lost our minds. Fortunately, we were able to attract several other highly qualified team members to manage the day-to-day planning and execution.

ARE YOU CRAZY?

During the preparation, we faced withering criticism from many Bank colleagues. One of them said, "The World Bank hires the best experts, so why do we have to waste our time inviting all these other experts to give us their ideas?" When we said we were not only inviting other so-called experts, but also anyone else who wanted to participate, including community leaders from the developing world, another person replied, "Listen, if those people have good ideas, then why are they poor?" One manager bet us that we would not receive more than 100 qualified applications. Those of us on the (much expanded) Development Marketplace team were too scared to accept the bet, especially since we had no idea how to market this event to people outside the World Bank.

We received few applications until the last few days before the deadline, increasing our fears. But on the last two days there was a flood, and by the deadline we had received 1,130 submissions, from over 1,000 organizations, based in over 80 countries spread across all continents.

Despite the doubts expressed, we went back to many colleagues outside the Marketplace team, and asked them to help us review the submissions and select a number of finalists to invite to Washington. They grumbled, but nearly 80 of them agreed to help. And when the initial review panel was over, we breathed our first sighs of relief, since those colleagues came out of the room with big smiles on their faces, saying things like, "Hey, those were some very cool ideas. Did you read the one about . . ." and, "Thanks for roping me into that; it was the most enjoyable thing I have done in months." Another said, "There were so many fresh ideas there. Some were totally impractical, but others have promise."

At the end of the review, we decided to invite 339 finalists to Washington. Again we faced resistance, with colleagues asking us how we expected people from developing countries to be able to afford a trip to Washington, D.C. "Well, they are not required to come," we replied, "We are just giving them the opportunity to come, if they can." In truth, again we had no idea what would happen. To be safe, we arranged for them to be present by videoconference, if they preferred.

Nearly 300 teams arrived in Washington, in early February 2000. Another 30 or so had arranged to present their ideas to the jury panel by videoconference. On the day before the event, I went out into the atrium to check on things, and make sure that the teams were able to set up their booths and had everything they needed.

THE MAYOR NEVER GAVE US THE TIME OF DAY

The first participants I saw when I entered were two older African women, who were sitting on the floor, looking dejected. I asked them what was wrong, and they said nothing, but just pointed to the crudely hand-drawn posters they had pinned up on their booth. They then pointed to a booth across the aisle that had beautiful satellite pictures. I sensed the problem, and told them that it was not their pictures that mattered but their ideas. It turned out they were from a rural village in Uganda and had never been outside of their home province. They ran a clinic for new and expecting mothers, most of whom had no money to buy the vitamins and medicines needed to keep their children healthy. These women had done some research and come up with a plan to start a micro-credit program, so the mothers could earn some money.

The mayor of the town had refused to help them, but one day staff from a Canadian NGO came by, told them about the Development Marketplace, helped them apply, and helped them buy tickets to Washington when they were selected as finalists. As the women told me their story, they slowly regained their confidence, and by the end of the story, they asked me, "Is it true that the World Bank president will be here, to listen to our proposal?"

When the women asked me that, I nearly broke down. After assuring them that the president would be there, I went into a side room to collect myself. I then came back out into the atrium and visited the booth with the satellite images. That booth was manned by a scientist from NASA who had never been to a developing country, but wondered whether NASA's astounding satellite technology could contribute to better agriculture practices by providing data on soil erosion.

Next to the scientist were two teams of supreme court justices from Latin America. One team wanted to launch an innovative program to train judges in how to adjudicate land rights cases brought by indigenous peoples in his country.

As the event unfolded, hundreds of extraordinary teams like these packed into the Bank's atrium. Over the next two days, it was like a carnival of ideas, and anyone who entered the atrium was swept up into the fray and given five tokens with which to vote for their own favorite ideas.

At the end of the second day, Jim Wolfensohn went to the stage and began announcing the winners. Forty-four teams were awarded a total of about

$5 million. The scientist from NASA failed to win, but he was thrilled to have had the chance to get feedback on his idea. One set of supreme court justices won and looked stunned but proud as they marched to the stage. One of the last announcements was the award to the Ugandan women, who were awarded about $80,000 to start their micro-credit clinic.[1]

I Didn't Win!

When the event was over, I was sitting in a chair near the exit, exhausted, talking to a few of my colleagues. A woman from South Africa, who I remembered from one of the booths, walked up to us and said in strong voice, "I did not win!" And I replied, "Well, I am sorry, but this is a competition, and not everyone can win." She retorted, "Well, I am telling you that my idea is a good one, and just because the World Bank did not finance it does not mean that there are not others out there who will finance it." She waited for a response, but we were all too tired to think of anything intelligent to say.

Over the next few days, a few of us became obsessed by what the South African woman had said. Although we called it the Development Marketplace, it was not really a full marketplace, because there was really only one buyer, and it was destined to be only a periodic event, rather than an ongoing market.

This led to two initiatives. The first was the creation of a full-fledged unit, devoted full time to the implementation of additional Development Marketplaces, as an ongoing activity within the Bank. The second was the departure of Mari Kuraishi and me from the World Bank to create Global-Giving, as an independent, online marketplace that provides a level playing field for both funders and those with project ideas. Both initiatives have extended the concept significantly.

World Bank Marketplace Goes Local

Within the World Bank, successive teams led new waves of marketplaces, both in Washington and in bank offices around the world.[2] There have now been five "global" marketplaces in Washington, funding nearly 200 projects, with about $25 million. Awards have ranged from $23,000 for a reforestation project in Peru, to $380,000 for a community-based health insurance scheme, based in the Philippines. Most recently, the global marketplaces are focusing on specific themes, such as water and sanitation.

Arguably even more successful have been the Country Marketplaces. Forty-three of these marketplaces have been held since 2001. The awards are typically much smaller, ranging from $5,000 to $25,000. A total of about $10 million has been provided to about 650 projects. These local marketplaces have helped bring the Bank much closer to the ultimate beneficiaries, and have, in several cases, also provided a forum for national governments to work more constructively with NGOs, with whom they were often at loggerheads.

The Development Marketplaces have not fundamentally changed the World Bank's business model. The Bank is making progress, but in many ways remains a top-down, ponderous, and closed system. Without question, the Marketplaces have provided a way for the Bank to better understand the real issues facing communities, at the grassroots level. It also surfaces many good ideas about what local people consider appropriate solutions and technologies. The Marketplaces have also finally provided a concrete way in which the Bank can work together with private companies, which are beginning to sponsor prizes and awards at some of the events.

And finally, nearly all Bank staff who are involved with these Marketplaces come out of the experience extremely energized—a key benefit for the many staff worn down by the bureaucracy over the years.

The degree to which the marketplace concept can change the Bank's overall way of doing business is constrained by many factors, including the bylaws of the Bank, which require it to lend almost exclusively to national governments. Time will tell whether the Development Marketplaces have had a profound effect on the World Bank's development model.

GlobalGiving Marketplace Goes Virtual

The "other" marketplace, GlobalGiving.com, is now in its adolescence and growing steadily. Mari Kuraishi and I left the World Bank at the end of 2000, to respond to the South African woman's demand for what was, in effect, a true marketplace for project funding. The idea was to build an eBay-like site, where any qualified person or group could list a project, and any person or organization in the world could fund it. Feedback loops, including ratings systems, would be implemented, so that the best projects could attract more funding, and successful project leaders could build a positive reputation, presumably leading to even more funding.

It took us over a year to design the beta version of the platform, which was launched in February 2002. Many project ideas were submitted from all over the world right away, but only a few scattered funders used the site initially. GlobalGiving really began taking off when Hewlett Packard employees provided over $100,000 to projects, using the platform during their annual giving campaign, alongside the United Way in November 2002 (see Exhibit 3.6).

Building on that experience, we totally revamped and relaunched in early 2003; since then, activity has steadily increased. Our research and increases in donation volume tell us that both experienced and novice philanthropists value the project-specific, tangible nature of GlobalGiving. Through mid-2006, several million dollars have flowed to over 700 projects. In addition to thousands of public users, employees and customers of companies such as VISA, the Gap, North Face, Applied Materials, and many others use the marketplace to fund projects.

One of the key challenges for GlobalGiving was scaling the vetting of projects at a low cost. The solution proved to be the creation of a network of "project sponsors," who vet projects before they are posted. A team led by Elizabeth Stefanski, formerly of Ashoka, has expanded this network to include about 40 sponsors, including leading NGOs—such as Acumen, Ashoka, Mercy Corps, the Open Society Institute, the Tech Museum, and Trickle Up; private companies, including Hewlett Packard and North Face; and even official agencies, like the World Bank and UN.[3]

EXHIBIT 3.6   TOTAL REGISTERED USERS— GLOBALGIVING FROM 10/04 TO 06/06

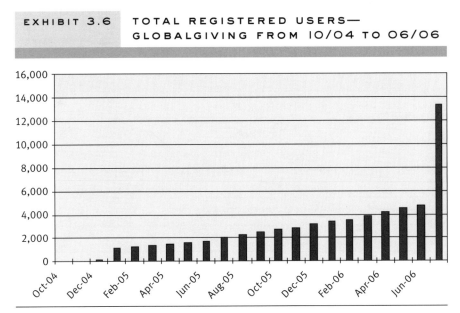

Source: GlobalGiving, 2006.

GlobalGiving is now experimenting with ways to open access to even more projects, via a system whereby the broader GlobalGiving community is able to nominate and vet projects. After two pilots, the results are encouraging, with almost a fourth of all projects coming via the open access channel (see Exhibit 3.7)

As the only true worldwide marketplace, GlobalGiving is helping lead a revolution in the philanthropic sector (see Exhibit 3.8). That means that we are providing a place for that South African woman to find the "others" who will finance her idea. And it means that we provide a place for funders to support similar high-impact initiatives all around the world.

THE FUTURE: AN EMERGING ECOSYSTEM

Almost $2 trillion has been spent on foreign aid over the past 50 years. While some progress has been made in improving living standards (especially in a few larger countries such as China and India), there is a general consensus that the money has had far less impact than hoped. One reason for this has been the lack of a market mechanism, for allocating resources to the projects with the highest impact. Instead, the aid system has been divided

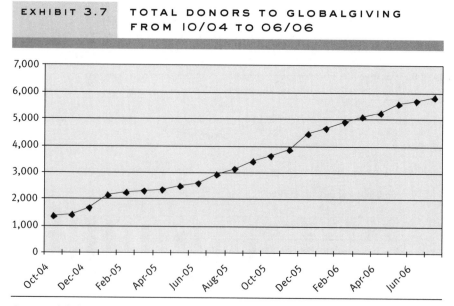

EXHIBIT 3.7   TOTAL DONORS TO GLOBALGIVING FROM 10/04 TO 06/06

Source: GlobalGiving, 2006.

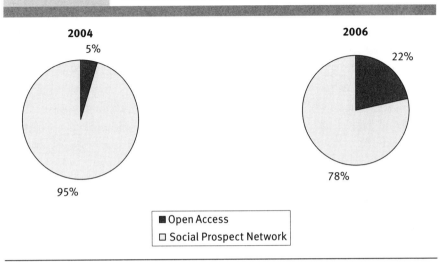

EXHIBIT 3.8   ORIGIN OF PROJECTS ON GLOBALGIVING

Source: GlobalGiving, 2006.

up among a small number of organizations, which allocate resources based on a top-down approach that bears some similarities to central planning in the former Soviet Union.

The Development Marketplace was one of the first major challenges to the existing system, and it is encouraging that it was launched from within the largest of the central planning–oriented institutions. GlobalGiving and other related initiatives were launched soon after, and many elements of a market system for international development are emerging. Some of these, such as Ashoka,[4] focus on grooming and networking "social entrepreneurs"—project leaders who have potentially world-changing ideas. Others, such as Acumen, focus on funding a small number of high-potential, socially-oriented start-ups. And organizations like GuideStar International and Keystone have begun developing accreditation systems. Finally, country-specific marketplaces similar to GlobalGiving are emerging in places like India (GiveIndia), Argentina (HelpArgentina), and South Africa (Greater Good).[5]

The challenge now is for these various actors to start collaborating much more intensely, in the manner of a real marketplace. One of the most useful analogies is to think about how successful start-ups get launched, and then grow, in the United States. There is an ecosystem of investors who specialize in different stages of growth.

"Angel investors" put in small amounts of money to help entrepreneurs develop an idea. If the business looks promising, venture capitalists come in to provide larger amounts of money to build a product and try to market it. At this stage, there is an entire industry of people who specialize in providing coaching, technical, and managerial support to start-ups. If the start-up can sell its products, a group of "mezzanine funders" provides additional capital. When the firm begins growing rapidly, it goes public, and sells shares on the NASDAQ or the NYSE, or private equity funds provide additional capital. Banks and other funders then provide loans for further expansion. At each stage, a whole industry of accountants and lawyers and others provide due diligence and analyze creditworthiness.

Such an ecosystem is only just now beginning to emerge in the international aid space. The speed with which this ecosystem develops will determine the pace at which promising new organizations will be able to get the funding or expertise they need to grow. But such a market-based system will also be a threat to larger, more established organizations, since it will expose them to greater transparency and competition. Just as in the private sector, the most nimble and well-managed of the larger organizations will survive and even grow, while others will shrink or even go out of business. The imperative is to ensure that resources are allocated efficiently, and that incentives are in place for innovation and impact. With total spending on foreign aid programs running close to $100 billion per year,[6] there is much at stake.

AUTHOR'S NOTE

The author wishes to thank Mike Kubzansky, Joyita Mukherjee, and Dan Crisafulli for their ideas and comments. Maria Whittle provided research assistance. The opinions expressed are those of the author, and do not necessarily represent the views of GlobalGiving, the World Bank, or any other person or organization. Any errors are the responsibility of the author, who may be contacted at dwhittle@globalgiving.com.

NOTES

1. For more details on the original Development Marketplace, see Robert Wood and Gary Hamel, "The World Bank's Innovation Marketplace," *Harvard Business Review,* November 2002.

2. Mike Kubzansky, Dan Crisafulli, and Joyita Mukherjee have been among the leaders of these teams, and each has introduced a new feature to expand the original concept.

3. For a full list, see www.globalgiving.com/aboutus/partners.html.

4. Ashoka deserves special mention, because it was established by Bill Drayton over 20 years ago. Drayton is responsible for seeding many of the ideas and concepts discussed in this article.

5. This is only a small selection of some the excellent organizations emerging; many others could have been included.

6. The numbers fluctuate, but about one-quarter to one-third of this $100 billion comes from private individuals, companies, and foundations; the remainder comes from official agencies, such as the World Bank, and from governments.

Analysis of Philanthropy for Science and Technology Part I: Pasteur's Quadrant

RODNEY W. NICHOLS

In the twenty-first century, potential patrons of science and technology sort through almost limitless opportunities. The research community's ambition knows no bounds—from atoms to the cosmos, from biotechnology to engineering. Moreover, compelling goals of the citizenry, in areas ranging from health and environment to energy and economic development, demand fresh approaches. Government does not do it all. Innovation still rests on the creativity of individual initiatives. This essay and the next, outline how to navigate the terrain, analyze choices, weigh results, and consider a variety of specific prospects for progress.

INTRODUCTION

"The best philanthropy," said John D. Rockefeller, Sr. in 1909, "involves a search for cause, an attempt to cure evils at their source."[1] He was discussing the purpose of his gift to found the Rockefeller Institute for Medical Research, now Rockefeller University. For Rockefeller and his advisors, the imperative was to support fundamental science in order to understand and conquer disease. Setting high standards of quality for staff was paramount. The mission was visionary: *pro bono humani generis*.

> The underlying incentives for patrons, and for their beneficiaries in science, were captured by Goethe: "To one man (science) is the highest thing, a heavenly goddess; to another it is a productive and proficient cow, who supplies them with butter."

After 100 years of modern biomedical research, utilizing private and public funds, the general case for providing resources — to build in-depth understanding, in an environment of freedom for open inquiry — remains robust. The achievements have been remarkable. Yet resulting technological changes in medicine have also brought unexpected frustrations, such as rising costs of science-based healthcare, and controversial applications like gene therapy and artificial organs. After World War II, enormous increases in government funding for medical research prompted the great twentieth-century foundations to withdraw almost entirely from the field, moving to other, mostly social priorities, including advocacy programs. This has been an important trend.

Comparable patterns appear in every field of natural science, engineering, and mathematics. Philanthropy stimulates long-range, basic work. When projects are led by creative investigators, and when results are continuously subjected to vigorous debate, research pays off. A century of pressing the frontiers in physics and engineering — supported largely during the past 50 years by government and businesses, not private philanthropists — created the "information economy." The resulting revolutionary advances increased economic productivity, creating powerful new means for every mode of transportation and communication throughout the world. Unfortunately, as in the life sciences, remarkable advances in engineering occasionally come with unexpected adverse consequences. The environmental effects of economic development are seen today in China and India, as they rapidly exploit modern technology.

Sometimes, as in World War II, urgency dictates that governments step in to assure rapid progress and instantly applied results. Often, private initiatives take the lead while public and private partnerships set the stage. For example, MIT, Chicago, Harvard, Caltech, Berkeley, and other universities were ready to accept war-time assignments, when deadlines demanded mobilization with surges of government support.

What course shall philanthropy take in the future? Is private philanthropy still relevant, with irrepressible technological change and innumerable opportunities across the sciences? Yes! In this essay I sketch a conceptual framework for considering how philanthropy may invest in science and technology. First, I consider the national context of governmental vis-à-vis private funding, then I review the models and motives for private support.

In the subsequent essay, I review a variety of "big questions" in research and illustrate the international trends that may drive future American philanthropy. I also emphasize the need to build greater capacity for sharpening assessments of results. Finally, I advocate greater consideration of the need for gifts that endow gifted people, programs, and institutions for the long term.

I am not a scholar of the "philanthropoid" community. And this is neither a survey, nor an evaluation, of all gifts to science by private sources. Yet I do have experience, having sought and received grants and contracts while serving as investigator and executive in the public and private sectors, as well as in universities. My aims in this chapter and the next are to lay out continuing issues and stimulate informed debate.

NATIONAL CONTEXT OF FUNDING

To display the themes under review in this chapter, I must first outline the process of identifying substantive objectives for philanthropy in science and technology. Then I summarize the past and current funding for science and technology from all national sources.

Process

Every donor today has undeniably greater awareness of worldwide needs than almost any donor could have had during past decades. Whether giving $1,000 to a local AIDS clinic, or $1 billion to a global AIDS campaign, donors today have greater access to reliable data. Through news accounts and the pleas of advocacy organizations, knowledge of needs has multiplied abundantly, often clamorously. Moreover, by using instant communications, donors can learn about grants by other donors, as well as information about at least some of the results of past and ongoing projects. In AIDS, for instance, widely publicized professional conferences, intergovernmental reports, and assessments from the private sector reveal why, after 25 years, an AIDS vaccine is still not feasible. Accordingly, a philanthropist interested in AIDS—whether the grant would be for research, medical care, or counseling—can frame highly specific and informed alternatives for possible action.[2, 3, 4]

Furthermore, the process of weighing alternatives in modern philanthropy—not just for science, but for all subjects—has been greatly enhanced by technology itself. Tapping into formal technical literature, checking data on public funding, inviting proposals, soliciting expert commentary, archiving the conclusions of prior reviews—these functions buttress reviews of grant applications. All can be accomplished with keener efficiency, and greater precision, using electronic communications. Offices of foundations are no more "paperless" than other offices. Yet, like most of the rest of the service industry, productivity in most support staff and administrative areas is high and rising. This enhanced capability ought to mean less overhead, and more impact per dollar of philanthropy. While this is obvious, few donors fully exploit the potential. Still, modern technology matters in the process of grant making. It can produce extensive gains over the coming years, multiplying the effective purchasing power of the philanthropic dollar.

Funding

What is the current funding? Exhibit 3.9 summarizes 2004 data, compiled by the Foundation Center, covering categories related to science and technology. Of the estimated total of $15.5 billion in grants, from about 1,000 major foundations, I have made "ballpark" totals showing roughly $1.8 billion dedicated to "science and technology," or about 12 percent of the total. This may well be an upper limit. My guess is that the actual funding for *research*—as the term might be defined by the National Academy of Sciences, or the National Science Foundation—was less than this amount. On the other hand, smaller foundations that often give at the local level may have helped fund scientists and medical projects.[5]

This estimate, however, leaves out sources that are not, by IRS standards, "foundations." For example, the Howard Hughes Medical Institute (HHMI) an "operating foundation," had annual research expenditures of almost $600 million in 2005.[6] This is roughly equal to the total of all other foundations' grants to health-related research. HHMI supports elite investigators in American biomedical research, through its own selection of "units" at established research universities.

Recall that the total budget of the federal National Institutes of Health (NIH) was about $28 billion in 2005, which dwarfs HHMI spending. However, HHMI's added funds for its investigators would not bear as much fruit without their having earned NIH support independently, in an open national competition. Still, HHMI's $15 billion endowment is crucial today for U.S. life sciences. Typically more flexible than federal grants, HHMI fosters the

EXHIBIT 3.9   SCIENCE AND TECHNOLOGY
FOUNDATION GRANTS (2004)

Category	$ Millions	Distribution of Science- and Technology-Related Foundation Grants (2004)
Environment*	170	
Health**- Specific Diseases and Medical Research	959	
Science and Technology	454	
Social Sciences***	214	
Total	1,797	

Science and Technology 25.26%

Social Sciences 11.91%

Environment 9.96%

Health 53.37%

*The total here was $675 million. Arbitrarily I assumed that 75 percent was "purely conservation of land and natural history," and thus only a quarter related to environmental science or research.

**Health category total was $3.4 billion. I included only the two subcategories most obviously possessing a strong science base. Other subcategories, left out in this narrower interpretation, are mental health and public health; both encompass some research, but comparatively little laboratory effort.

***Includes social science, economics, and interdisciplinary work; I interpret the last category as encompassing interactions with natural science and engineering, or with computer models.

Source: Foundation Center.

independent flair of productive scientists. However, for sound legal and historical reasons, HHMI does not appear in the public compilations of "giving." It does appear in federal tabulations of "nonprofit research and development performers," along with institutions such as the Mayo Clinic and Sematech, which raise funds to support their "intramural" research and development.[7]

Along similar lines, many donors make comparatively small gifts (say, $1,000 to $50,000) to support pre- and doctoral investigators, such as in immunology through the Irvington Institute, or to cancer research through the American Cancer Society. Often, such diverse lines of nationwide funding neither come from nor go to "foundations," so they are neither easily nor necessarily counted. Presumably, these diverse gifts are encompassed by the aggregate "charitable giving," compiled by Giving USA, which estimated that total private gifts for all purposes reached about $250 billion in 2004.[8]

To arrive at a grand total, assume that in addition to the funding for science and technology from recognized foundations—as shown in Exhibit 3.9, a total of almost $1.8 billion—we add $600 million from HHMI, along with an estimated $100 million from sources that somehow slip through the national data collection. We then come to a grand total of $2.5 billion—roughly one percent of all national giving.

For 2004, the national context looked like this: Philanthropic funding was equal to about 2.5 percent of the total federal research and development (R&D) budget of roughly $94 billion. Looked at another way, donors supported about 0.75 percent of the total national R&D spending, which was about $312 billion in current dollars. About 64 percent of the overall national R&D investment came from industry, a little less than 30 percent from the federal government, and the balance from independent academic funds, state and local government, foundations, and nonprofit institutions.[9]

From the standpoint of most university laboratories, private funds may appear to be a mere sliver of revenue. But private funds are, in fact, frequently the baseline for start-ups, representing the seed money, without which the American research community would be less nimble, less innovative, and more risk averse. Scores of examples across the country confirm this phenomenon. When federal and corporate budget hawks crack their whips on spending, and shorten their time horizons for gauging returns on investments, private support is crucial at the margin. Many private donors, large and small, with diverse purposes, permit fresh ideas to flourish.

MODELS AND MOTIVES

With this background on the process of grant making for science and technology, in a national context, I will show how to analyze the territory. Philanthropists inevitably depend on mental "models" to learn how their possible actions might produce the results they passionately desire.

One criterion for many sponsors (individuals, corporate donors, and major philanthropists) is the time they believe is available, or appropriate, for the work to be done. Consider the simplified timeline in Exhibit 3.10, for a range of needs. If the sponsor's goal were urgent—say, relief from a disaster or drought—the time allowable is very short. Such a goal demands immediate action; and achieving that goal often requires technology, as in the airlifting of supplies to citizens trapped by flood or earthquake. If the goal were complex—say, understanding the origin of the cosmos, or unraveling the nature of the unconscious—then the allowable time for the work would

EXHIBIT 3.10   FUNDERS', SPONSORS', OR
                SCIENTISTS'/ENGINEERS' VIEW TIME

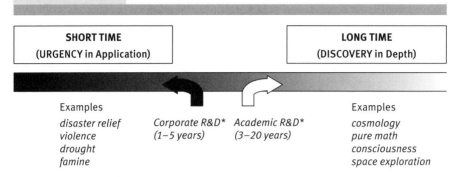

SHORT TIME	LONG TIME
(URGENCY in Application)	(DISCOVERY in Depth)

Examples   Corporate R&D*   Academic R&D*   Examples
disaster relief   (1–5 years)   (3–20 years)   cosmology
violence   pure math
drought   consciousness
famine   space exploration

*The time frames for much of both academic and especially corporate research have short-
ened during recent years. Government support encompasses the entire time spectrum, but
the vast majority of government funding goes to "development" (D), not "research" (R).

be much longer. Such goals for discovery demand patience and extraordinary talent; as achieving them frequently requires both originality in thought
and novelty in means, as in confirming Einstein's predictions.

Today most corporate R&D and most corporate philanthropy tend
toward the short term. Most academic R&D, and private philanthropy to
campuses, tend toward longer-range outlooks. Should the present emphasis on "businesslike" (or "venture") philanthropy continue—a section in the
next essay considers that angle—the United States would run the risk of
under-investing in those deep problems that rarely yield to an insistence
on a short-range focus. Moreover, as the U.S. economy must base its future
on innovation, given the challenge of global competition from China, India,
and others, the base of research must not be thinned out by excessively
short-term investments.

The once-popular idea of a linear model—supporting the notion that
science feeds technology, which then produces new products and services—
is largely a misconception.[10] Instead, the realistic dynamic, as confirmed by
vast experience, is shown in Exhibit 3.11. Science does feed technology, but
the flow can also be seen to go the other way. For example, the development
of the electron microscope created the possibility for dazzling explorations
in cell biology; and the elaborately insightful engineering design of modern
observatories and satellites created the capability for breakthroughs in
astronomy.

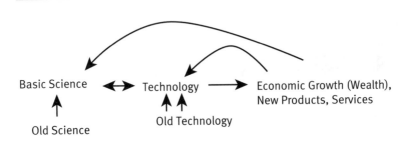

EXHIBIT 3.11   MODEL OF DYNAMICS IN SCIENCE AND TECHNOLOGY

Science and technology are in many ways autonomous, each building on itself. For instance, the hard-won understanding, bit by bit, of the physics and chemistry of materials was essential for—as work in materials science and engineering remains crucial for—translating fundamental knowledge into consumer electronics and energy-efficient manufacturing processes. And, of course, the feedbacks in the process of wealth creation underlie the entire premise of this book: New philanthropy drives progress in science and technology. The feedback loops are in all directions.

Now I turn to a more sophisticated model. It shows and integrates the motives for an ensemble of philanthropists, sponsors, and investigators. Exhibit 3.12 is adapted from the late Donald Stokes's discussion of basic science and technological innovation.[11]

To introduce this model – and to reveal its relevance to philanthropy – recall Pasteur's remark: "No, a thousand times no, there does not exist a category of science to which one can give the name applied science. There are science and the applications of science, bound together as the fruit to the tree which bears it." In the words of Stokes, Pasteur's drive in basic research was "use-inspired." He had two powerful motives: to understand phenomena as deeply as possible and to control the results as fully as possible. These twins are rare.

But what about a quest for fundamental understanding that is not driven by any consideration of use? What about Einstein? He sought to uncover the most basic empirical patterns, frame theoretical principles, and test explanations of order. When Einstein said, "The eternal mystery of the world is its comprehensibility," he was moved by the exhilaration of fathoming nature's complexity. He did not envision the benefits an answer would supply. Such intellectual challenges hold a potent attraction for investigators.

EXHIBIT 3.12   ILLUSTRATIONS OF MOTIVES OF
SPONSORS AND INVESTIGATORS
FOR RESEARCH

Inspired by Need For Use

	NO	YES
YES **Inspired by Need for Fundamental Understanding**	**"Pure" Basic Research** *Investigator: BOHR* *Sponsors: Guggenheim,* *Kavli, NSF, Carnegie Institution*	**"Mission-Oriented" Basic Research** *Investigator: PASTEUR* *Sponsors: RF, Bell Labs, NIH, HHMI*
NO	**"Particular Phenomena"** *Investigator: PETERSON* *Sponsors: Science Museums, Conservationists/Preservationists, Naturalists*	**"Applications" Research** *Investigator: EDISON* *Sponsors: FF, Gates, CGIAR, Intel*

Source: Adapted from Donald E. Stokes [note 11], p. 73.

For many donors, however, there is a question: Although applied science is certainly not "impure," should its practice command respect as a separate category? Of course it should. Edisonian approaches to discovery, for instance, with their incremental improvements, do pay off, often handsomely. Yet the idea that applied science is the only reliable investment for R&D dollars infects the thinking of many patrons of science, engineering, mathematics, and medicine.[12] Now I will explore the deceptively simple ideas in Exhibit 3.12, which illustrates the motives of sponsors and investigators in four domains of activity.

Bohr's Quadrant

In the upper left-hand quadrant, we find Niels Bohr, an extraordinary pioneer in the physics of atomic structure. Like Einstein, he was not interested in, nor inspired by, social or economic needs or applications. Instead, his was the domain of total dedication to fundamental understanding. During recent years, Fred Kavli, a physicist and philanthropist, has followed the philosophy of this quadrant by spending about \$100 million to establish a number of basic, independent, research institutes, in fields such as cosmology.[13] For many years, Guggenheim Fellowships have taken a route through this quadrant, by selecting the best individuals from an array of fields, each aiming to push the envelope of knowledge for its own sake. The National Science Foundation and the Carnegie Institution follow this course and purpose.

Edison's Quadrant

In the lower right-hand quadrant, we find Thomas Edison, intensely determined to produce incremental advances without much concern for theory or general principles. His brilliant successes in fulfilling practical needs produced revolutionary societal benefits; and he assured both firm and lucrative patent protection. But his results yielded little deep understanding because that was not his goal. During recent years, the Ford Foundation's aims show this character, of incremental advances, sought avidly. So have the goals of the World Bank's Consultative Group on International Agricultural Research (CGIAR). The remarkable achievements of Intel have pushed and validated Moore's Law, to perpetually drive down costs, and relentlessly increase the power of semiconductor chips; this, too, is an example of great talent dedicated to practical goals in information-handling.

Phenomenological Systems

A third quadrant, in the lower left-hand corner of Exhibit 3.12, is more diffuse. In this domain, determined investigators—say, Roger Peterson, with his *Guide to the Birds of North America*—systematically document particular phenomena without much, if any, concern for either enriching a conceptual framework or pursuing a concrete application. Similar aims characterize the professional curators at science museums and the trained conservationists affiliated with art museums and historic sites. Donors to such efforts share the curiosity that energizes the investigators, and they appreciate beauty and craftsmanship. But neither practical purpose, nor search for originality in knowledge, is their motive.

Pasteur's Quadrant

The upper right-hand quadrant encompasses what should, in my judgment, engage more future philanthropists. Pasteur aimed for depth as well as utility, as I mentioned in opening this section. His "germ theory of disease" arose from use-inspired research, aimed at solving the everyday problems of breweries and milk suppliers. Going back to the 1930s, the Rockefeller Foundation followed this notion, giving birth to efforts researching applications in molecular biology," and in the 1950s, spawning the "green revolution." Bell Labs, the National Institutes of Health, and HHMI have all subscribed to the philosophy of this mission at one time or another. Core commitments pivot around excellent people, freedom of inquiry, and long-range objectives, framed in terms of gaining *both* deeper understanding as well as significant use.

Dynamic Research

While Exhibit 3.12 clarifies many static features of the science and technology landscape, it cannot capture the dynamic realities of investigators moving from one quadrant to another. For example, Charles Darwin began his systematic observations in the lower left-hand quadrant. He documented particular phenomena. Then, as patterns emerged and his interpretive conjectures had sufficient evidence, he migrated to "Bohr's quadrant," discovering evolution, what most regard as the most fundamental theory of biology (along with Mendel's genetics). His work was, in part, privately supported. Would a philanthropist today bet on such an open-ended study?

Comparable examples come from many fields; as Pasteur said, "chance favors the prepared mind." Most clinical investigation might be placed in Edison's quadrant. Yet perceptive, clinically oriented biomedical scientists see, really "see," conditions (i.e., aberrations) in patients that lead back to the bench. Avery, MacCleod, and McCarty's seminal discovery, in 1944, that DNA is the fundamental genetic material, grew out of work similar to Pasteur's, to prepare a vaccine against pneumonia.

Social Sciences

The social sciences can be included in this schema. For instance, Nobel Prize–winning economists John Maynard Keynes, Robert Solow, Paul Romer, and Milton Friedman have been occupants of "Pasteur's quadrant." Their discoveries arose from deeply probing the causes of economic depression (Keynes), the roles of technology in economic growth (Solow and Romer), and the consequences of dynamics in monetary supply (Friedman).

Because government policy often fights the last economic or social crisis, private funding in the social sciences is all the more necessary to contest conventional wisdom. The Brookings Institution, the National Bureau of

Economic Research, and Resources for the Future are among the institutions sustaining independent economic research. The Manhattan Institute's seminal work on policing, counterterrorism, welfare, educational reform, tort reform, and immigration shows the value of a "think tank" pushing the public policy envelope with empiricism and insight.

Space

In the 1960s, NASA's program belonged in "Edison's quadrant." It was, in most respects, a striking case of incremental advances, orchestrated sagely by stunning "rocket science," but nonetheless having a clear-cut objective — getting a man to the moon and back. There was little time or taste for in-depth "discoveries." Yet that mega-project, with its governmental-financed technology, rode on the back of mostly privately funded experiments in rocketry, going back to the 1920s. Much of the earlier engineering work by Robert Goddard was almost as open-ended as Pasteur's.[14] Furthermore, contemporary observatories in space, like the Hubble telescope, make possible new scientific research. Space science beautifully illustrates the feedbacks shown in Exhibit 3.11.

The space "program" suggests a deeper question that most donors and philanthropic advisors face frequently. Joshua Lederberg posed it in his probing 1987 speech to the Association of State Universities and Land Grant Colleges: *Does Scientific Progress Come from Projects or People?*[15] No one knows the truth about answering this question. Circumstances matter. For "little science," such as a line of experiments on the genetics of autism, excellence of the investigator is almost the entire story. While reviewing an investigator's recent record and proposed work is a good idea, diligence assures confidence. For "big science," such as the space program, or an experimental facility in particle physics, the overall enterprise necessarily is a collective involving hundreds of people. Nonetheless, such projects must have gifted, determined, resilient leaders. When they do, Nobel Prizes recognize the organizational success of those leaders, as well as their originality.

On balance, and always at the margin, donors should bet on people. If the issue at hand is heart disease, run a competition to address the issue, then avoid the fashions of a new cure or intervention and pick the best talent.

CONCLUDING NOTE

Francis Bacon, the great seventeenth-century philosopher of science, anticipated twentieth-century thinking about science policy when he sharply demarcated "experiments of light" from "experiments of use."[16] The former aim to expand and deepen understanding; the latter try to solve pragmatically significant problems.

A comparable distinction may be made among philanthropists. The Gates Foundation could be regarded as a hybrid of the Edisonian and Pasteurian quadrants. It aims to muster and master new scientific means, as necessary, to conquer the long-standing scourges of malaria, tuberculosis, and AIDS. But its shorter-range, problem-oriented focus is paramount, which may explain why the entrepreneurial, results-oriented Warren Buffet chose to join Gates's program.[17, 18]

In contrast, the donors of many leading scientific prizes are in Bohr's quadrant. The Nobel in Physics, Chemistry, and Medicine; the Wolff Prize in Mathematics; the Inamori Foundation's Kyoto Prizes in Basic Science and Technology; and the Weizmann Award for Women in Science—all aim to recognize individuals who have made exceptional achievements in "experiments of light."

At intermediate points along this spectrum are foundations, such as W. M. Keck, which encompass *both* "the forefront . . . a potential for breakthrough" *and* a "compelling need."[19] Thus, Keck's projects concentrate on the Bohr and Pasteur quadrants.

When great wealth emerges as philanthropy in the twenty-first century, motives will be as diverse as in the past. The projects supported—and their consequences—will reflect the complexity of the systems described here as well as the range of opportunity described. The underlying incentives for patrons, and for their beneficiaries in science, were captured by Goethe: "To one man (science) is the highest thing, a heavenly goddess; to another, it is a productive and proficient cow, who supplies them with butter."

■ NOTES

1. Raymond B. Fosdick, *The Story of the Rockefeller Foundation: Nineteen Thirteen to Nineteen Fifty* (New York: Harper & Brothers, 1952).

2. Anthony S. Fauci, "Twenty-Five Years of HIV/AIDS," *Science* 313 (5786), 2006: 409.

3. Lawrence K. Altman, "Gateses to Finance HIV Vaccine Search," *New York Times,* July 20 2006, late ed.: A15.

4. "Stand and Deliver," *The Economist,* August 19 2006: 66; Bjorn Lomborg, ed., *Global Crisis, Global Solutions* (Cambridge: Cambridge University Press, 2004).

5. Foundation Center Statistical Information Service, 2004. The Foundation Center's data encompasses 1,172 foundations, a sample that includes the largest grant makers. But Sara Engelhardt, in a private communication (9/30/06), reminded me that the Center estimates national giving, by about 66,000 foundations, to be $32.4 billion. Most of the smaller foundations are oriented toward locally "charitable" purposes. Uncertainties abound because of varied definitions, multi-year gifts (or intentions), incomplete data, and possible double-counting.

6. Howard Hughes Medical Institute, 2005 Annual Report. Retrieved November 28, 2006 from http://hhmi.org/home/HHMI_AR05.PDF.

7. National Science Foundation 01-318, data brief, February 15, 2001.

8. Giving USA Foundation, *Giving USA 2006,* Glenview IL: Giving USA Foundation, 2006.

9. American Association for the Advancement of Science, Report XXXI: Research and Development Fiscal Year 2007 (Washington, D.C.: American Association for the Advancement of Science, 2006).

10. See, for example, Terence Kealey, *The Economic Laws of Scientific Research* (London, Macmillan: 1996): 219, and the many other references to analysis, such as Harvard's Harvey Brooks.

11. Donald E. Stokes, *Pasteur's Quadrant* (Brookings, Washington, D.C.: 1997): 73.

12. Excerpted in part from Rodney W. Nichols, "What Drives Discovery," *The Sciences* (New York Academy of Sciences: July/August 1999): 4.

13. See www.kavlifoundation.org/Support for Kavli Institutes at Stanford, Delft (Holland), Yale, Columbia, Chicago, MIT, CalTech. A recent gift by Kavli in China, at Peking University, was announced in *Science* 30, June 2006.

14. See highlights of Goddard in *A Century of Innovation* (Joseph Henry Press: Washington, D.C.: 2003).

15. Joshua Lederberg, "Does Scientific Progress Come from Projects or People?" *Current Contents,* 29(48), 1989: 4–12.

16. Francis Bacon, *Of the Advancement and Proficienci of Learning* (London: 1674).

17. "The New Powers of Giving," *The Economist,* July 1, 2006: 63–65.

18. S. Beatty, M. Chase, and G. Naik, "How $60 Billion Behemoth Will Affect the World of Charity," *Wall Street Journal,* June 27, 2006, Easter ed.

19. See www.wmkeck.org.

Analysis of Philanthropy for Science and Technology Part II: Opportunities in Funding Science and Technology

RODNEY W. NICHOLS

In analyzing the motives of patrons and researchers in science and technology, clear categories emerge. Those patterns shape thinking about the future.

In this essay I illustrate specific choices for philanthropic investment and offer recommendations. Then I explore international perspectives, the assessments of results, and larger dilemmas about grant making for endowments to institutions.

NEEDS AND OPPORTUNITIES

Consider three broad opportunities: frontiers in the "hard" sciences; goals for more effective linking of science and technology with social and economic needs; and possibilities that turn on major long-term commitments.

The American "innovation system"—when primed by government, private, and philanthropic capital—is flexible. It will exploit invention anywhere. It will thrive whenever and wherever new findings emerge. Just as protectionism is the enemy, over time, of economic growth, intellectual isolationism is the enemy, over time, of discovery.

FRONTIERS

The Physical Sciences

Science magazine presented "125 Questions," based on a survey of research leaders.[1] These difficult questions—in a sense, a powerful measure of our present ignorance of the natural universe—might be answered within 25 years. As the editors note in their introduction, "some, such as the nature of dark energy, have come to prominence only recently; others, such as the mechanism behind limb regeneration in amphibians, have intrigued scientists for more than a century."[2]

The queries go on. What is the nature of black holes? What is the biological basis of consciousness? How are memories stored and retrieved? What are the limits of conventional—and quantum—computing? Can fusion replace oil, and when? Chemists have their big questions, too; and the Clay Institute posed six profound, arcane questions for mathematicians.[3]

Such mysteries may catch the fancy of a few philanthropists. To justify the investment in solving them, "patient capital" is essential. And immediate social need or benefit is not—and cannot ever be—the criterion for success.

Biomedical Sciences

So-called "orphan diseases" are comparatively rare, and thus cannot command priority by major pharmaceutical companies (or, for that matter, by taxpayers). Examples follow:

- Spinal cord injury, which has been publicized effectively by the Christopher Reeve Foundation, producing a new wave of research focused on this crippling condition: Reeve exemplified the way in which a public figure can draw attention, and funds, to advance the science necessary to produce cures and relieve suffering.

- Amyotrophic lateral sclerosis (ALS), better known as "Lou Gehrig's disease," is also receiving greater public attention and fresh research initiatives, through the energies of an expanding national ALS Association and its regional/city chapters, devoted to research and care for this fatal, neurodegenerative condition.

Each of these diseases has no effective treatment. And each is a powerful opportunity for philanthropy, not only in terms of specific human need but also in terms of frontiers in neurosciences.

A broad domain in the biomedical sciences is the emergence of cross-disciplinary fields encompassing biotechnology. Today, however, despite much brighter prospects for clinical benefits from genetics, the pace at which they arrive may remain frustratingly slow. Physician and essayist Jerome Groopman, of Harvard Medical School, described gene therapy as "a roller-coaster ride for virtually all those involved: suffering patients and their desperate families; laboratory scientists and clinical researchers; university hospitals and their ethical oversight committees; biotechnology companies and their investors; the Food and Drug Administration; the National Institutes of Health; and Congress."

Medicine and Hope

This roller-coaster ride is powered by a desperate hope for miracles. The persuasive appeal of gene therapy is temptingly direct—just identify and fix the defective gene. But large obstacles must be overcome before the technology's safety and effectiveness can be assured. Scientists and physicians will solve those problems. But then, how will we use the technology? Fix every genetic flaw? What exactly is a "flaw"? What are the broader implications for humanity? An Orwellian future? Eugenics? The original impulse in research that drove the effort to understand the genome cannot determine humane choices for individuals and societies.

Think about the entirely unprecedented choices flowing from the use of genetics in medical diagnosis, or "personalized medicine," as many observers now call it. As U.S. Supreme Court Justice Stephen G. Breyer says, "We are not truly used to the idea of knowing, in advance, who will and who will not develop a deadly disease like cancer." Will diagnostic accuracy be high? What about the impacts of other disease-causing factors, and of diagnostic errors? Who should receive genetic information, and what are the proper controls to ensure privacy? Breyer adds, "We are a little like late Victorians, asked to predict the social consequences of the automobile."[4]

The upshot is that two clusters of magnificent opportunities exist for future philanthropy in biotechnology: funding the path-breaking laboratory and clinical research, and funding the scholarly and public dialogues about the social consequences of applying the results. Specifically, for instance, the contemporary debate about frontier research with embryonic (and adult) stem cells reaches to the core of the relationship between religion, humane values, and science; thus, the research itself, and the debate about its conduct and consequences, merit more resources.

SCIENCE IN PUBLIC POLICY

Education

Perhaps the most urgent and long-running challenge is to improve elementary and secondary education in science and math.[5] *Endless Frontier,* the legendary report that Vannevar Bush submitted to President Truman, in July 1945—almost two generations ago—made a strong assertion. "Improvement in the teaching of science is imperative."[6]

Yet for 60 years the performance of the nation's K–12 educational system for science and math has drifted downward, despite episodic surges of fanfare, funding, and flawed fixes. During the past 20 years, as this national-disaster-in-the-making was exposed, and as various nations demonstrated superior educational systems, a few corporate executives and philanthropists joined state and national legislators, to try to make fundamental changes.

For instance, a brilliant new experiment in New York City, called Math for America—privately financed by James Simons, his foundation, and other donors—presses for two private-sector tenets: Select math teachers for their high competence, and then pay them for their performance.[7] This experiment should be tried around the country, by philanthropists who recognize the powerful connection: The skills of teachers drive the competence of the workforce, and hence the productivity and growth of the economy, and ultimately the competitiveness of the country. National and local government, along with teachers' unions and school boards, might be convinced to change as the experiments succeed.

Systems for National Innovation

Another opportunity for private initiatives is the challenge of how to ensure a vigorous national system of innovation. President Bush's "American Competitiveness Initiative," announced in his 2006 state-of-the-union message, grew out of two assessments in 2005, from the Council on Competitiveness ("Innovate America") and the National Academies ("Gathering Storm").[8] These convincing studies showed that the United States must raise the priority on research and education to ensure economic growth. Achieving this goal is not just the responsibility of the public sector. Philanthropy will be indispensable.

The metrics for weighing alternatives and setting national priorities, however, are murky. Which research and development (R&D) relates in what ways, and how and when, to, say, rises in productivity? Jack Marburger, White

House Science Advisor, reviewed the past 30 years of chronic tensions about metrics for allocating federal funding for R&D. He bewailed the $2.7 billion in "earmarks" on appropriations bills (i.e., special allocations to projects that are not screened for comparative merit) insisting that the scientific and engineering communities must play even larger roles in guiding federal priority rankings.[9] These much-neglected policy questions demand social and economic analysis, in interdisciplinary, long-term efforts. Private philanthropy could fulfill its self-designated role as an "independent sector," by stepping up support for science and technology policy centers at universities and think tanks.

INTERDISCIPLINARY STUDIES

Institutional endeavors on long-range issues will require long-term substance across disciplines.

Few foundations, for instance, invest meaningfully in area studies of Islam or the cultures of the Middle East and the underlying social, global sources of resistance to technology-based modernity. Why don't more foundations recall the enormous successes—in conducting research and in nurturing talent—that flowed from the Carnegie Corporation's 1947 creation of Harvard's Russian Research Center? During the Cold War, the United States benefited from robust work by privately supported analysts of Soviet military and society. Now, the federal government and the nation clearly need more research into the past and future in Asia, the Muslim World, Africa, and Latin America.

Such interdisciplinary examples span every major component of the nation's activities. Domestically, consider the Food and Drug Administration (FDA) and, for example, the challenge to modernize the "critical path" to drug development.[10] There are far too few independent studies of the FDA's goals, resources, and problems. Yet this agency regulates a fifth of the American economy, and plays a key role in our defense against disease, or bioterrorism, directed at the food supply.

For three generations, the Council on Foreign Relations has planted seeds of fresh options in almost every dimension of foreign policy, including probably the best and most stimulating analysis of presidential options on climate change.[11] Where is the philanthropic derring-do these days, to make long-term commitments to such twenty-first-century issues?

All of these interdisciplinary problems—on social, economic, foreign policy, or regulatory issues—require, in varying degrees, expertise in science and technology. Although this might imply the need for major endowment grants, on the scale that created the large foundations a century ago—after all, the issues are likely to persist for decades—even small to mid-sized foundations can play a surprisingly important role. The Richard Lounsbery Foundation, for example, made pioneering start-up grants to a global "marine census," and to the first exchanges of U.S. and Iraqi science faculty.[12]

This leads us to international opportunities.

INTERNATIONAL PERSPECTIVES

Clarity and charity for American philanthropy begin at home. But a world-wide perspective has always inspired action.

Carnegie was dedicated to searching for paths to international peace. Rockefeller made commitments to eradicate the world's infectious diseases. Knowledge of global issues—the urge to study them and to resolve them whenever possible—has long been a base for programmatic grant making and institution building. So it is today. To the extent that such U.S. philanthropy also advances national interests—which is often the case—grants bring dual benefits and engender both gratitude and backlash.

The Scope of the International Endeavor

For any philanthropist reckoning with global issues, the scope is daunting. The Gates Foundation may seem to have sufficient resources—many billions of dollars, granted over the past five years—and has the experienced staff to target the pervasive scourge of AIDS and other diseases, in Africa, Asia, and Latin America. Yet even Bill Gates is forthright in saying "the leverage in our developing-world work is greatly advanced by the basic funding (over many past years) from the NIH."[13] Few philanthropists have either the boldness or the funds to tackle such grand challenges, as outlined by Gates, and now reinforced by the added resources from Warren Buffett.

Making matters worse, unfortunately, the chaos in many of the poorest developing countries—notably, Africa—also has made U.S. philanthropy hesitant to consider long-term commitments abroad. Studies and conferences are fine. An occasional short-term project is fine. Humanitarian relief is, of course, needed. But generally, as many foundations and donors see the scene, the environment in the so-called third world is too messy and too corrupt for enduring engagements. Isn't it time to rethink this attitude?

For instance, the State Department and the Agency for International Development would benefit from independent intellectual centers—

emphatically *not* from the often stale, predictable contractors—with disciplined and dedicated analysts, who can explore original concepts for dealing with, say, punishing shortages of water and energy. Colin Powell called for "science and statecraft [to] work together."[14]

In the late 1980s and early 1990s, David Hamburg conceived and nurtured far-reaching studies by the Carnegie Commission on Science, Technology and Government. Several of the distinguished task forces insisted that the federal government could, and must, conduct more scientifically and technologically informed activities, with respect to international affairs, including economic development and the environment.[15] Sadly, however, the federal government did not act broadly on the commission's recommendations. Nor did private philanthropy step in, except in a few cases. The need and promise remain.

Asia Rising

The newest potential source for major private philanthropy will spring up in Asia. Chinese and Indian entrepreneurs are rapidly reaching the level of assets of the great American philanthropists of 100 years ago. Tata in India is an important example of the historically influential donors to world-class science. Hong Kong's Li Ka-Shing is a recent example of a major donor to medicine. Accordingly, and especially in terms of their own national interests—in the environment, for example, as urbanization and industrialization proceed—Asians soon could lead globally relevant philanthropy.

Furthermore, in light of the large resources of several European foundations—such as IKEA (about $30 billion) and Wellcome Trust (about $20 billion)—major U.S. foundations dedicated to either scientific frontiers or concrete applications should encourage the rising Chinese and Indian wealth to enter into global "syndicate" of patrons. One focus could be on resolving cross-border problems, such as infectious disease. Some analysts refer to these as "global" because they demand concerted international action going beyond what any country could accomplish alone. A different focus could be on conducting comparative experiments to address the conservation of water or K–12 education, problems that, though shared by many countries, usually arise in locally distinctive ways. Analysts refer to such problems as "universal" in that solutions require special local adaptations.

Given global concerns, the United States should not shirk its role in cooperative endeavors. In fact, American philanthropy should lead. Could there be new U.S.-led institutional mechanisms linking the American non-profit sectors? If so, such projects may stimulate the for-profit sector, to discover new modes for larger investments. Which U.S. foundations are ready to explore such a cooperative path, in a long-range commitment, perhaps with Asian partners?

I realize that this sounds like Glendower's, "I can call spirits from the vasty deep." To which Hotspur replied, "Why, so can I, or so can any man; but will they come when you do call for them?"[16] International philanthropy may yet begin to take on the character of a "globally integrated enterprise," as IBM CEO Samuel Palmisano underscored for the private sector in discussing the 35-year trend in exploiting information technology to "improve the quality and cut the cost of global operations."[17] He added that the "twentieth-century corporate model is no longer optimal for innovation."

> I doubt whether the twentieth-century U.S. foundation model is optimal for coping with future global demands and constraints, much less for doing so innovatively. Establishing trust will be crucial in conducting cooperative experiments of the kind I suggest.

Similarly, I doubt whether the twentieth-century U.S. foundation model is optimal for coping with future global demands and constraints, much less for doing so innovatively. Establishing trust will be crucial in conducting cooperative experiments of the kind I suggest. The Rockefeller Foundation achieved exactly such trust, and an extraordinary success, in creating the "green revolution" for agriculture decades ago. In the same fashion, globally minded American entrepreneur-philanthropists may be able to collaborate with their counterparts abroad, in a more trustworthy mode than can intergovernment negotiators and bureaucrats.

Resources and Mechanisms for International Initiatives

Is this feasible? In terms of assembling the overall resources, while drawing on competence in science and technology, it is. Carl Dahlman, at Georgetown University, has compiled data on the performance of China and India as "emerging technological powers." For 2003, Chinese R&D spending reached almost $100 billion (in purchasing power parity [PPP] terms), and India reached $29 billion.[18] China was then third in the world, after the United States and Japan, with India in the top 10. Both countries are continuing to move ahead aggressively, toward increasing the share of GDP allocated to R&D. Many projections suggest that China's GDP (in PPP terms) will overtake the United States' within a decade, and India is accelerating its growth. The U.S. private sector community must contend with this competitive reality. And so must the philanthropic sector.

A modest recent example of building broader-scale, public-private partnerships is the U.S.-India Science and Technology Forum.[19] With start-up funds from each country's government, the forum stimulates exchanges and workshops for young and mid-career investigators. The topics range from space to agriculture, and from disease-relevant genetics to science education. The mechanism works well, and it can scale up.

Too often in the almost madcap surges of commercial investments in India and China, it is easy to lose sight of the large stakes in the long-range problems all societies share. These problems, according to long-standing American traditions, should not be left entirely to governments. After all, the "independent sector" is important, not only for building and expressing a "civil society" in political and social terms—human rights, democracy, and the rule of law—but also for shoring up socioeconomic building blocks—health, education, agriculture, transportation, communications, energy. All these depend on science and technology.

To those who might argue that for the United States to "cooperate too much" in these fields with India and China—our new global "competitors"—would run the risk of suffering economic disadvantages, I say, nonsense. We must invest first, and prudently, in our own research and education. If we do, we will gain, and we will gain even more as the Chinese and Indians also succeed in science.

As Frederick Seitz, former president of the National Academy of Sciences, wisely put it: "The larger the number of competent minds engaged in work at the frontier of science the greater will be the expectation of new discoveries."[20] The American "innovation system" is flexible when primed by governmental, private, and philanthropic capital. It will exploit invention anywhere. It will thrive whenever and wherever new findings emerge. Just as protectionism is the enemy, over time, of economic growth, intellectual isolationism is the enemy, over time, of discovery.

ASSESSMENTS AND BENCHMARKS

How shall "success" be measured? It is vital, of course, to gauge prospects in weighing the opportunities for philanthropy. And it is mandatory to pay attention to actual past results. But I approach these central questions with diffidence. The ideals of "doing good" or "trying hard" often mask ignorance of cause and effect. Good intentions often induce defensiveness or even secrecy about past decisions. Even worse, difficult choices can create confusion about current priorities, and lower standards in evaluations of past work. It is hard to face all the consequences.

The Imperative of Priorities

The initial choice of strategy must be derived from some calculus of priorities, however fuzzy. But that is a challenge. Any donor has interests, preferences, and inclinations about the subjects to be blessed with gifts. But that is the beginning of a strategy. After all, as Pascal said, "the heart has its reasons that Reason cannot know."

To push the thinking deeper, however, an analysis of choices, and a cost-effectiveness evaluation wherever appropriate, can be added. On science-related global issues, for instance, a pioneering economic prioritization (i.e., the goal was to quantitatively estimate the economic costs and benefits) was organized by Bjorn Lomborg. An expert group came to the conclusion that measures to prevent communicable diseases had a much higher benefit–cost ratio than any other global challenge, including hunger, trade, water, governance, and climate change.[21] Other observers and donors may come to different conclusions. But my point is to master the evidence, contrast a range of choices, and face the likely implications—because resources are always scarce, whatever a donor's intuitive and subjective inclinations may be. How can it detract from philanthropy to be explicit about the alternatives?

As Fosdick asserted, "foundations face the necessity of constant self-examination and reappraisal, to ensure their adaptability to conditions that time is constantly altering."[22] However, at a pessimistic extreme, one scholar of the economics of philanthropy said, "Donors to charities, it seems, do not behave rationally. Increasing evidence shows that donors often tolerate high administrative costs, fail to monitor charities, and do not insist on measurable results—the opposite of how they act when they invest in the stock market."[23]

One reason for this situation, especially when grants are for science and technology, is that activities can be confounded by jargon, complicated by a search for legitimating credentials, and blurred by the mindless critiques or hopes of the envious or flaky. Assessments, diligent and continuing, reduce those dangers.

Accountability and Peer Review

A core issue is accountability. Foundations, as tax-exempt entities, of course are accountable to the IRS, an agency acting on behalf of taxpayers who, in a direct sense, pay part of the bill. For the modern large foundation, accountability also runs, in a profoundly important way, back to the original donor. What did that donor aim to accomplish? What risks would that donor be willing to run?

Setting aside any concern for illegal or unethical behavior on the part of a foundation's trustees or executives, whenever grants support science and technology *per se,* or finance projects that depend heavily upon scientific expertise, certain well-established patterns can assure more transparent accountability, and enhance reliable decision making designed to assure high quality.

One effective means for quality control turns on peer review. All scientists and engineers understand this process. If a donor aims to focus on, say, nuclear power—either the technology or the environmental consequences or the economics—advertising openly for proposals will lead to alternative projects (see MIT's report, *The Future of Nuclear Power,* 2003, for a superb introduction). These alternative projects can then be evaluated by relatively disinterested panels of experts.

Occasionally, of course, arbitrary or politically motivated decisions will be made, for example, playing favorites or going with fashions, as occurs with the wasteful and notorious federal "earmarking."[24] Yet if the process were more competitive and transparent—not necessarily public, just visible to all of the foundation's principal participants—the donor and advisors would see more vividly the choices as well as the trade-offs.

Furthermore, conducting preliminary feasibility studies can clarify promising topics, show important uncertainties, and identify talented leaders.[25] Such a study can be the starting point for subsequent open competitions. In fact, this is uniformly regarded as a "best practice."

The Complexity of Competition in Science and Technology

In thinking about competition through peer review, especially among research universities, Stigler points out that "competition is not a goal: it is a means of organizing activity to achieve a goal."[26] Unfortunately, owing to the pluralistic and political character of faculties, some of the apparent competition within academic research may not achieve the goal of pushing toward higher quality. Instead, as Prewitt ruefully noted, one historian and university administrator cynically says, "a vast majority of the so-called research turned out in the modern university is essentially worthless."[27]

In Henry Rosovsky's sparkling *The University: An Owner's Manual,* the former Harvard Dean of the Faculty of Arts and Sciences says that "fundraising will always be the leitmotif of academic life . . . and asking for money is an excellent way to test the free market."[28] That is the essence of the competition among universities for donors. Accordingly, most donors confront solicitors who are brimming with chutzpah.

Given the brawling intellectual marketplace of ideas, how can donors judge what is excellent, what is most relevant to their goals, or how long to wait for results? Confident answers to those questions, even after a fair competition, are hard to attain. Making analysis more difficult, historical and longitudinal data are shaky about the past financing and results in philanthropy.[29] Taking a rigorous retrospective view is almost as difficult as predicting future outcomes.

Accordingly, the pragmatic process of evaluation in philanthropy for science-related efforts must depend on—indeed, will mainly depend on—qualitative assessments of: the overall coherence of an applicant's plans; the acumen of the project's leader; the "fit" of the applicant with respect to the donor's goals; and the respect for the institutional setting of the project. All of these criteria demand judgments. All demand consistent due diligence. The assessments, as noted above, can be sharpened by peer review. This is plainly feasible for projects in science and technology.

Still, donors and their advisors ought to be unsettled, even inspired, by recalling the remark of the physicist Lord Kelvin: "When you cannot measure it, when you cannot express it in numbers, you have scarcely advanced to the level of science . . . whatever the matter may be."[30]

ENDOWMENTS AND INSTITUTIONS

Throughout history, most charity is a day-to-day, year-to-year activity: soup kitchens, shelters for the homeless, church groups binding communities, and summer camps for urban children. Individual donors and many family foundations still focus on these traditional activities, operating through tried-and-true organizations, managed cautiously by earnest and experienced professionals.

But 100 years ago, when a few philanthropists accumulated great wealth and became more ambitious, they saw that "radically new approaches would require new institutional forms."[31] The new institutional approach was the endowment, accompanied by a "scientific approach" to continuing social progress.

Foundations with endowments adopted an "investment strategy"—"it was elitist through and through"—"to identify the best research institutions" and "to support and enhance what they were doing."[32] As Stanley Katz interprets philanthropic history, over most of the early twentieth century— especially the 1920s—these foundations had a "very long-term" view. Their founders and leaders recognized that big problems could not be solved quickly. Biomedical research was, and is, a compelling case. Accordingly, Katz adds, they were "prepared to develop long-term relationships with their grantees," were "highly tolerant of failure," and they "defined their grants broadly."[33]

Big Science, Philanthropy, and Government

Times have changed. Any fundraising office concerned with science and technology will say that grants for endowment are increasingly difficult to obtain. A long-term view by donors is rarer. What has happened? Where are the great endowers of yesteryear?

A critical turning point came after World War II, when the federal government began to greatly increase support for science and technology. Exhibit 3.13 shows this trend. The total national R&D spending is more than $300 billion today, and industrial funding has increased to more than double the federal funding. The sheer scale of the enterprise seems well beyond the ability of any science-interested foundation to influence in any significant way. As mentioned earlier, this is the reason many private foundations moved farther away from the natural sciences.

Little Science Matters

This is a far different situation from the first half of the twentieth century. Then federal, and most other support, for science was puny. Hence, private philanthropists could be the leaders in many domains of research. Exhibit 3.14 is a snapshot of academic physics departments' budgets long ago, in 1939–1940. Note that the dollars are in *thousands*!

Compare those historical data with the trends in Exhibit 3.15 (more recent indicators of budgets for physics, compared with budgets for the life sciences). For the past generation, the resources for the physical sciences

EXHIBIT 3.13   U.S. R&D EXPENDITURES

Year	Total	Federal	Industry	Nonprofit
1953	28.3	15.3	12.3	0.3
1963	80.4	53.4**	24.6**	0.9
1973	97.2	52.0	41.8	1.3
1983	138	63	69.4	1.9
1993	187	68	109.2	3.8
2004*	288	86	183.9	7.9

*2006 total was about $315 billion in current dollars.

**Note shift over 40 years in federal vis-à-vis industrial funding: Federal was twice corporate in 1963, and the relationship reversed by 2004.

U.S. R&D Expenditures

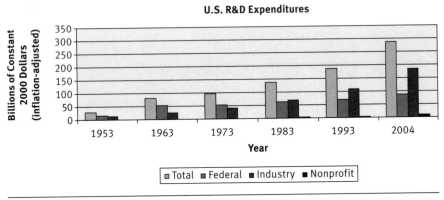

Billions of Constant 2000 Dollars (inflation-adjusted)

Year

□ Total   ▪ Federal   ▪ Industry   ▪ Nonprofit

Source: National Science Board, *Science and Engineering Indicators 2006,* Vol. 2, NSB 06-01A, Table 4-6, p. A4-9.

have been growing more slowly, and often more haltingly, than for the life sciences.

Yet frontiers in physics are bristling with potential—some in Bohr's quadrant, and some in Pasteur's and Edison's quadrants (as defined in the previous essay). Examples of fruitful fields include nanotechnology, energy, particle physics, astrophysics, and materials. Many of these fields are interdisciplinary, blurring the boundaries across all disciplines. It is time for private patrons and first-rank physicist-pioneers to complement Uncle Sam, in far-reaching fashion—to help restore vigor to these areas.

I must add here that I do not argue for reducing support for the life sciences. Quite the contrary, NIH's funding should continue to increase; recent cuts in constant dollars jeopardize one of the U.S. jewels of innovation. I do contend that the nation needs "balance"—hard to measure and always debatable—in its research priorities. Overall, in fact, the United States

EXHIBIT 3.14	HISTORICAL SNAPSHOT: ACADEMIC PHYSICS DEPARTMENTS IN 1939–1940

	# Prof. Staff	Prof. Salaries ($ thousands)	Total Budget ($ thousands)	% Res. Funds from Non-Univ.	Ph.D. Awarded
Large Private University	35	106	169	29	7.6
Large Private Engineering School	56	148	245	33	10
Large State University	47	79	123	0	8

Source: Adapted from Science—The Endless Frontier, Vannevar Bush, 1945, republished by National Science Foundation, 1990, NSF 90-8, p. 127.

should aim to increase total R&D from 2.6 percent to about 3 percent of GDP (see Exhibit 3.15). This would mean increasing federal funding for all fields, in line with national long-range interests and priorities. That policy would align with, and compensate for, business support which inevitably reflects market opportunities and cycles.

EXHIBIT 3.15	INDICATORS OF CONTEMPORARY FUNDING FOR PHYSICS, COMPARED WITH LIFE SCIENCES AT UNIVERSITIES

- Share of all academic R&D in 2003: Physics 8% compared with Life Sciences: 59%
- Share of all academic R&D from 1973–2003: 4% decrease in Physics compared with Life Sciences: 6% increase
- Millions of net assignable sq. ft in 2003: 20.4 for Physics compared with Biological and Medical Sciences: 70.9%

Source: NSB 06-01, Section 5.

Expenditures (millions of constant 2000 $)				Expenditures for Research Equip. (millions of constant 2000 $)		
	1973	1993	2003		1983	2003
Physics	538	1,065	1,338	Physics	56	130
Life Sciences	4,932	12,287	22,931	Life Sciences	322	767

Source: NSB 06-01A, Tables in Section 5 Appendix.

After all, the great fortunes built in recent decades often were based on technologically savvy entrepreneurs (in fields like semiconductors or telecommunications)—who, one might suppose, would be game to support research in the physical and engineering sciences. Some do. However, the most visible case of an entrepreneur in information technology is Gates; and his philanthropy—almost all in the life sciences—finances mid-range projects. Few major grants by the newly rich philanthropists are for endowment, or large projects, in physics, chemistry, mathematics, and engineering. Very few are large enough to create—or even significantly enhance—institutions, as the early twentieth-century foundations aimed to do.

The Case Against Endowment Giving

Why are so few donors endowing science and technology? Here is a list of reasons:

- Modern entrepreneurs steeped in "business culture" sharply focus on targets and milestones, year to year, even quarter to quarter. Most research is too open-ended, donors surmise, and so it is wise to keep the scholars lean and hungry.

- The "megawealthy," with billions in net worth, are reluctant to invade a large fraction of their hard-won capital; their gifts are from earnings and income, because if their capital were given away, it might not be managed well. Especially in light of the poor returns earned on portfolios, and the high overhead absorbed by some institutions, donors hold their funds and make commitments only to operating expenses, and only for short spans of time.

- An unsettling distrust of the influence of academicians and university administrators means that a donor cannot be confident that long-range purposefulness in the substance of the work will be sustained. Even worse, donors may believe that "politically correct" views will trump objective inquiry, when choices about programs or faculty must be made.

- Some prospective donors question whether universities and nonprofit research institutes really need more capital (after all, several campuses already have multibillion-dollar endowments) for their long-range mission. If they do, ask the alumni, or create especially compelling "naming opportunities," usually in the $1–$5 million range, such as professorships. Of course, this objection does not apply to the goals for raising capital for construction of laboratories and hospitals, partly because this need is so specific, and partly because donors receive name-recognition.

- Other prospective donors have no taste for starting new institutions, entailing large risks, when the U.S. research enterprise already engages so many people who may, in fact, duplicate each other's work. These doubts often overlap with the concern that endowment-guaranteed tenure may breed complacency.

- Hanging over all of these reasons for hesitation is the 800-pound gorilla, Uncle Sam, with his huge resources for R&D, combining both the capacity as well as the responsibility, to serve the nation's interests by ensuring a strong base of science and technology. So let the feds do it.

The Compelling Rebuttal in Favor of Endowment Giving

Is there a case for rejecting some or all of these arguments? I think there is.

- Much of the federal government's funding for science and technology (setting aside military development, and the space program) is in short-range grants of two to five years, with highly specific objectives. This slow-moving, bureaucratic, somewhat risk-averse, highly professional system allows little flexibility. Durable lines of private support are the best way to assure nimble attacks whenever serendipity strikes, new leads emerge, or interdisciplinary insights arise.

- The need for flexibility is especially acute for the start-up phase of a young investigator's career, and for meeting the gaps in funding that occur all too often (even in the best laboratories), when government budgets slip, or the competitive review process leads to a brief hiatus of support. Research institutions with financial reserves can back the best young talent on a continuous, rolling basis.

- As Vannevar Bush emphasized 60 years ago, first-rank research needs capital for facilities and equipment. Yet during recent years, the federal government has reduced its support for laboratory construction and instrumentation, relative to its funding for personnel and supplies. Some private support has been forthcoming for this purpose—the names of new donors on scores of science buildings and hospitals across the country confirm the reality. But every decade brings a renewed wave of such goals as demands grow in science labs.

- In the social sciences and related interdisciplinary subjects (area studies) only long-term, patient, private support can produce the depth and subtlety of independent scholarship. This is essential, not only for graduate education, but also for a base of savvy public policy, whenever changing political, economic, diplomatic, and social problems surface.

- Corporations have shortened the time horizons for R&D in their in-house labs; the Bell Labs' shrinkage in scope, and perhaps quality, is the exemplar. Thus, they are even less likely to favor longer-range support for their external academic and nonprofit "partners."

- A direct way to fulfill a donor's intent is to require liquidation of a foundation's assets, as was the case for the Lucille Markey Trust. The assets in an original endowment could be distributed in large enough units to assure ongoing activities at one institution (or several), already committed to the donor's or foundation's initial objectives.

I believe a strong case can be made for twenty-first-century American philanthropy to renew the ideas of the great endowers of yesteryear. After all, the early twentieth century's philanthropic strategy produced great returns. A century later, the path is similar. Donors should evaluate long-range scientific, technological, social, and economic problems. Then, weigh whether to put down big bets on excellent leaders at the best existing institutions, or to create new institutions with endurance, as well as leaders with the originality to make a difference—a dazzling difference. Endowments must be an option.

John C. Whitehead recently underscored the theme I have emphasized. "Revolutionary discoveries have occurred in the last decade . . . it will take vast amounts of money, and many more trained scientists, to develop the products that will create huge potential benefits for mankind." And he added, "More and more of the hundreds of billionaires are realizing that it's not how much you make that counts; it's what you do with it that really matters."[34]

The "innovation system" in the United States depends upon private initiative, individual drive, a creative environment, and authentic venturing. I urge attention to the Chinese proverb: "Be not afraid of going slowly; be only afraid of standing still."[35]

NOTES

1. *Science* 1, July 2005: 75–102.
2. Ibid., 75.
3. "What Chemists Want to Know," *Nature* 3, August 2006: 500–502; see also www.claymath.org/millennium.

4. Rodney W. Nichols, "Biotech in the Clinic," *The Sciences* (New York Academy of Sciences, Sept/Oct 2000). See recent review of biotech and pharmaceutical industry by Frederick Frank, "Lehman Brothers," *Bay Bio 2006* (San Mateo, CA: June 2006).

5. For a review, see Rodney W. Nichols, "From Jefferson to Feynman: U.S. Aspirations for Science and Technology Education," *Science Education,* ed. Peter Csermely (Amsterdam: IOS Press, 2003). Recent data are in "The Nation's Report Card: Science 2005," www.nationsreportcard.gov; and "Results from the Trends in International Mathematics and Science Study: 1995, 1999, and 2003," http://timss.bc.edu/.

6. Vannevar Bush, "Science—The Endless Frontier," *National Science Foundation* 90-8 (National Science Foundation, 1945): 26. The full sentence reads: "Improvement in the teaching of science is imperative, for students of latent scientific ability are particularly vulnerable to high school teaching which fails to awaken interest or to provide adequate instruction."

7. See www.mathforamerica.org. The Newton Fellowship Program started in June 2004 and has the support of the NYC Dept. of Education and, particularly noteworthy, the partnership with the NYC United Federation of Teachers. Also see "Finding Common Ground in the U.S. Math Wars," *Science* 19, May 2006: 988; and www.maa.org/common-ground.

8. Innovative America: National Innovation Initiative Summit, Council on Competitiveness, Washington, D.C., 2005; *Rising Above the Gathering Storm: Energizing and Employing American for a Brighter Economic Future* (Washington, D.C.: National Academies, 2005).

9. John Marburger, "2006 AAAS Policy Forum," Washington, D.C.: April 20, 2006, mimeo, from OSTP, EOP; also see Neal Lane, *Science,* June 2006: 1847, re. "focus" on innovation; a formal announcement of the Federal "R&D Budget Priorities" is in a memo (M-06-17) from Marburger and OMB Director Portman (White House: June 23, 2006); see follow-up letter by Marburger, to the *New York Times* on "research budget," September 17, 2006: BU 9.

10. Robert Goldberg and Peter Pitts, "Prescription for Progress: The Critical Path to Drug Development," Manhattan Institute for Policy Research (New York: June 2006). This discussion paper sets a baseline for trying to modernize the Food and Drug Administration; includes background on FDA's charter and budget.

11. David G. Victor, "Climate Change: Debating America's Policy Options," Council on Foreign Relations, New York: 2004. This brilliant assessment has stood the test of time; includes key appendices on the science base as well as references to literature. For an update aimed at general audience, see "The

Heat Is On: A Survey of Climate Change," *The Economist,* September 2006: 24.

12. See www.rlounsbery.org. The mission was reevaluated and sharpened a few years ago. The purposes, unusual for a foundation these days, focus on science and technology policy.

13. *Business Week Online,* interview with Bill Gates, May 5, 2003; *Science,* July 2005: 33; also see www.grandchallengesgh.org.

14. Colin L. Powell, "Exploring the Role of Science in Foreign Policy," *APS News,* October 2002: 8.

15. See "Concluding Report of the Carnegie Commission on Science, Technology and Government," Carnegie Corporation of New York: April 1993. Two of the Commission's task forces were Science and Technology in International Affairs and Global Development.

16. *Henry IV, Part I.*

17. *Foreign Affairs* 85(3), May/June 2006: 127–136.

18. Carl Dahlman, at a Georgetown University seminar presentation at Council on Foreign Relations, April 24, 2006.

19. See www.indousstf.org for a review of activities.

20. Frederick Seitz, *The Science Matrix* (New York: Springer-Verlag, 1992): 68.

21. Bjorn Lomborg, ed., *Global Crises, Global Solutions* (Cambridge, 2004); see interview with Lomborg, *Wall Street Journal,* July 2006: A10.

22. Fosdick, Ibid., p.18.

23. Tyler Cowen, *Wall Street Journal,* June 2006: C3.

24. The literature on, but unfortunately not the public exposure of, "earmarks" is enormous. The sharp increase over the past decade, from 3,000 to 13,000 earmarks, and to $67 billion for 2006, is discouraging. For recent commentary on attempts to curb their waste, see interview with Congressman Jeff Flake, *Wall Street Journal,* June 29, 2006: A4; also see *New York Times* editorial (June 25, 2006) and John Fund, *Wall Street Journal,* September 18, 2006: A19; President Bush featured the problem in a June 27, 2006 speech on the line-item veto. For federal science and technology in 2006, earmarking set a record of $2.4 billion, a 13 percent increase over 2005; given tight funding, agencies recently must cut into their core, competitive programs to find the money for what most observers regard as second rate projects, and Congressional "pork." However, for an exposure of the ambivalence at universities, see *Science,* September 8, 2006: 1374.

25. Saul Benison, "Simon Flexner: Evolution of a Career in Medical Science," *Institute to University* (Rockefeller University, 1977): 21; he explains that John

D. Rockefeller, Sr. conducted a wide-ranging feasibility study before founding the Rockefeller Institute for Medical Research.

26. Stephen M. Stigler, "Competition and the Research Universities," *Daedalus*,
Fall 1993: 157.

27. Kenneth Prewitt, "America's Research Universities Under Public Scrutiny,"
Daedalus, Fall 1993: 89.

28. Henry Rosovsky, *The University: An Owner's Manual* (New York: Norton,
1990): 255.

29. Peter Dobkin Hall and Colin B. Burke, *Historical Statistics of the United States*,
chapter on "Voluntary, Nonprofit, and Religious Entities and Activities,"
Hauser Center, Kennedy School, Harvard University, working paper #14,
November 2002.

30. Rodney W. Nichols, "Kelvin's Injunction," *The Sciences* (New York: New
York Academy of Sciences, July/Aug 1996): 4; for a sometimes pained and
consistently sophisticated set of essays on a full range of issues in philanthropy, including accountability, see H. Peter Karoff ed., *Just Money: A
Critique of Contemporary American Philanthropy* (TPI Editions, 2004); in this
volume, for example, Joel Fleishman says, "foundations have almost always
been unwilling to evaluate rigorously the social impact of philanthropic
dollars." (p. 105) and Stephen A. Schroeder says, "foundations tend to over-
emphasize strategy at the expense of execution." (p. 185).

31. Barry D. Karl and Stanley N. Katz, "The American Private Philanthropic
Foundation and the Public Sphere: 1890–1930," *Minerva* XIX, 1981: 244.

32. Stanley N. Katz, "Whatever Happened to the General Purpose Foundation?
And Who Is Thinking About the Big Problems?," speech at Nielsen Seminar, Georgetown University, October 19, 2001: 8.

33. Ibid, p. 9.

34. John C. Whitehead, private communication, August 29, 2006.

35. For assistance and comments on earlier drafts of this chapter, and the preceding chapter, I thank: Florence Arwade, Jesse Ausubel, Walter Baer, Jennifer
Bond, Katherine Eldridge, Alexander Forger, Richard Foster, Frederick
Frank, Marnie Imhoff, Joshua Lederberg, Christopher Nichols, James Piere-
son, Richard Rifkind, Frederick Seitz, George Schillinger, Marilyn Simons,
Darwin Stapleton, John C. Whitehead, and Herbert Winokur. Most importantly, I thank Susan Raymond for inviting me to contribute to this volume;
she is an extraordinary professional.

When Philanthropy Isn't Just About Philanthropy: Cause-Related Marketing and Cause-Branding

NANCY NEMECEK CRUME

A gift is a pretty straightforward concept. There is a recipient, hopefully a worthy one, and the giver willingly bestows the gift upon them, with no thought of receiving something in return. However, in the case of corporate philanthropy, "gifts" have long come with a string firmly attached for all to see—the expectation, if not the outright need, of getting something in return.

In fact, prior to 1936—when Franklin Roosevelt passed his famous tax act, allowing corporations to deduct charitable contributions of up to five percent of pretax profit from their federal income taxes—corporate giving had to be proven a legitimate business expense, with direct benefit to the company or its employees. But when a New Jersey supreme court ruling in 1953 eliminated that direct-benefit requirement, it also ushered in the notion that corporations have a social responsibility to the entire community. In that case, A. P. Smith Manufacturing Company was sued by a shareholder after the company donated $1,000 to Princeton University. Fifty-three years later, education continues to be the number one recipient of corporate giving.

Whereas philanthropy is a "gift" and cause-related marketing tends to be based on a point-in-time promotion, Cause Branding is a long-term

(continues)

exchange. At its most turbocharged, Cause Branding can be characterized as a continuous, 365-day-a-year association with a cause through both internal and external programs.

Today, corporate philanthropy accounts for about $12 billion in the United States—only a small fraction of the nearly $250 billion in American giving (see Exhibit 3.16). But an increasing number of dollars and resources, human and in-kind, are changing hands between corporations and non-profits. And it is not coming only from traditional philanthropic channels, such as corporate foundations. It is coming from a much more unlikely place—the marketing department.

The first time the term *cause-related marketing* was used was in 1983, by American Express, when it launched its campaign to fund the Statue of Liberty centennial celebration restoration. American Express had been a "cause marketer" for almost 100 years by then; they had raised money through employees, in 1885, to fund the statue's original pedestal.

In 2004, American Express underwrote a Martin Scorsese documentary for the History Channel, to solicit individual donations for the statue's renovation. In addition, the company donated a penny for every purchase made on their cards, and raised close to $19 million. That same year, the American Express Foundation made more than 600 grants, totaling $20 million (according to the Form 990 filed with the IRS), worldwide—an average of about $28,000 per recipient.

EXHIBIT 3.16   DISTRIBUTION OF SOURCES OF PHILANTHROPY

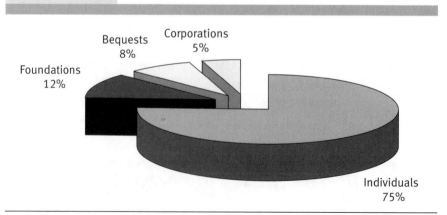

Bequests
8%

Corporations
5%

Foundations
12%

Individuals
75%

Source: Giving USA 2006.

John Hayes, American Express chief marketing officer, put it this way in a conversation with the Cause Marketing Forum, "We choose to support causes that are important to our cardmembers, and to our merchant partners. . . . Working with merchants, we can extend the scope of our programs, thus touching more lives and raising more funds." Those programs are typically separate from the foundation's targeted causes.

"Cause-related marketing" or CRM (not to be confused with the direct marketing term *consumer-related marketing* or the sales term *customer relationship marketing*), is the catchall moniker that actually includes a variety of practices, including:

- Media-facing CRM, or message promotion
- Customer fundraising (also known as "customer-facilitated giving")
- Sponsorships and licensing agreements
- Transaction-based CRM

A good example of a *media-facing CRM* program is the 2006 Halo Award-winning "Change Your Clock. Change Your Battery" campaign. (Yes, there are even awards for CRM.) The campaign is jointly promoted by Energizer Max brand batteries and the International Association of Fire Chiefs.

The consumer proposition is simple: When setting clocks back from daylight saving time, change your smoke alarm batteries. National and local public relations strengthen community awareness programs, executed by the 5,800 fire departments that adopted and support this program. It's been a lifesaving campaign for 18 years running. And it sells a lot of batteries.

What about those solicitations from businesses that facilitate giving to a charity or even to its own customers? This is called *customer-facilitated giving or customer fundraising*. Take TXU Energy, in Texas. The scorching heat of Texas summers threatens the lives of seniors and the infirm each year. In 2001, the "Check on Your Neighbor" program was executed, as a partnership with Meals on Wheels of Tarrant County, in Fort Worth, and the Visiting Nurse Association Meals on Wheels, in Dallas. The core message was for people to check on neighbors who may be at risk. But the solicitation was to TXU customers. In addition to donating $5 million in summer heat assistance in the summer of 2001, TXU offered to match up to $2.5 million in monetary donations from customers.

Is TXU providing future assistance or eradicating unpaid balances for people who still will not be able to shoulder their energy bills when temperatures rise above 100 degrees? The distinction is unclear, and the answer is "probably both."

In any case, utilities widely use these approaches—phone companies, energy companies, water utilities—just check your monthly statement envelope; there is sure to be a solicitation in there somewhere.

Sponsorships and licensing agreements simply leverage an asset or an event to promote an end. The Hyundai Hope on Wheels campaign provides an apt example. Hyundai Motor America and CureSearch National Childhood Cancer Foundation teamed up for a 30-market tour, to raise awareness of Hyundai and CureSearch, its "partner in the fight against pediatric cancer."

Hyundai SUVs were taken to local hospitals, where children fighting cancer put their brightly colored handprints on the trucks. Hyundai and its dealers raised $1.5 million—enough to fund 97 clinical research positions, 500 enrollments in clinical trials, and other medical investments.

Probably the most familiar form of CRM is *transaction-based,* which is characterized by promotions that seek a spike in sales to generate funds for a cause during a promotional period.

A few successful examples include some of the most well-regarded brands in America:[1]

Coca-Cola: In 1997, Coca-Cola donated 15 cents to Mothers Against Drunk Driving for every case of Coca-Cola bought during a six-week promotion in Wal-Mart stores. Coca-Cola sales in these stores increased 490 percent during the promotion.

Calphalon Corporation: Beginning in 1995, Calphalon entered a partnership with Share Our Strength. The company co-branded several of its poorly selling pans with the Share Our Strength name and logo, and donated five dollars to the nonprofit for every such pan sold. Sales of the previously unpopular pans increased 250 percent.

Yoplait: While Yoplait keeps confidential the impact of cause-related marketing on its sales, it has documented consumer shifts from Dannon to Yoplait because of the Save Lids Save Lives program, through which Yoplait donates 10 cents to the Susan G. Komen Breast Cancer Foundation for every specially marked, pink yogurt lid mailed in by consumers. The specially marked lids appear on containers every September and October.

Traditional cause-related marketing tends to look at opportunity as point-in-time promotional matching—in other words, matching the characteristics of a company with the ability to best raise money for a cause in a finite time period.

Exhibit 3.17 illustrates the types of cause marketing described, as well as some fictional examples.

EXHIBIT 3.I7   CAUSE MARKETING ILLUSTRATIONS

Examples—Illustrative Only	Transactional	Customer Fundraising	Message Promotion	Sponsorship/Licensing
Consumer Direct		amazon.com Education and Donation Online		MBNA Co-Brand Card
Physical Location Contact	McDonald's Buy/Donate	THE HOME DEPOT In-Store Solicitation		
3rd Party Distribution	ONE A DAY Save Children by Taking Your Vitamins	Coca-Cola Collect Cans for Hunger	Campbell's On-Air Tie-Ins	
Recurring Payment	MasterCard Bill Round-Up	verizon Bill Insert		

As illustrated, cause-related marketing tends to match corporate strengths with a cause, then uses point-in-time promotion to raise awareness, funds for the cause, and both sales and goodwill for the company. A company with a physical location can easily use transactional methods at particular locations, whereas a company without a physical location will use sponsorship or licensing mechanisms with direct consumer contacts.

Beyond the promotional essence of cause-related marketing, a more integrated method of linking causes with corporations has emerged over the last 20 years. This method, trademarked as Cause Branding by Carol Cone, founder and chairperson of the Boston consultancy, Cone, helps companies and nonprofits integrate values and social issues into brand equity and organizational identity. More and more leadership companies are finding that the benefits to both parties are far more robust when the cause becomes a part of the corporate DNA.

Whereas philanthropy is a "gift," and cause-related marketing tends to be based on a point-in-time promotion, Cause Branding is a long-term exchange. At its most turbocharged, Cause Branding can be characterized as a continuous, 365-day-a-year association with a cause, through both internal and external programs. In its purest form, a brand brings its core values to life by supporting a cause or nonprofit partner that embodies those same values. Such an approach requires the commitment of the senior management to apply its corporate muscle—not just money, but talent and expertise—to a targeted social need that it feels passionately about helping solve. This requires both the commitment to promote the fight and raise awareness of the cause, as well as ensuring the company's role as advocate and "resource raiser."

As Exhibit 3.18 makes clear, the best Cause Branding effort is a long-term, committed association, leveraging as many channels, assets, and dimensions of a company as possible, to raise awareness and funds in the fight for a specific cause. These comprehensive tactics yield the most productive strategy.

The trend toward Cause Branding is being fueled by many market forces: the desire to behave honorably in a time when so many corporations are misbehaving; fierce competition; retention of staff; and the need to create genuine, sustainable differentiation.

The question, as always, is "Does it pay"? There are many cases that serve as evidence that sophisticated strategies lead to increased revenue during a cause-related promotion. What about a longer-term Cause Branding affiliation?

A 2004 study from the Graziadio School of Business and Management at Pepperdine University[2] shows empirically that investments by a firm in corporate responsibility yield tangible financial benefits. The study used event

EXHIBIT 3.18   CAUSE BRANDING ILLUSTRATIONS

Fictional Wireless, Inc.	Transactional	Consumer Fundraising	Message Promotion	Licensing/ Sponsorships
Consumer Direct	$X for online sign-up during promotional period Text "networking" for cause	Bill insert with info for donations Link for donations "Round-up" the bill Texting donations	Bill inserts with information Links to xyz.org XYZ blog Vcast ** content on the phone	Co-branded phone card Wallpaper for your phone XYZ-related ringtones (world music)
Physical Location Consumer Contact	In-store promotion; sign up for a plan or buy in store	In-store donation collection "Round up" the bill in store	In-store signage	Skins on the service fleet
3rd Party Distribution	Consider whether it meets the brand values test (Best Buy, mom/pop)	Partnership with Univision "Give Back Home" to fund LAC projects	In-store signage Supply chain program to all hardware suppliers (Motorola, Ericsson, Nokia)	Functional wireless sponsorships with NFL teams
Employees	$.01 for every call made as a donation to cause	Event volunteerism	On-site informational booths, signage Paycheck stuffers Volunteer "spread the word" involvement	Pregame party for volunteers/givers Ongoing team events

study methodology and looked at 416 firms; they also flipped the question to, "Specifically, is there a 'crisis' value to a firm's reputation for social responsibility, in which the benefit of social responsibility comes not from increases in financial performance, but rather from insulation from negative financial performance?" Examples they cite include Johnson & Johnson, coming out of the Tylenol tampering cases in the 1980s relatively unscathed, due to the goodwill built up over the years from honorable corporate citizenship.

Cone vociferously agrees. According to Cone, this is not about marketing, "It's about programs that have deep social impacts that benefit both parties—and not just financially." She suggests that Cause Branding creates a "goodwill bank, recruiting retention, strong business partner relations, and a license to operate." To illustrate the latter, she pointed to the 1992 Los Angeles riots, during which $775 million of property damage occurred. However, Cone notes significantly, "McDonalds [restaurants] were not touched. It would have cost more than $2 million a store to rebuild, but it did not happen." Could it have something to do with their reputation?

In best-practice cases, Cause Branding leverages a multiplicity of company assets, and the strengths of the cause, to create powerful societal impact. In each case, common themes are evident: size, scale, multiplication, innovation, and sustainability. Target's "Take Charge of Education" initiative is a great example of sustainability. More than $170 million has been raised since 1997, for more than 100,000 K–12 schools. Not only is the entire organization involved, Target actually provides fundraising tools (fliers, clip art, press releases, etc.) to the schools to get the word out.

The Avon Breast Cancer Crusade has basically been a self-fulfilling prophecy, making Avon exactly what its tagline "Avon, the Company for Women" suggests. The crusade focuses on the medically underserved, to advance access to care, and fundraising to find a cure. Since 1992, more than $400 million—from 50 countries—has been donated for medical research, access to treatment, screening, support services, and education. This is unique, in that it supports a network of research, medical social service, and community-based organizations. Avon has awarded grants to more than 1,000 nonprofit, community-based breast health programs, in all 50 states and the District of Columbia; 100 of these are funded annually. Again, size, scale, multiplication, innovation, and sustainability combine for success.

One of the most amazing Cause Branding examples is that of the Pittsburgh-based PNC Financial Services Group's "PNC Grow Up Great" campaign. This is Cause Branding at its best. Spearheaded by CEO James

Rohr, "PNC Grow Up Great" is a $100 million commitment to prepare young children (from birth to age five) for school and life. What makes "PNC Grow Up Great" so powerful?

- *CEO ownership and focus:* PNC had dedicated millions of dollars and volunteer hours to multiple children's causes. But James Rohr wanted to align the company with a cause that focused prior giving and advanced the PNC goal. Many companies have grand goals but then relegate the job of integration to a middle manager, who may have the responsibility but is not granted the cross-functional authority so critical to success.

- *Corporate integration against a measurable goal:* In the case of "PNC Grow Up Great," the goal is to reach 2.8 million children over a 10-year period, with a primary focus on school readiness, including improved cognitive, social, and emotional ability. And it's not only money that's being given—23,500 PNC employees are focused on this goal and granted time off to volunteer. Media channels are used by PNC to educate parents and caregivers, and grants are made to similarly focused nonprofits.

- *Strong partnerships:* PNC partnerships include Head Start, Sesame Street, and Family Communications.

These examples begin to demonstrate an important trend in corporate investment in society, outside of the traditional philanthropic channels. They also illustrate the big difference between pure philanthropy (gifts), cause-related marketing—in which a promotion benefits two parties in the short term—and Cause Branding.

Short-spurt promotion can raise appreciated funds, but it doesn't fundamentally change the brand. Cause Branding, done well, changes everything.

Ben and Jerry's brand was built on what it calls "values-led marketing," and a commitment to invest seven and one-half percent of pretax profit to bettering the world through eco-friendly strategies. At Ben and Jerry's, it is hard to tell where the giving begins and the business ends, because they are their causes. In fact, they call their consumers "fans." And of course, their fans are advocates of the causes Ben and Jerry's stands for.

And who can think of Sears now and not hear Ty Pennington's, "Move that bus!" and see the tears of gratitude as a family's dreams for a home come true each week? The association between Sears and ABC's *Extreme Makeover: Home Edition* is a powerful tactic in the Sears arsenal—and a $100 million, multiyear commitment to strengthen families, homes, and communities through Sears's "American Dream Campaign."

In 2004, Norm Marshall and Associates, a California-based entertainment and marketing company, brokered the partnership, which was created to build brand platforms, and drive Sears's business objectives. Of course, the American Dream Campaign in aggregate continues to aid many people in the process.

Google has committed to investing $1 billion—or one percent of its stock value over the next 20 years, as well as one percent of profits—to solve social ills. Larry Page and Sergey Brin, Google co-founders, vowed to create a company "that does good things for the world, even if we forgo short-term gains." In fact, in the company's annual report, Brin stated, "We hope someday this institution may eclipse Google itself in terms of overall world impact, by ambitiously applying innovation and significant resources to the largest of the world's problems."

Granted, not all companies subscribe to this philosophy. ExxonMobil, the $340 billion energy giant, contributed only $106.5 million last year. A lot of money, to be sure, but less than one-third of a percentage point of profit, from the company that reported the largest profit in the history of U.S. business ($36 billion). The company also fell near the bottom of the Reputation Institute's 2005 corporate rankings, at number 53 (out of 60), while Google was ranked third.

By and large, however, the trend is in the other direction; companies still give generously through their foundations. In addition, more and more companies are engaging in partnership associations. From companies that strategically participate in cause-related marketing and Cause Branding, to those whose fight is the brand, like Ben and Jerry's and Avon, it appears companies are continuing to crusade for what they believe in—and stand for. They are raising money for causes, and benefiting themselves, in much more powerful, visible ways than if they had simply written a check.

AUTHOR'S NOTE

The author gratefully acknowledges the contributions and research assistance of Cori Cunningham and Jessica Stannard-Friel, of Changing Our World, Inc.

▨ GENERAL SOURCES

American Express, Return of Private Foundation 990-PF 2004 Federal Tax Filing.

Brandchannel.com; "Can Branding Save the World?" (2001); Ron Irwin, Cape Town, South Africa.

CNN.com: Los Angeles at a Glance.

Cause Marketing Forum, Conversations with Cause Marketers, John Hayes, Chief Marketing Officer, American Express.

Cause Marketing Forum, 2006 Halo Awards.

The Foundation Center, "50 Largest Corporate Foundations by Total Giving," (2004).

Giving USA Foundation, "AAFRC Trust for Philanthropy," (Giving USA, 2005).

Google.org.

Mothers Against Drunk Driving (www.madd.org).

Personal Interview, Carol Cone, Chairperson, Cone, Inc. (June 23, 2006).

Sears American Dream, (www.searsamericandream.com).

Share Our Strength (www.strength.org).

Reputation Institute 2005 Corporate Rankings; RQ scores.

Jessica Stannard-Friel, of Changing Our World, Inc.

■ NOTES

1. See also J. Stannard-Friel, "Proving the Win-Win Strategy of Cause Related Marketing," www.onPhilanthropy.com, November 5, 2004.
2. K. E. Schnietz and M. Epstein, "Does Corporate Social Responsibility Pay Off? Evidence from the Failed 1999 WTO Meeting in Seattle," The George L. Graziadio School of Business & Management (Pepperdine University, July 9, 2004).

Going to Scale: Realizing the Potential of the New Philanthropy

HOWARD HUSOCK

T he announcement, in June of 2006, that significant portions of two of the greatest fortunes in modern America—those of Berkshire-Hathaway's Warren Buffet and Microsoft's Bill Gates—would be largely merged under one philanthropic umbrella not only points out the stunning growth of contemporary philanthropy but reminds us how different the nonprofit sector is from the for-profit world in which the two accumulated the wealth the Gates Foundation will now dispense. Buffet, as the ultimate canny investor, would long have had access to candid and specific research reports about the firms in which he considered putting his capital. Similarly, Gates profited by the fact that private research, and required public reporting, allowed capital market investors to recognize the strengths of Microsoft and thereby fuel its growth.

> The advent of good stock market–style research on nonprofits will not happen simply because it's a good idea. It must rely, like any good research, on someone's willingness to pay for it. Providing incentives for that to happen will require broader changes in nonprofit finance or in the behavior of major donors.

But to the extent that, wearing their philanthropists' hats, Gates and Buffet or their agents might wish to "invest" in ways comparable to the approaches of their for-profit selves, they will find doing so difficult. Savvy investors such as Buffet especially like to spot top performers deserving of capital, as well as to identify up-and-comers with the potential to provide innovative services efficiently and effectively—and to grow, or "go to scale." In the nonprofit world, Buffet and Gates face quite a different playing field. Available forms of information about nonprofits are limited, and may not tell potential "investors" much at all to guide their decision making. Indeed, it is far easier to find out about the merits of an organization's mission, and how important it is to the society, than whether the organization is actually effective in ameliorating a problem or uplifting those it assists.

Moreover, there are virtually no financial instruments that can bring capital to the "social entrepreneur" that are at all comparable to the vast variety offered by capital markets, for the for-profit firm. Even those existing systems designed, in part, to steer funding reliably to successful nonprofits (such as the United Way and its predecessor, the Community Chest movement) are in decline.

Yet the need for some means to advise those who would support promising and effective nonprofits has never been greater. Before us today is a prospective wave of philanthropic giving, of unprecedented proportion, famously estimated by the Boston College Center on Wealth and Philanthropy to reach some $6 trillion (between 2003 and 2050), coupled with public spending constraints, and failures by government to serve as an effective provider of social services. This makes clear the need to find new methods to match philanthropic dollars with those who can best put them to use, and to do so on a large scale.

The ways and means to help social entrepreneurs "go to scale," however, will not be easy to assemble. The advent of good stock market–style research on nonprofits will not happen simply because it's a good idea. It must rely, like any good research, on someone's willingness to pay for it. Providing incentives for that to happen will require broader changes in nonprofit finance, or in the behavior of major donors.

It's worth keeping in mind that the impulse to know which organizations make the best use of philanthropic funds before distributing them is far from a novel idea. Indeed, the idea that significant pools of philanthropic capital might be directed toward effective organizations, based on research by intermediary organizations, was part of the original motivation of the late nineteenth-century Community Chest movement. In turn, the Community Chest was the forerunner of the United Way unified fund-raising campaign for local charities so familiar in American cities. Those movements are best known today for having sought to take the burden of fundraising off individual agencies, by serving as an umbrella, volunteer-based community effort, led by respected local citizens, to raise funds and then distribute them (more recently with the help of an extensive professional staff). From the outset, the Community Chest movement embraced the idea that those organizing the central fund-raising should also be free to invest in new agencies, which they believed showed promise.

In J. P. Brander's 1941 monograph *The Community Chest and Chest Council System: Central Financing and Planning of Charities,*[1] reference is made to a previous, undated study of the early movement in England ("Community Chests and the Co-Operative Raising of Funds for Charitable Purposes," by E. I. Black, of Liverpool University). "It was proved," the Black study is quoted as saying, "that a certain number of individuals were prepared to welcome the recommendations of some responsible body, with regard to the distribution of their subscriptions." Indeed, six years after its founding in Liverpool in 1873, as a central fund-raising initiative, there was added, says the Black paper, "an unappropriated fund," which, Brander writes, "was available for distribution at the discretion of a responsible committee." Thus, one can see the Community Chest and United Way as precedents for intermediary organizations, which would become familiar with promising agencies—in ways that would go well beyond audited financial statements and estimates of administrative costs—at a point where they were seeking to grow.

The approach served American cities well for a long period of time. It cannot, however, be considered adequate any longer; based crucially on localism—local agencies relying on local philanthropy, and later a combination of public and private funds disbursed by local provincial elites, it remains useful today, as far as it goes. But in recent years, it might be said that the philanthropic market has turned its back on the United Way. The combined United Way share of U.S. charitable dollars has, in fact, been falling precipitously. Research conducted by United Way of America indicates that while the dollar value has risen from \$120.4 billion to \$248.52 billion, the share of total U.S. philanthropy channeled through the United Way has fallen from 2.56 percent of the total in 1994, to just 1.45 percent of the total in 2004 (see Exhibit 3.19).

A number of explanations for the decline come to mind. We live in a less "local" world. Both philanthropists, and those social entrepreneurs starting new social service organizations, may well set their sights on problems that transcend the local, aspiring to start organizations that operate in more than one locality. Consider the example of Ashoka Fellow and Manhattan

EXHIBIT 3.19   UNITED WAY SHARE OF PHILANTHROPY

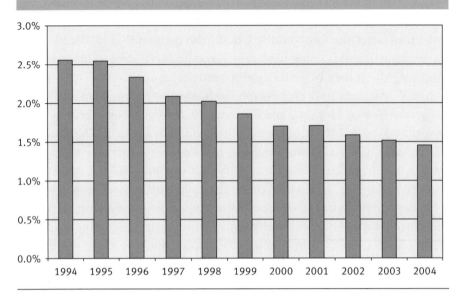

Source: United Way of America.

Institute social entrepreneurship award winner J. B. Schramm, whose College Summit organization provides disadvantaged students—mainly black and Hispanic—with intensive assistance with the college application process. The organization began in Washington, D.C. From the start, however, Schramm sought to extend it across the United States. By 2006, the College Summit was in 14 states. Similarly, the KIPP Foundation, which funds and supports charter schools by the same name, spread during the 2001 through 2006 period, from one city (Houston) to more than 40. The same decline in localism, which characterizes the commercial world (i.e., the replacement of the mom-and-pop store with chain stores), is taking shape in the nonprofit world.

Vehicles for philanthropy research, which might serve to attract capital to help such organizations go to scale, have not yet caught up to this change. Those rating services for nonprofits which do exist tend to examine organizations narrowly, looking at easily determined measures such as the percentage of an organization's revenue devoted to administrative costs as compared to that which it spends directly toward its mission. Such measures are not without merit. They are revealing and relevant for those charities, for instance, whose professed mission is that of raising funds for disease research. In such cases, the extent to which funds are spent on overhead, less can be dispensed. The same focus on overhead costs also reflects the growth, over the past generation, in policy advocacy groups—organizations that are not providing a tangible service to individuals but rather are seeking to influence public debate, and the political process

Indeed, a review of *Giving USA,* the definitive compendium of U.S. philanthropic giving, compiled by the American Association of Fundraising Counsel, reveals that over the period 1964 through 2004, grants for work aimed at influencing public policy (e.g., civil rights)—so-called "public-society benefit" grants—grew from two to five percent of all giving, increasing from $2.38 to $12.96 billion in constant dollars. To the extent that such groups must spend large portions of their budget on fundraising, donors will be justifiably interested.

Such scorecards are far less relevant to groups that provide tangible services, and which are seeking to go to scale. Spending on personnel is, after all, exactly what is called for. To understand the record and prospects of such groups, one must bore in deeply and creatively. What is the service being provided, and how can its success or failure be determined? For instance, a college counseling service might be judged, not only on whether those it assisted were admitted to college, but on their record after matriculation. What is the cost per individual served? Such measures are not readily available from the perusal of audited financial statements. Nonprofit "investors" will either have to do such research themselves (an effort also known as "venture philanthropy") or somehow provide support for new intermediary organizations, which will undertake the sort of in-depth research that stock market analysts routinely provide for the Gateses and Buffets of the world in their commercial lives.

But again, such research—arguably a key to catalyzing an organization's efforts to go to scale—is inevitably costly. It is heartening, however, that imaginative thinkers, experienced in the for-profit sector, are beginning to address the question of how nonprofits might go to scale, and how assistance for doing so might be financed. One such is George Overholser, a founding partner of the Capital One financial services firm, who in a paper entitled "Building Is Not Buying," published by the New York–based Nonprofit Finance Fund,[2] points out that nonprofit accounting itself makes it difficult to raise investment capital. In contrast to for-profit counterparts, nonprofit accounting does not include a way to distinguish between funds meant to help a start-up agency get going (growth capital) and revenue from donors who like an already-established service and want to support it ("buy" funding, which includes earned income for services provided). Writing about the need for donors to determine whether an agency has established an effective service delivery mechanism—which Overholser terms reaching "take-off"—he observes, "The commingling of investments and revenues in standard nonprofit accounting makes it very difficult to determine whether take-off has been achieved."

Overholser has suggested that segregating growth capital from other forms of revenue, for nonprofit accounting purposes, could lay the foundation for new forms of nonprofit investing, which would help support research that would identify promising new agencies. He goes on to suggest that some donors might specialize in providing growth capital, and that such donors might enter into agreements with donors who prefer already-established agencies, with a track record of effectiveness. The two types of donors could make a deal, says Overholser, something like a bond agreement, which would stipulate that if a start-up agency proves its effectiveness after five years, the first donor would be repaid by the second, with interest. This would not only allow venture donors to replenish their capital but would create a market for research; somehow, the effectiveness of a new agency would have to be objectively determined, and the cost of doing so could be part of the agreement between the two donors. In other words, contrary to tradition, it is not impossible, says Overholser, for financial instruments to be devised to build profit into the support of nonprofits and, in the process, to highlight both those which perform well and those which fail, albeit in a good cause. Indeed, should a start-up nonprofit fail, the venture donor would be out of luck.

Another model for going to scale has been suggested by former Goldman Sachs vice-chairman Robert Steel, who suggests a sort of hedge fund approach. Steel, in remarks made on a panel sponsored by the Manhattan Institute's Social Entrepreneurship Initiative,[3] envisioned a small group of extremely high-net-worth donors, who would satisfy themselves that a nonprofit has what it takes to undertake a major expansion successfully. That small group would then approach other high-net-worth donors—not, Steel emphasizes, friends or members of the same business and social network, but rather individuals who would be convinced strictly by the performance measures, and business plans, of the nonprofit being promoted (or, one might say, "going public"). Again, research would have to be undertaken, perhaps supported by the original circle of donors, that would demonstrate the agency's effectiveness.

Steel has already led a successful fundraising effort of this sort for the College Summit, and believes there is just a "small number" of nonprofits that really have what it takes to go to scale. In order to help identify them, there should develop "organizations that do all the things that Goldman Sachs does for the for-profit marketplace, helping the not-for-profit marketplace over time. It is merger advice, it's research, it's corporate-finance work, and it's finding the cheapest place to get debt."

One can imagine such a goal being realized through the effort of a consortium of major foundations, supporting common research on nonprofits, in much the same way as the stock market supports commonly available equity research. For this to occur, however, various forms of culture change will be necessary. Not all, or even most, philanthropy is predicated on specific results being achieved. As Peter Frumkin has observed, for many donors, the act of giving is an end in itself. Many foundations may be reluctant to give up their own internal review processes, even if they might not be effective as an organization dedicated to performance measurement.

The broader point is this: The stars are aligned for a new, golden age of nonprofit growth, for a new generation of effective nonprofit providers of key social services—many of a type heretofore unimagined—to emerge in American society, and perhaps beyond. But for that potential to be realized, effective methods will have to emerge to identify those agencies whose missions are actually accomplished, to get them the funding they deserve.

▨ NOTES

1. J. P. Brander, *The Community Chest and Chest Council System: Central Financing and Planning of Charities* (London: George Allen and Unwin, 1941).

2. G. Overholser, "Building Is Not Buying," in *Nonprofit Growth Capital: Defining, Measuring, and Managing Growth Capital in Nonprofit Enterprises* (working paper, presented to the Boston Foundation Nonprofit Forum, June 1, 2005).

3. R. Steel, "Going to Scale: A New Era for Funding Nonprofits," *Manhattan Institute, Civic Bulletin 39*, March 2006.

Private Philanthropy and Government: Friends or Foes?

GLEN MACDONALD AND ANDRÁS SZÁNTÓ, PhD

An abandoned gas station is not a pretty sight. But for Allison Rockefeller, it is a suburban oasis waiting to be reborn.

A few years ago, Allison had a vision: What if she could convert some of the 180,000 unused gas stations around the United States into small parks and community centers? Thus was born Cornerstone Parks, a new twist on the kind of historic preservation for which Allison's extended family is known.

The project had clear, tangible benefits, but no government agency was mandated to support it. So Allison, an unsalaried commissioner of parks in New York state, began to raise private capital and look for public partners. "In terms of collaborators for me, I really need government," she said at a panel on community revitalization organized by the Wealth & Giving Forum. "So I made government my friend."

> Government can draw strength from the injection of energy and creativity that philanthropy can provide. Philanthropists can act with greater confidence and impact when governments stand behind them. In the process, we may start to appreciate affinities between the two spheres that are often missed.

"Make government your friend" is a motto philanthropists everywhere should take to heart. For all the talk about public-private partnerships these days, the relationship between government and philanthropy remains awkward and incomplete. They are usually portrayed as opposites—two sides of a coin at best, adversaries at worst.

Philanthropists are wary of government for many reasons. Ineffectual government bureaucracy is one. The fact that private charity often steps in where government is seen to have failed is another. Even so, government and philanthropy need each other. Together, they can engineer positive outcomes that neither could achieve alone.

Each sphere is uniquely equipped to tackle certain tasks, and each has its own particular weak spots. Government works on a massive scale. It can, at times, impose its will on the community, by changing the laws if it must. It can put a stamp of legitimacy on projects, garnering public support and attracting other sources of funding to the cause. Government can do what individuals cannot do, no matter how rich or famous they are.

On the downside, governments tend to be cautious, incremental, and dependent on a cumbersome, arduous, and sometimes corruptible process that recipients of aid view with mistrust. Because they are spending taxpayers' money, public officials are restricted in ways that private philanthropists rarely need to worry about.

Private philanthropy, by contrast, is quite nimble and responsive. Individuals spending their own money aren't hounded by lobbyists, lawmakers, or the press. They can operate under the radar, without having to compromise. If a donor makes a mistake, she can go back and try again and again, as long as a solution is found. Moreover, the individual donor can build trust, respect, and decency into the giving process, in ways that government is not inclined to do.

The flip side of charity is its diffuse, uncoordinated, sometimes redundant, or ill-conceived approach to asset allocation. Lack of oversight can lead to suboptimal results or worse. Too much philanthropy is motivated by the search for status or the impulse to jump on the latest fashionable bandwagon. Philanthropy's main weakness is tied to its chief strength, insofar as it relies solely on the donor's willingness to give and his understanding of the problems being addressed.

How, then, can these two disparate spheres come together to solve problems? The answer lies in how each exerts its power. Simply put, what governments do first and foremost is govern, whereas individuals achieve their goals through innovation and influence.

Only government can enact laws and set national agendas. Individuals, however, are able to sway the policy consensus. Time and again we see private individuals, though their philanthropic endeavors, raise awareness of certain problems, and suggest courses of action that government may adopt. People of unfettered vision and resources, like Warren Buffet and Bill Gates, have the capacity and privilege to take risks and get behind innovations. Where they and other visionaries go, government will likely follow.

Think of Buffet's proposal, backed by $50 million of his own money, to create an independently monitored international stockpile of nuclear power–plant fuel. It is an untested notion, but it could change the texture of international affairs by enabling small nations to peacefully adopt nuclear technologies—an "investment into a safer world," as the Omaha investor put it. Or think of Sir Richard Branson's pledge, announced at the Clinton Global Initiative in October 2006, to direct $3 billion into new technologies to combat global warming. Over time, the policy implications of his work are likely to be profound.

Branson's and Buffet's philanthropic strategies can shift perceptions, and propose novel approaches to social and environmental problems. In short, they can shape government agendas—all the more so as they are likely to rally other donors to their causes. Working on a small scale, in concert with local government agencies, private philanthropists everywhere can act in similar ways as agents of change.

Examples abound of private individuals who have used their financial resources, or their charisma, to spur government to action. Frenchman Hubert Leven's Sacti Rashi Foundation, for instance, has seeded youth-at-risk programs in Israel that are deliberately designed to be deployed in places where government is unable or reluctant to go. His foundation pilots initiatives that can then be scaled up into large-scale government programs. Kate Anderton, the indefatigable, long-time executive director of Save the Redwoods League, showed that you don't need huge wealth to make a difference, even in the resource-hungry realm of forest preservation. Deft alliance building and marshaling of public support can go a long way.

When it comes to celebrities, an individual's capacity to shame and cajole public officials into taking action is multiplied a hundredfold. Look at what Bono, lead singer of the Irish rock band U2, has done to mobilize the arcane policy arena of debt relief. This one individual's determination to influence lawmakers may do more for the people of Africa than a generation of activists and bureaucrats had done before him.

At the other end of the philanthropic spectrum, institutional grant makers, spearheaded by entities like the Ford and Rockefeller foundations, cannot, by law, lobby government. But targeted research, or the support of cause-oriented organizations, can stimulate public dialogue and prod government action on specific issues. An especially encouraging sign in recent years has been the appearance of former government officials, notably former U.S. Presidents Carter and Clinton, on the philanthropic stage. These highly visible figures are able to exert vast influence through philanthropy, as a means to seed collaborations, and concentrate funds toward the alleviation of systemic crises at home and abroad.

The kinds of problems we are confronting today—from worldwide epidemics to imbalances in education or access to potable water—are such that neither government nor philanthropy can really go it alone. In the final analysis, the real question is not whether these two sectors will collaborate, but whether they will arrive at terms of engagement that avoid redundancy, waste, and unnecessary turf battles. If both stay squarely focused on the task at hand—namely, problem solving that yields sustainable solutions—their joint efforts may very well succeed.

But some questions do need to be answered before such collaboration develops on a massive scale. Will philanthropy leverage public agencies, or will it interfere with them? Will private money amplify government's problem-solving capacity, or will it deflate political will and undermine policy commitments? Last but not least, how long can we expect cash-starved governments to encourage private philanthropy, if by doing so they risk losing tax revenues?

Despite these dilemmas, there is reason to hope that interactions between government and philanthropy will improve and accelerate in the future. In the process, we may start to appreciate affinities between the two spheres that are often missed. After all, both government and philanthropy operate outside the marketplace. Both are called upon to address the market's blind spots and imbalances. Because of the lack of a bottom-line focus, both sometimes act in similar ways. They can be whimsical and unpredictable, more susceptible to mood swings and power shifts than the cool, rational marketplace.

Government can draw strength from the injection of energy and creativity that philanthropy can provide. Philanthropists can act with greater confidence and impact when government stands behind them. The one outcome we need to fear is that philanthropy will repeat the mistakes that often plague large institutions. As it grows larger, more assertive, and more powerful, philanthropy may become bureaucratic and process-oriented, and less imaginative and responsive to the needs of the constituencies it serves. In short, it may end up looking a lot like government.

Two years ago, at the Wealth & Giving Forum's inaugural gathering, Vaclav Havel, the Czech dissident writer who led the Velvet Revolution and became president of the free Czech Republic, gave an inspiring address, in which he praised Western democracies for allowing their citizens to pursue both their affluence and their personal passions. He contrasted that sense of opportunity with life in totalitarian states, where people are forced to become overly reliant on government. Such dependence on a paternalistic state, Havel argued, saps individuals of their energy and steals from them the joy of exercising responsibility. It dampens the human spirit.

In the West and other parts of the globe, philanthropy plays an increasingly vital role as a counterpart, and countervailing force to government. Let's hope that, as it succeeds, an increasing number of accomplished individuals will be encouraged to direct their resources, imagination, and ingenuity toward the common good.

The Political Dimensions of Change: Philanthropy as Power in the Corridors of Foreign Policy

SUSAN RAYMOND, PHD

As philanthropy expands, and as large nonprofits grow stronger and diversify their funding strategies, an extraordinary level of resources will be put into play on the social and economic playing field of the United States and, to some extent, the broader world. For example, in June 2006, Warren Buffett made the single largest financial commitment to philanthropy in U.S. history. The $37 billion transfer to the Gates Foundation doubled the size of what was even then the largest private foundation in the world, which doubled its annual giving. At the same time, Buffett infused the foundations of his children with billions in additional assets, catapulting their philanthropy to national leadership.

This is the first of what is likely to be a stream of extremely large philanthropic gifts from new wealth. Unlike their forebears, new economy leaders appear to have decided that the best way to ensure that philanthropy conforms to your desires is to give the money away while you are alive. These new leaders are personally involved, not only in making their wealth, but in giving it away. The resultant philanthropy will be wielded by the donor—not surrogates for the donor's intent—in pursuit of firmly held purposes toward privately defined ends.

The bigger the private philanthropic dollar becomes, the more policy may turn on its presence, and the more say it may have in policy. It does not stretch credulity to speculate that there may be questionable lines to be crossed, in such areas as education, healthcare, and foreign policy, where the electoral accountability of public policy may not align well with the largely unaccountable private wishes of billions of philanthropic dollars.

At the same time, those huge inflows of resources to philanthropy will have to find organizations scaled to accept them as grants. It would be difficult to on-grant the required five percent of $37 billion ($1.85 billion) in $10,000 increments. At that rate, the donor would have to select, process, and fund 185,000 grants each year and probably fervently hope that annual stock market growth never exceeded five percent!

So, organizational scale will be important, and the likely bias will be to move large amounts of money to large organizations. Concentration already characterizes the American nonprofit sector. Revenue for nonprofits with income of $10 million or more per year represented 80 percent of all nonprofit revenues, and 65 percent of all receipts from private philanthropy, while they account for only eight percent of all nonprofit organizations (see Exhibit 3.20).

With billions of new philanthropic dollars to be allocated each year, it is likely that this concentration will increase. The future, then, will see very large nonprofits and very, very large philanthropies, moving significant resources onto the public commons.

All manner of problems may ensue. When money is the pull in organizational direction, mission can be left on the cutting room floor. This is exactly the problem that the Salvation Army faces in utilizing the $1.5 billion left to it by Joan Kroc, wife of Ray Kroc, founder of McDonald's Corporation. The Kroc community centers now planned across the country are providing unprecedented resources to local communities, but their size and scope are quite different from either the Salvation Army's culture and mission or its style of operations. Yet the gift was made, and results will follow.

The second problem is to be found in the corridors of public policy. Very large organizations—wielding very large sums of money, with very large (even global) networks—can seriously influence public policy, even though they were elected by not a single voter. Of course, there is nothing historically unusual about this, in principle. Domestically, the twentieth century

EXHIBIT 3.20   DISTRIBUTION OF NONPROFIT FINANCE AND ORGANIZATIONS BY SIZE (2004)

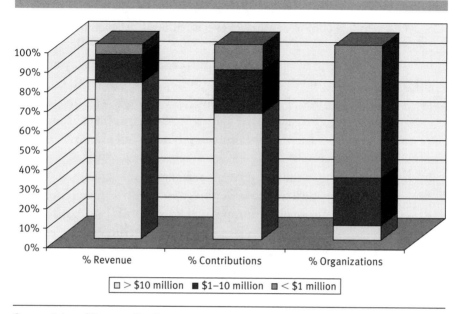

□ > $10 million   ■ $1–10 million   ▨ < $1 million

Source: Internal Revenue Service.

saw many policy-leading roles in America's large philanthropies, from Carnegie to Ford to Rockefeller to the Mott and Markle foundations. The Civil Rights Movement, public television, legal services for the poor, the environmental movement, and affirmative action were all inspirations for— and in some cases the offspring of—the nation's philanthropies. That involvement, and the resources brought to bear in each area, paved pathways directly to public policy.

More recently, funding from the Bradley Foundation, the Smith Richardson Foundation, and the Scaife Foundation has seeded the research and analysis that, in turn, has given birth to much of the current conservative leadership on policy issues in the United States.

Internationally, the historical record of influence is similarly present, but with a much, much smaller policy footprint. In the early years of the twentieth century, the Rockefeller Foundation was the driving force behind the creation of U.S. tropical medicine capacity. Its research and treatment funding provided the base for removing yellow fever and hookworm from the Americas. Lesser known was the role of private support for the work of Albert Sabin, on polio vaccines, which was carried out in close collaboration with Soviet virologists even as the Cold War raged. With the tacit approval of the Eisenhower Administration, Sabin and the Soviets proceeded to collaborate on testing, and a freeze-drying technology resulted.

Since the mid-twentieth century, however, things have changed. Domestically, there is growing acceptance, for better or for worse, that private effort, through private nonprofits, occupies center stage in many areas of social initiative. The role of government is more widely debated than was the case four decades ago. Private initiative, and the variety of approaches and solutions to problems that private initiative brings, are accepted and even valued, as bringing malleability to complex problems and responsiveness to local cultures and priorities.

The current theme of "public-private partnerships" characterizes most, if not all, community initiatives around the country. Government not only tolerates the role of private philanthropy in problem solving, it actually seeks out and even cultivates it. Indeed, federal and local government agencies are creating whole new categories of private foundations, affiliated with them and consciously seeking to ensure that private philanthropy embraces public initiative. That such strategies open the door to private philanthropy, in making policy about public initiatives, appears to trouble few if any of the leaders involved. Far from seeing private philanthropic funders as "meddling in" or influencing the decisions of elected officials, these new partnerships are seen as defining the playing field of collaboration between government and private initiative.

Of course, the bigger the private dollar becomes, the more policy may turn on its presence, and the more say it may have in policy. It does not stretch credulity to speculate that there may be questionable lines to be crossed, in such areas as education and healthcare, where the electoral accountability of public policy may not align well with the largely unaccountable private wishes of billions of philanthropic dollars. Where there is a questioning of the role of government to begin with, the shadow of doubt will likely work in favor of private philanthropy.

The international scene provides a different twist to this problem in two dimensions: the nature of the government role and the size and concentration of philanthropic flows.

While there is wide debate and disagreement about the importance of government policy and initiatives in many areas of domestic life, there is near universal agreement that government (specifically the federal government) has both responsibility for and authority over national defense and foreign policy. The will of the electorate, expressed at the ballot box, establishes the ultimate accountability for government action in both arenas.

Giving for international causes and issues has more than doubled in real terms in the last 15 years (see Exhibit 3.21). While it still represents a fraction of all U.S. philanthropy, it now tops $6 billion per year.[1] This is the cash portion of flows and does not include gifts-in-kind (goods and services), which have been estimated to total about $5 billion.[2] How much is $11 billion? This is an amount equivalent to the annual budget of the U.S. Agency for International Development, the federal agency charged with moving U.S. public resources to programs in the developing world, which support economic and social development and humanitarian affairs, and by association, U.S. foreign policy. Hence, the private giving stream of cash philanthropy plus goods and services rivals the size of official U.S. government transfers for development.

Where does this leave us? Today, the economic development landscape—which concerns foreign policy (an acknowledged area of government responsibility)—is as populated with private philanthropic dollars as it is with public dollars. For many years this has been the case with commercial

EXHIBIT 3.21   CONTRIBUTIONS FOR INTERNATIONAL AFFAIRS

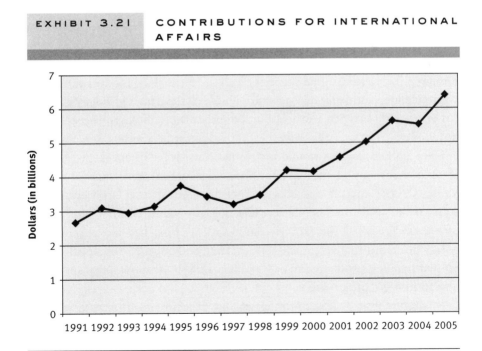

Source: Giving USA 2006.

resources, like trade and direct foreign investment; it is now true for private philanthropy.

What is different here, as compared to the domestic policy scene, is concentration. From 2000 through 2004, the four largest U.S. funders on the international scene accounted for over one-third of all U.S. international grant making, if measured by dollar value of grants. Of that total, the Gates and Ford foundations accounted for the overwhelming majority.

This is not necessarily a problem. Private initiative is to be valued, especially where the track record of performance of international public foreign assistance is so poor. Progress in global development and poverty alleviation can only benefit from fresh ideas and fresh approaches. However, potentially useful new money is destined to cross paths with public policy that guides the nation through foreign relations and national security.

The path, of course, is not one way. Foreign policy and U.S. foreign relations impact private philanthropy. The push for an HIV vaccine provides a prime example. While the Gates Foundation can fund the research and trials, the political, commercial, and trade barriers to the dissemination of any privately funded potential product can be smoothed by the diplomacy and negotiating power of the U.S. government.

We face, then, a problem that is also an opportunity. One can easily imagine the emergence of a few large private foundations, whose donors—alive and well and pursuing their personal priorities—provide resources in areas that are of significant importance to the larger public interest (specifically, foreign policy and national security) for which the federal government has acknowledged authority. The resulting Clash of the Titans in Foggy Bottom is a policy drama, with a script steeped in conflict, in which there will be no winners. It is a script, however, that need not be written.

To negotiate such potential problems in its other interests, the United States government has created a number of advisory mechanisms. The President's science advisor oversees a panel of scientists and engineers—the Advisory Council on Science and Technology—to help understand scientific advance, educate the executive and legislative branches, and help mediate policy decisions that affect the U.S. science and engineering community. Similar panels exist for many policy areas, ranging from women and business to historic preservation.

It is time for an analog in foreign policy. It is time for the State Department to reach out to American philanthropy involved in foreign affairs and international development. The objective is not to co-opt private effort to serve public policy, because that policy is, in part, driven by electoral politics. Rather, the purpose would be to open communication channels, to ensure that in this time of global insecurity these new, major actors on the international stage can share their perspectives and decisions with those charged with public policy responsibilities; and that public policy must share its perspective with philanthropy. The philanthropic institutions of America are moving major resources on the global scene, and moving them into areas that are of direct consequence for national security and foreign policy. Pluralism of resources is to be applauded. Pluralism, however, does not necessarily have to come with a price tag of confusion and surprise.

Establishing an advisory council mechanism, at the level of foreign policy and government foreign assistance, does not suppress pluralism. Indeed, by prompting the exchange of information and perspectives, it may generate an even greater range of viewpoints. That such an exchange will also generate disagreements is self-evident. There are disagreements on all advisory panels. If there were not, then the panels would not be serving their purpose. But disagreement born of communication is infinitely preferable to disagreement born of isolation. Ignorance on either side is not bliss.

▨ OTHER SOURCES

S. Strom, "New Wealth Leaves the Salvation Army with Worries Concerning Its Mission," *New York Times,* August 4, 2006.

T. E. Wirth, "The Need for Philanthropic Advocacy," remarks at the Global Philanthropy Forum Conference on Borderless Giving, Stanford University, June 6, 2003.

Y. Noguchi, "Bill Gates' World of Possibility," *Washington Post,* June 21, 2006: D01.

P. J. Hotez, "Vaccines as Instruments of Foreign Policy," EMBO Reports 2:10, 2001: 862–868.

▨ NOTES

1. *Giving USA 2006* (Giving USA Foundation: 2006): 209.
2. *Index of Global Philanthropy* (Washington, D.C.: Hudson Institute, 2006): 24.

The Reactions: New Rules for a New World

OVERVIEW OF THE ISSUES

Seldom does any major action occur without a reaction. No less can be expected for changes occurring in the philanthropic and nonprofit sectors. If American society continues to turn to the nonprofit sector to address social needs, and if the sector responds with the significant growth that has characterized the last decade, and if philanthropic expansion continues to be at least part of the fuel that powers that growth, then all types of institutions will take note. Scrutiny will follow.

> As the size and the public profile of the nonprofit and philanthropic sector grows, so will awareness, and with awareness will come examination, and with examination will come exposure, of any and all weaknesses as well as strengths.

Citizens and communities, while valuing the central role of charities, will begin to ask hard questions about the scope of their operations, about their accountability, and about the taxes displaced by their tax-free status. Indeed, such questions are beginning to be raised even now, especially in communities where property taxes form the basis of municipal finance, and where increasing numbers of properties are removed from the tax rolls due to charitable ownership. The citizens' burden grows with every such action, so their reaction is inevitable.

Government itself has turned an increasingly skeptical eye on nonprofit growth. Anything that becomes 10 percent of the national economy will not escape the notice of government. Senator Charles Grassley (R. Iowa), as chairman of the Senate Committee on Finance, held hearings on the abuse of the tax-exempt status given to charities and other nonprofits, and is one of the leading champions for reform of the rules and regulations governing charitable giving.

But the federal government is not the only skeptic. States' attorneys general have shown even more aggressive interest in nonprofit trends, in part because it is at the state level that the tax effect is concentrated. At the state level, the attorneys general pursue cases, ranging from the tax-exempt status of organizations to scams and the improper use of donations. The Supreme Court's ruling in *Madigan v. Telemarketing Associates* (2003) only damaged the reputation of nonprofits, and validated the aggressive pursuit of nonprofits.

Of course, the courts are also to be found in the mix. Recent decisions may affect the reliability of bequests. Indeed, the concept of "donor intent" has been widely upheld, with significant limitations on the freedom of the nonprofit sector to allocate donated resources to current needs, even when those resources were donated a generation ago.

Finally, of course, all of this exposure and debate can entail a high price in terms of public trust. Work by Paul Light at the Brookings Institution has indicated that, as recently as 2004, public trust in nonprofits had not recovered from the doubts sown by the flow of funds after the tragedy of September 11, 2001. When monies do not flow as donors intend, when nonprofit profiles include financial scandal, when headlines bare poor decisions, and when questions of salaries and perquisites out-shout profiles of good deeds, then the public doubts. It does not matter that the problems cast in the spotlight exist within a tiny minority of nonprofits; it does not matter that the preponderance of evidence is on the side of dedicated servants of the societal good. As the size and profile of the nonprofit and philanthropic sector grows, so will awareness, and with awareness will come examination, and with examination will come exposure.

The new rules of public expectations, and public relations in the nonprofit sector, will drive nonprofits and philanthropy in one of two directions. On the one hand, they might create a desire to close off and to withhold information for fear of misinterpretation, to become increasingly opaque so as not to be a target of public examination. This would be an unfortunate result, in part because it is not in keeping with the public trust, and in part because it will not work. On the other hand, increased public awareness may create a commitment to transparency in the nonprofit sector and leadership in the nonprofit sector favoring openness that has been missing in many other sectors of the economy. This would be a fortunate result for the sector and for the nation.

The Tax Man Cometh: Should Nonprofits Pay?

SUSAN RAYMOND, PHD

There are over a million nonprofits in the United States, of which 850,000 are public charities and some 70,000 philanthropic foundations, all of which have tax-exempt status. In the last two decades, the growth of the tax-exempt sector has outstripped the growth of commercial entities. There are advantages to growth, to be sure. But growth also creates visibility all the more as household names from the world of mega-wealth enter the philanthropic field. The visibility created by growth has not only raised the interests of academics and social observers, it has put the nonprofit sector firmly in the crosshairs of those responsible for public finance. With visibility comes attention.

> The visibility created by growth has not only raised the interests of academics and social observers, it has put the nonprofit sector firmly in the crosshairs of those responsible for public finance. With visibility comes attention.

At the same time, there are 87,000 local units of government in the United States, encompassing 19,000 municipalities, 16,000 townships and towns, 3,000 counties, more than 13,000 school districts, and 35,000 special districts (see Exhibit 4.1). The interface between the financial base of this complexity of government and the complexity of rising numbers of nonprofits is destined to become more strained.

EXHIBIT 4.1   DISTRIBUTION OF LOCAL GOVERNMENT
UNITS IN THE UNITED STATES (2003)

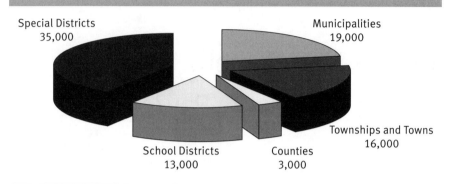

Special Districts
35,000

Municipalities
19,000

Townships and Towns
16,000

School Districts
13,000

Counties
3,000

Source: Bowman, *Land Lines,* 2003.

Overall, the percentage of local government resources received from federal sources has declined, from over 26 percent to 20 percent.[1] In New York
state, federal aid has fallen, from 18.4 percent of local budgets to 12.4 percent, since 1975. State and federal aid to New York's local governments has
fallen, from nearly half of local government funds to just over one-third.[2]

As a result, the local tax base, at all levels of local government, is increasingly reliant on local taxation. On average, 40 percent of the revenue for
school districts and special districts derived from property taxes in 2004 (see
Exhibit 4.2).

There are many elements behind the erosion of the tax base, not the least
of which is mobility inherent in globalization, and the decline in purchasing power inherent in demographic aging. A growing factor is also the
"nonprofitization" of local economies. The rate of growth in the number
of nonprofits is outpacing that of commercial organizations. Moreover, not
counting religious organizations, the nonprofit sector's benefits from tax
exemptions are valued at something on the order of $1 billion per year,
about half of which accrue to hospitals and educational institutions.

There is growing unease in government corridors in many communities
over that trend. No central data are available, but a scan of media coverage
hints at the gathering clouds.

In the counties that make up North Carolina's high-tech Research Tri-
angle Park, property removed from the tax rolls in the last three years has
increased by 15 percent. Its total value exceeds $15 billion.[3] In Connecticut,
47 percent of the land in Bridgeport, 50 percent in Hartford, and 74 percent

EXHIBIT 4.2   NEW YORK LOCAL GOVERMENTS'
REVENUE BY SOURCE (2004)

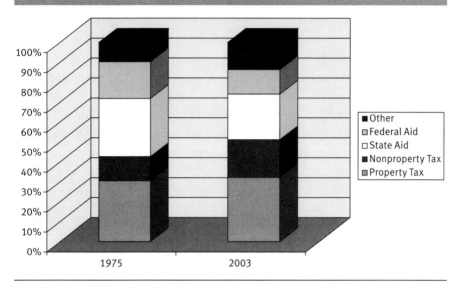

Source: New York State Office of the Controller.

in New Haven is tax-exempt. Local tax assessors have responded by questioning all but the most charitable uses of nonprofit properties, levying taxes on churches, universities, and nonprofits when facilities are used for conferences or conventions.[4] Indeed, in Fairfield County, Connecticut, the IRS has even come after the parent-led local youth soccer league for taxes and fines.[5]

New York State Legislator John Bonacic estimates that one-third of all land in New York is tax exempt and off the tax rolls, shifting that burden to homeowners and small businesses.[6] In Baltimore, Maryland, one out of every five jobs is in the nonprofit sector, and the nonprofit price tag to local taxation is nearly $70 million per year. That sum is larger than the projected 2004 general funds deficit in the city's tax coffers.[7]

In Berkeley, California, the tax loss from exempt properties (including the university) was two-thirds as large as the amount of taxes actually collected.[8] In recent months, in cities as diverse as Pittsburgh, Buffalo, Wichita, San Francisco, Houston, Tulsa, Meriden (NH), and Augusta (GA), nonprofit petitions to take properties off the tax rolls have roiled political waters. In part, those controversies have been because the nonprofits seeking the exemptions wanted to use the infrastructure to provide goods and services that actually made money—in some cases millions of dollars—competing with local nonexempt businesses to open, for example, fitness centers, parking lots, laundry services, and medical billing offices.

It is a tenet of dogma that, by definition, nonprofits should not pay taxes. That principle has its roots in early English law, which exempted governments from taxing themselves for their own land. The extension to charities was made in the theory that charitable institutions, and by extension their property, carried out functions that would otherwise be carried out by government. The inherent social contract is that, in exchange for nonprofit provision of a public good not available in the marketplace, the rest of society—households, individuals, and businesses—will bear the extra tax burden. The emerging problems are threefold. None of them bodes well for the relationship of trust between philanthropy and the American public.

First, what constitutes a nonprofit service on the public commons? A fitness company that seeks tax-exempt status for its new gyms, with the rationale that they are engaged in a public health battle to fight an epidemic of obesity, may seem an extreme example. Reading recent press accounts on the topic you will see that it is not. One fears that the whole rationale for the designation "tax-exempt nonprofit" may be losing its meaning, as the number of nonprofits spirals upward.

Second, what constitutes the value of the service provided on the public commons? Studies in Pennsylvania and California have called into question, for example, the magnitude of uncompensated care provided by nonprofit hospitals, relative to the taxes foregone. A recent study by Kane and Wubbenhorst found that when the total of all bad debt and all free care was measured against the value of tax exemption for nonprofit hospitals, fully a third of hospitals still had excess tax benefits. Since some bad debt is not related to indigence, if only half of bad debt and all of free care is compared to the value of tax exemption, over half (55 percent) of hospitals enjoyed excess tax benefits.[9]

Education has not been spared the same type of analysis. Some commentators, in cities with large academic institutions, have argued that there is nothing particularly "nonprofit" about a university that can charge $30,000 per year per student in tuition. "Voluntary" payments for colleges and universities, and other large nonprofits, to municipalities are relatively common ways for institutions to assist local government without compromising their tax status.

The level of these payments has often come into dispute, as the costs of government services rise, and more property moves off tax rolls. In Boston, for example, the $23.2 million collected in voluntary payments, from 40 nonprofits, represents only a small portion of the taxes lost annually. In Pittsburgh in 2005, the $12 million voluntarily paid by 83 nonprofits is measured against what the city council estimates is $55 million in taxes lost.[10]

These are troubling trends. Whether or not they are accurate—measurement is always a thorny issue—the fact that studies of relative value are there and have gained the ear of local government and regulators means that nonprofits must pay attention to the question. And they would best do so with open dialogue, rather than cries of indignation, because the taxpayer is paying attention.

Third, how shall local governments relate to nonprofits? It is certainly not in the best interests of nonprofits (or for-profits, for that matter) for local government to be in fiscal crisis. Neither is it in the best interests of local government to have major employers in a financial bind, whether they be nonprofit or for-profit businesses. The sharing of tax burden is a fundamental part of self-interest on all sides of democracy's many-sided table. Some cities and states have negotiated payments in lieu of taxes (PILT) with major nonprofits, notably universities. But these are few and far between.

Because a nonprofit's current status is tax exempt does not make it a future guarantee. The ability to take advantage of publicly funded resources (such as roads, police and fire departments) without having to shoulder the burden of their cost is not a right; it is a privilege. Hence, the relationship between local government and nonprofits (even the most powerful, universities and hospitals) must reflect the needs of the community in its entirety, not simply the needs of the nonprofit's balance sheet.

Moreover, concern does not stop at the level of local government, although the always-heated topic of property taxes makes the subject of tax burden particularly lively there. Federal research is also under way to assess nonprofit tax behavior. For example, Omer and Yetman completed a study in 2005, which found that nearly one in five of the nonprofits in their sample *evaded* income taxes, and that the overstatement of taxable expenses was, on average, around 30 percent.[11] That is a powerful finding. Tax avoidance is legal; tax *evasion* is not.

There are no clear answers to any of the three questions. What is stunning, however, is that the questions are not being raised *at all*. This is a mistake. Nonprofit, philanthropic, and government leaders should be actively discussing these issues broadly and honestly. The possible need for change should be confronted and admitted. Governments need to be treated as partners; in turn, local governments need to treat nonprofits as partners.

Silence is not a strategy. Simply saying nothing, while hoping the issues of service content, value, and taxability will go away has only one certain outcome. Nonprofits exist to serve the public; their credibility derives from willing, public recognition of that role. Silence in the face of divergent viewpoints about that role and public finance is not an option. It will erode trust; and nonprofits erode public policy and taxpayer trust at their own peril.

■ OTHER SOURCES

J. Grover, "Cash-Strapped Governments Seek More Funds," *American City and County,* May 1, 2004.

T. Bonnett, "Is the New Global Economy Leaving State-Local Tax Structures Behind?" National Conference of State Legislatures, March 15, 1999.

P. Lakamp, "Pittsburgh Shares Woes of Constrained Tax Base," *Buffalo News,* July 6, 2004.

D. S. Levine, "Nonprofit Hospitals Take Tax Break and Run," *San Francisco Business Times,* November 21, 2003.

R. Salee, "Council Weighs Tax Break for Hospital System," *Houston Chronicle,* July 7, 2004.

"Sale of $200 Million in Tax-Exempt Bonds to Buy Apartments Raises Concerns," Press Release of Representative Russ Roach, Tulsa, Oklahoma.

S. Cooper, "Group Wants Tax-Free Property," *Augusta (GA) Chronicle,* June 15, 2004.

G. Campbell, "Leaders Worry that Meriden, NH Senior Housing Project May Drain Town Money," *Eagle Times,* June 27, 2004.

D. Lefler, "Genesis Asks Tax Break for 3 Gyms," *Wichita Eagle,* July 11, 2004.

P. Leland, "Giving and Getting: Charitable Tax Exempt Status at the Local Level," comments at the Center for Community Development and Family Policy, University of Delaware, Winter 2001.

■ NOTES

1. H. W. Bowman, "Reexamining the Property Tax Exemption," *Land Lines* 15(3), July 2003.

2. Special Report on Municipal Affairs, New York Office of the State Controller, 2004.

3. Associated Press State and Local Wire, "House Committee Clears Bill to Exempt UNC-Related Nonprofits from Property Tax," June 29, 2004.

4. J. Gordon, "Playing Tough with the Tax Exempt," *New York Times,* May 7, 2006.

5. T. Kelley, "It's Goalkeeper vs. Bookkeeper as IRS Discovers Youth Soccer," *New York Times,* June 25, 2006.

6. P. Breakley, "Bonacic Talks Nonprofit Tax Exemption," *Daily Star Online,* April 10, 2003.

7. J. S. Hopkins, "Nonprofit Growth Creates Quandary," *Baltimore Sun,* June 21, 2004.

8. P. Brenneman, "City Tax Burden Skips UC Properties," *Berkeley Daily Planet,* May 11, 2004.

9. N. M. Kane and W. H. Wubbenhorst, "Alternative Funding Policies for the Uninsured: Exploring the Value of Hospital Tax Exemption," *Milbank Quarterly* 78(2), 2000: 185–211.

10. R. Lord, "City's Nonprofits Don't Plan to Up Their Contributions," *Pittsburgh Post-Gazette,* October 18, 2005.

11. T. Omer and R. Yeltman, "Tax Evasion and Avoidance by Nonprofit Organizations," mimeo, September 2005.

We the People: Public Trust and Expectations

ANNE F. GLAUBER

The front-page headline of a July 2006 *Wall Street Journal*[1] tells a familiar story. "Scrutiny of Gifts Threatens Charitable Movement" describes how the Nehemiah Corporation, which donates down-payment funds to the working poor, enabling hundreds of people to become first-time homeowners, is now at risk. The article details the multiple allegations of how the founder of Nehemiah Corporation personally profited from these gifts. Although the news article focuses only on the allegations, and not on any admission or judgment of guilt, the result is the same. The message is conveyed that there is yet another nonprofit that cannot be trusted.

This narrative of nonprofit missions gone bad seems familiar, because it is. Americans are not surprised to read another article about nonprofit malfeasance, because we do so with great frequency. In fact, a 2004 study by the Washington-based Independent Sector reported that, over the course of 16 months, it compiled more than 350 news articles on nonprofit organizations' problems with governance, stewardship, and integrity.[2] That means Americans were reading more than 25 negative articles a month about how nonprofits are managed and operated. Had this been a public relations campaign to change perceptions, it would have been a rousing success. The quantity and continuity of negative coverage during this time could only have served to undermine public trust.

> If public trust is ebbing, the nonprofit sector runs the risk of losing the most important asset it has.

No wonder only 1 in 10 Americans strongly agrees that charitable organizations are ethical in their use of donated funds. According to a Harris interactive survey, conducted in January 2006, roughly one-third of U.S. adults (32 percent) has less than positive feelings about charitable organizations. And the same number also believe that charitable organizations are "off in the wrong direction." What is striking about the data is that the closer Americans get in age to being those who will transfer wealth, the less they trust the nonprofits who seek to receive that wealth (see Exhibit 4.3).

Yet despite the significant number of Americans who have doubts about the direction and ethics of nonprofit organizations, according to this same survey people are still donating. More than 90 percent of adults report that they or members of their household have given to charities.[3]

But a closer look at how, and to whom, people are giving actually reflects how public distrust of nonprofits influences the thrust of their charitable donations. More than half of all contributions were given to local religious organizations, where there are strong personal community ties and involvement.

If, according to the Harris poll, public trust is ebbing, the nonprofit sector runs the risk of losing the most important asset it has. Working actively to

EXHIBIT 4.3   ATTITUDE TOWARDS CHARITABLE
ORGANIZATIONS

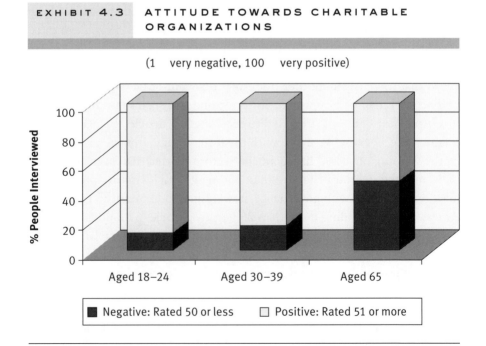

(1   very negative, 100   very positive)

Negative: Rated 50 or less   Positive: Rated 51 or more

Source: Harris Interactive.

build relationships and trust has to be the top priority of management and leadership. The task is difficult for several reasons.

First, the relentless availability of information complicates the communication process of building public trust. Nothing is hidden. Google places a magnifying glass on our world, detailing past and present behaviors, alliances, and actions, in ways that can impede the best abilities of organizations to shape and deliver messages. Bloggers take advantage of innuendo or rumor to pursue stories that would have been ignored by the conventional press. Once their stories are completed, bloggers widely disseminate their findings, virally or through the mainstream media. Disgruntled employees, whistle-blowers, and disheartened donors now have many more communication vehicles and information outlets than at any other time in history, to describe alleged failings or mismanagement. This is a new and ever-expanding source of negative news—just the news that the mainstream media wants to replicate.

Every blogger is a potential investigative reporter, serving the print and broadcast media, whose ratings and revenue are typically based on the power of negative news to engage audiences. Simply, the negative bias of the media, which now has a lot more negative fodder to use, complicates efforts to build public trust.

Second, high-profile cases of malfeasance, inefficiencies, and corruption that do receive inordinate amounts of publicity and media attention are sticky. Shaking these negative stories from people's minds takes significant resources and time; and mitigating their impact is a significant challenge. A study by the Washington-based Public Agenda in October 2005 found that people have a long memory for scandal and waste when it involved nonprofits. Focus groups taking part in the study consistently said that they took past misdeeds "quite personally, and the breach is nearly impossible to repair."[4] Although the Red Cross rebounded after 9/11 to receive the bulk of contributions for Katrina, the massive coverage of its mishandling of 9/11 left a scar. In 2005, when Guidestar.org, the Web site that tracks nonprofit finances and contributions, asked its newsletter readers whether the public has more or less confidence in nonprofits than in the past, the results clearly reflected the public sense of distrust. Of those readers, many of whom were affiliated with nonprofits and philanthropy, a 58 percent majority believed the American public has less confidence than ever before.[5] Several reasons were cited for the decline in public confidence. The most overarching reason was the belief that corruption, lies, and scandals permeate all sectors of society. Basically, no organization is immune from skepticism and distrust, and organizations in the nonprofit sector have demonstrated that they are no more ethical than other sectors.

The third reason that it is increasingly difficult to change perceptions is the evolving nature of nonprofits. The growth of social entrepreneurship has drawn a sharp line between slow-moving, bureaucratic organizations and the nimble, entrepreneurial effort that engages donors and supporters in designing and participating in programs, where direct impact is personally experienced. New philanthropists are insisting that their money be directed in different ways, and they are looking to match strategies of the capital markets in addressing social problems.

As a different type of philanthropy emerges, one that seeks to apply the best elements of business to the nonprofit world, there is an entirely new vocabulary emerging as well; terms like *venture philanthropy, social investing,* and *philanthrocapitalism* are but a few. This jargon sets up a whole different approach to measuring results, and holding nonprofits accountable to their missions and activities, thus increasing the pressure on traditional nonprofits to communicate more effectively about how they are managed.

When contrasting the perspective of old philanthropy versus the new, as *The Economist* magazine did in a major February 2006 feature story, the old was typically described as top heavy, plagued with excessive salaries, and unaccountable, while the new was increasingly viewed as smart, creative, and effective.[6] Conventional nonprofits must work even harder to regain the public trust, as they compete for funds and support against the new model of philanthropy. Indeed, in that same story, Harvard Business School professor and management guru, Michael Porter, made a stunning assertion when he said, "Nonprofit scandals tend to be about pay and perks, but the real scandal is how much money is [frittered] away on activities that have no impact. Billions are wasted on ineffective philanthropy."

What is a traditional nonprofit organization to do in the face of this skepticism and distrust? They must find new ways to communicate authentically to audiences, and they must make strategic communication a priority. Although the communication strategy will be different for each organization, there are several components that are essential for any type of communication effort.

KNOW YOUR AUDIENCE

The first step in developing a communication campaign that aims to change public opinion and increase understanding is to assess the perceptions and attitudes of the audience the organization seeks to reach. Thus, any campaign needs to begin with a communications audit, to determine how the organization is perceived by its multiple constituencies. A communications audit goes beyond conducting focus groups. It consists of an extensive internal and external review of all media, communication tools, and information vehicles, including Web sites, brochures, and newsletters, to analyze the current communications, and positioning of the organization, to compare this positioning to the image that the organization has in the media.

In addition, interviews are conducted with management, staff, and board members of the organization, as well as supporters, donors, journalists, prospects, and interested members of the general public. The goal is to determine whether there is a discrepancy between how an organization sees itself and how it is seen. This perception gap is then utilized to build a communication plan that not only shapes words but actions. Based on the findings of a communications audit, organizations are able to understand what they need to do to reshape governance, management, and programs to strengthen public trust and support.

Once specific actions are taken to narrow the perception gap, a communication plan can be developed that focuses on delivering details and educating the public, simply and openly, about the organization's work. That leads to the next tactic.

BE THE FIRST TO COMMUNICATE TOO MUCH

Given the role of the Internet and the availability of information, organizations must take the lead in being as transparent as possible. Indeed, organizations need to provide more information than they think the public wants or needs to know. This should not be done in a defensive way; once accepting the fact that every action taken can be the potential fodder for bad publicity, organizations need to focus their communication on all the processes, accountability procedures, and self-regulation practices they conduct.

Organizations need to provide their public constituencies and supporters with complete detailed information on the structure, implementation, and impact of these practices, in order to educate and engage constituencies in this effort. Thus, in addition to implementing new ways to govern and manage, organizations also need to develop effective communication tools to educate their audiences about these specific changes. These can include sections on the Web site devoted to financial management, frequent newsletters that provide a realistic assessment of the progress and impact of programs, and conference calls and public forums to describe and communicate efforts that did not succeed or meet expectations.

This is particularly true for bad news. Hearing negative news directly from an organization's own leadership is one of the most important ways to renew and retain public trust. Admissions of mistakes and problems are accepted and forgiven more readily if leadership takes immediate responsibility, openly delivers the details, and communicates a plan of action. But strategically, communications also should serve to enhance the positive and break through the media barrier that blocks the positive from being reported.

WORK CREATIVELY AND PERSISTENTLY TO FIND STORIES THAT REINFORCE THE NONPROFIT'S MISSION

By accepting the fact that the media prefers to report on the negative story, organizations need to concentrate on how to surmount that bias. This means investing in efforts that will identify and design new creative ways to galvanize positive responses from journalists, bloggers, broadcasters, and the general public. It is not as simple as it sounds. Nonprofit organizations need to walk a fine line between investing in public relations programs that will evoke a positive response and implementing a plan that will turn people away because of distaste for contrived marketing programs.

One of the key ways to surmount this challenge is to build emotional connections among audiences through stories. Stories serve to create relationships. People want to read about people. Reporters want to write a good story. Nonprofits need to find them and personalize the impact of their programs in ways that build and strengthen relationships and empathy. This is not the superficial summary of people in distress or need; rather, communications experts need to identify and develop in-depth stories that go into detail about people's experiences, aspirations, and struggles, making the people and the organization come alive for the public. By identifying the right stories and sharing the experiences, the media evolves into a partner. Media then provides a third-party endorsement for the importance and impact of these organizations, and can strengthen public trust. Other third-party experts can do so as well.

BRING IN THE THIRD PARTIES

Any effective communication campaign utilizes the testimony and credibility of third-party experts to endorse an institution and say things the organization cannot. Through the growth of social venture funds, analysts now exist who, like to their counterparts in the capital markets, assess the prospects, mission, and impact of the nonprofit sector. These analysts reach a critical audience, as their influence and insights can impact significantly how nonprofit organizations can be viewed and measured. Nonprofit organizations need to reach out to them and engage them in their mission and efforts to improve accountability and transparency. Academic, corporate, and public policy leaders can also all provide the third-party support to build public trust; key influencers need to be among the key audiences of any communication campaign.

At the other end of the spectrum, one of the most effective third-party supporters of an organization is the celebrity. Finding the right celebrity to endorse and support a nonprofit's mission can take an organization from complete obscurity to international prominence, with strengthened public trust, in the time it takes *Access Hollywood* to record a sound bite. This writer's recent experience involving Brad Pitt in the work of a small environmental organization demonstrated overwhelmingly that the power of celebrity could cut through cynicism, skepticism, and distrust effectively and easily.

Yet clearly, celebrities are a short-term and superficial communication tactic. The hard work is in sustaining honest, transparent communication to the public, who ultimately is the most important third-party endorsement. When it is clear that the work of the nonprofit sector fills a social and economic void and accomplishes what it seeks to do, trust is strengthened by the authenticity of results.

■ NOTES

1. M. Corkery, "Scrutiny of Gifts Threatens Charitable Movement," *Wall Street Journal,* July 5, 2006: B1.

2. Cited in speech by William H. Donaldson, Chairman, U.S. Securities and Exchange Commission, Chicago, IL, November 8, 2004.

3. "While a Third of Adults Think the Nonprofit Sector in the United States Is Headed in the Wrong Direction, a Vast Majority of Households Donated to Charities in the Past Year," *PR Newswire,* April 27, 2006.

4. "Americans Becoming Wary of 'Slick' Charity Marketing," *NonProfit Times,* October 25, 2005: 1.

5. http://www.guidestar.org/news/features/public_confidence.jsp.

6. "The Business of Giving," *The Economist,* February 23, 2006.

American Philanthropy and the Drive for Results: A Plea from the World of Ideas

SUSAN RAYMOND, PHD

Three passions have governed my life:
The longings for love, the search for knowledge,
And unbearable pity for the suffering of [humankind].

Love brings ecstasy and relieves loneliness.
In the union of love I have seen
In a mystic miniature the prefiguring vision
Of the heavens that saints and poets have imagined.

With equal passion I have sought knowledge.
I have wished to understand the hearts of [people].
I have wished to know why the stars shine.

Love and knowledge led upwards to the heavens,
But always pity brought me back to earth;
Cries of pain reverberated in my heart
Of children in famine, of victims tortured
And of old people left helpless.
I long to alleviate the evil, but I cannot,
And I, too, suffer.

—Bertrand Russell

This indeed is the tension. The world of ideas, the pursuit of knowledge for the sake of knowledge, is often seen as being at odds with the practical solution of immediate problems. Knowledge is academic; action is imperative. Whether that pursuit of knowledge is in the halls of America's colleges and universities or at the benches of its research laboratories, tension between funding knowledge and funding action is always present. It is also increasingly dangerous, because the pace of change is so rapid that knowledge and action must increasingly be harnessed together.

> The pace of change is so rapid that knowledge and action must increasingly be harnessed together. In philanthropy, too, one sees a risk of the divergence between support for knowledge and support for action that will undermine the role of philanthropy itself on the social commons.

In philanthropy, one also sees a risk of the divergence between support for knowledge and support for action, that will undermine the role of philanthropy itself on the social commons. The two diverging trends are a changing society and the approach to portfolio design in philanthropy. It is a divergence that risks separating philanthropy, not only from its core purposes but also from its critical, and perhaps unique, utility in the face of what is truly complex social and economic change in America. That change requires that we have a more robust world of ideas.

The topic can be approached in three steps: first, by illustrating the pace and implications of change in America; second, by reviewing the implications of current priorities in philanthropy; and third, by suggesting some areas in which, returning to its root purposes, American philanthropy has the potential to lead the nation in defining our future economy and society.

First, then, let us toss ourselves about on the seas of change.

The easiest, but far from the sole, place to find illustrations of change is, of course, science and technology. The number of patents issued in the United States has increased more than threefold since 1963 (see Exhibit 4.4). We have sequenced the human genome. We, as a species, now have the blueprints for constructing a biological entity. Huge benefits can accrue from that knowledge: personalized medicine, tissue and organ engineering, neural and sensory implants, cures for the incurable, hope for those who have had to face only despair since history has been recorded.

EXHIBIT 4.4   U.S. PATENTS ISSUED (1963–2004)

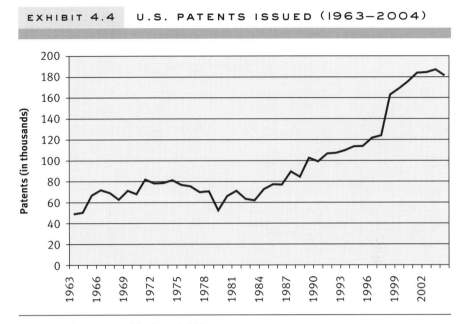

Source: U.S. Patent and Trademark Office.

Nanotechnology—creating machines on the atomic and molecular scale—is on the verge of revolutionizing approaches to materials design. Clothes, for example, will monitor vital signs and deliver medicines; buildings will adjust to weather; bridges and roads will sense cracks and repair themselves.[1]

Change is measured, however, not just by its trajectory but by its speed. Rates of change have been exponential, not linear. In the last decade of the twentieth century, more technological progress occurred than in the previous nine decades of that century. And the first decade of the twenty-first century will see more change than we experienced in all of the last century.[2]

Moreover, change is not elite, but is broadly accessible to society. A three-minute phone call from New York to London, in 1960, cost $60.42 in 2000 dollars; now, it costs less than 50 cents. A computer and peripheral equipment in 1960 cost $1,869,004; today a more powerful computer costs less than $1,000.

Change is also rapid outside of technology.

Globalization provides a marked illustration. In 1965, the value of world merchandise trade was $1 trillion (see Exhibit 4.5). In 2003, it was $6.7 trillion. Trade now accounts for a quarter of global GDP, compared to just seven percent in 1965. In the last two decades, developing countries that lowered

EXHIBIT 4.5   U.S. MERCHANDISE TRADE IN VOLUME TERMS

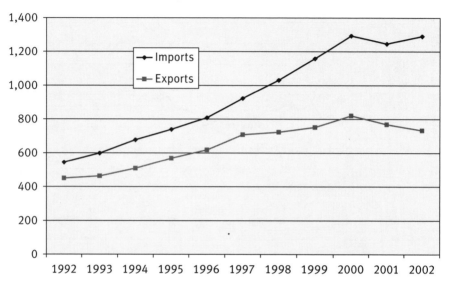

(Billions of Chained 1996 Dollars)

Source: World Trade Organization.

their barriers to trade had over twice the rate of economic growth of industrialized countries.[3] Growth is not just about industrialized markets anymore. In 2005, General Electric CEO Jeffrey Imelt predicted that, by 2010, 60 percent of GE's incremental revenue growth would come from developing countries. And the view from Wall Street? Goldman Sachs responded, "The developing world is GE's best option for delivering sustainable, double-digit growth." The developing world, no less!

Innovation and the world of ideas are also increasingly global. In 1963, 18 percent of all patents granted in the United States were to foreign entities. By 2004, that proportion was 48 percent. Transportation also illustrates the globalization of U.S. society. Between 1990 and 2000, the total number of passengers flying from U.S. airports to foreign destinations increased by 70 percent, and the top 20 routes accounted for only 16 percent of the passengers. Moreover, the highest rate of growth was not in New York, but in Detroit, Chicago, and Orlando.

Internally, America is also changing. We are better educated than ever in our nation's history. In 1940, only 4.5 percent of Americans over the age of 25 were college educated; today, nearly 30 percent are. In 1940, less than a quarter of Americans over the age of 25 had earned a high school diploma; today 85 percent have.

Up until 2005, immigration rates had been higher than the nation had experienced in a century. In 1959, immigration accounted for six percent of U.S. population growth. Now it accounts for 40 percent, and without immigration we would have an absolute decline in the population of working-age individuals.

As recently as 1970, 60 percent of immigrants to the United States were from Europe. Now, fewer than 10 percent are. In turn, we have become more religiously diverse. The number of Muslims, Hindus, and Buddhists in America has more than doubled since 1990. Together, these three religions now have more adherents than the Jewish faith in America.

These are but a few examples of the nature and pace of change to which our individual and collective stars are hitched. That change will create new social pressures and opportunities whose dimensions the nation only poorly comprehends.

What of philanthropy? It is here that one begins to be concerned. Unquestionably, discipline, rigor, accountability, impact, and transparency are fundamental characteristics that underpin trust in both public and private endeavors. The societal contract, between the American taxpayer and philanthropies and nonprofits, absolutely requires adherence to the highest standards in these areas.

However, there is a price to those standards, and an unsettling one. As philanthropy becomes more concerned with impact, and more consumed with structure, measuring results, and ensuring the effectiveness of its money, there is a growing danger of making philanthropy risk averse. When philanthropy seeks the sure, when it makes decisions on the basis of probability of success, it becomes mechanical. Philanthropy becomes like the mortgage business; add column A, subtract column B, and if the result is positive, make the loan. If it is negative, if it entails risk, deny the loan.

Is that what philanthropy is supposed to be? Are philanthropists mortgage brokers, or are they visionaries? An absorption with the details—of return on investment and measurement of impact, however important these considerations—will lead us to the safe and secure, the comfortable and quotidian, and will thus lead us away from the complexity and unpredictability, but also away from the rewards of risk.

Health provides an apt example. A decade ago, 22 percent of healthcare philanthropy flowed to research (see Exhibit 4.6). Today, the estimate is eight

EXHIBIT 4.6   RECIPIENTS OF U.S. HEALTH
PHILANTHROPY

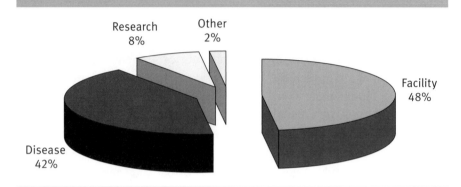

Source: Sample by Giving USA.

percent. Yet in 2005, Changing Our World surveyed 18 independent, non-profit, biological research institutes for fiscal 2003. Private contributions represented 40 percent of total revenue, and half relied upon philanthropy for 50 percent or more of their revenue.

When research cannot guarantee results, let alone impact, what happens to the philanthropic revenue stream for research? True, the federal government's biomedical research investment totals $30 billion. How big is $30 billion? That resource flow is greater than the combined annual grant payout of all private foundations for all giving sectors. So, philanthropy is a very minor part of the total, American research-resource pool.

But measurement of the relative size of the philanthropic dollar misses the point. On the landscape of change just illustrated, the philanthropic dollar is unique, which is why it is so important. Unlike any other dollar, it can have two characteristics.

First, it is "hunch money." Because one of the core purposes of philanthropy is to invest where markets cannot or will not because of the uncertainty of financial return, philanthropy can work on the edges of understanding. Even relative to government money, it can tolerate a degree of failure and intellectual risk that the taxpayer will not (and, arguably, ought not) tolerate in the federal budget.

Where we truly do not know the answers, where we truly do not know the implications of change, where we truly do not know the impact, it is *there* that the philanthropic dollar has its most unique, and therefore its highest, value.

Second, the philanthropic dollar is, or ought to be, politically neutral. This, of course, is not the reality. All too often, philanthropies do not stand above political alignments.

Nevertheless, there *ought* to be at least some core of philanthropy, or some walled-off part of philanthropy's portfolio, that is independent of ideology and politics. Being objective and independent does, of course, take courage, especially when voices are loud, debate is heated, and partisanship is bitter. But it is essential if philanthropy is to hold true to its purposes.

If it can muster the courage to be politically neutral, the philanthropic dollar brings huge value to our world of change. You do not have to read the newspapers every day (once a week is sufficient) to appreciate how much change has roiled the waters of American society. Jobs are lost, beliefs are questioned, strangers move in, girls come to class with their heads covered, and choices about aging and death that were never needed before become necessary. What can be begins to separate from what has comfortably been.

There is, amidst change, a need for the exploration of ideas, for a searching for new expressions of bedrock values, for robust examination of all views, in neutral and mutually respectful space.

Finally, then, let us examine but one illustration of where the philanthropic dollar can provide such a unique value amidst change.

Progress in biomedical research will break through even the current knowledge boundaries. That progress will create opportunities to act on problems or prevent consequences of problems never imagined in human history. But taking action on that knowledge may conflict with what all, or part, of American society believes. Questions of life and death, of treatment modalities, and of privacy will all become not theoretical but immediate.

Left unanticipated, the dilemmas will quickly become controversies. And, as always, controversies will quickly become the stuff of evening talk shows and political rallies. Once inserted into politics, controversies cannot help but become partisan and therefore divisive.

The unique value of philanthropy is that it is the only money that can anticipate and seed the dialogue about change in advance of, and independent from, politics and ideology. It is the only money that can be a positive, productive center of gravity, around which alternative views can coalesce with mutual respect and carry out a searching dialogue about the implications of change for American society.

Biology is not the only example, of course. Trends in religious diversity, economic dislocations associated with globalization, perhaps even roads that self-repair and shirts that morph into raincoats—all are changing our nation.

What the nation needs are ideas about adapting that are as good, as creative, and as sophisticated as the changes themselves. Changes in reality have far outpaced changes in social institutions. Changes in social institutions have far outpaced our understanding of change. Leadership from the world of ideas is critically needed.

Perhaps a modest proposition for the nonprofit world is in order.

Every nonprofit should reformulate its programs and priorities, to devote 10 percent of its effort to understanding, projecting, and planning for the consequences of change in its environment. Economic, technological, demographic, social, intellectual, ideological, religious, cultural—the trend line of all change requires ideas on two levels: ideas about how change will impact an organization, and, perhaps more importantly, ideas about how organizations can do more than react. Rather, how can they anticipate and shape change, so that it contributes to our nation's strength, vitality, and prosperity? Being out in front is always better than running to catch up.

In alignment with these efforts of nonprofits to be more future oriented, every philanthropy should adjust its giving portfolio to devote 10 percent of its resources to funding this world of ideas, without politics and without ideology. Look for the best, most interesting questions being asked about the future. Encourage and support those who are probing the edges of our knowledge and understanding. Allocate 10 percent of your portfolio to intellectual risk, to questions for which we can now only vaguely discern answers, to projecting implications of change before society is overwhelmed by it. Come back to the world of ideas, even though there will be no immediate proof of impact.

If only half of all philanthropies took up this challenge, well in excess of $1 billion per year would flow to understanding and anticipating the social consequences of the changing national environment. This will not buy all the answers, but it will buy the beginnings of understanding, and strengthen us as a people as we move forward into the brave, new world of the twenty-first century.

There are two alternatives. We can sit back and let the social implications of change surprise us. In such cases, surprise is almost never a good thing. The price of surprise will be divisiveness.

Or we can try to understand and anticipate change and seek out the best ideas and insights to prepare for it.

The philanthropic and nonprofit sector bears both the burden and the privilege of that choice.

▓ OTHER SOURCES

"U.S. International Travel and Transportation Trends," Bureau of Transportation Statistics, U.S. Department of Transportation, 2005.

World Trade Report, 2005 (Geneva: World Trade Organization, 2005).

National Center for Education Statistics, U.S. Department of Education.

U.S. Bureau of the Census.

"U.S. Patent Statistics," U.S. Patent and Trademark Office, 2005.

▓ NOTES

1. S. Regetar and E. Eiseman, *Anticipating Technological Change: Combinatorial Chemistry and the Environment* (Rand Science and Technology Division, April 2001).

2. K. P. Nyguen, "Emerging Technologies and Exponential Change: Implications for Army Transformation," *Parameters,* Summer 2002: 86–99.

3. "Globalization: The Story Behind the Numbers," *Finance and Development* 39(1), March 2002.

When Charities Behave Badly: State Attorneys General on the Case

KATHERINE C. JEWELL

In today's world, there are a multitude of organizations competing for the charitable dollar of each American household. It is not uncommon to receive a phone call during the dinner hour or a pamphlet in the mail, asking for a contribution to a particular cause. Many American citizens must decide which charity or nonprofit they will give their dollar to. Should they choose an organization with which they have a personal connection, or should they give to a popular, global cause? More importantly, however, is the following: Wouldn't it be nice to know that your charitable dollar is going to help the people the charity serves, rather than the people who serve the charity? Wouldn't it be nice to know that the organization you are giving to makes appropriate and legal decisions on where your donation goes?

> This is not just an opportunity for charities to suddenly stop unlawful practices (although that would be ideal), nor is it a time for the state attorneys general to strictly limit the actions of nonprofit organizations. Rather, this is an opportune time for both parties to work together, to create a common ground and a framework, in which these organizations can be permitted to carry out their business free from harsh or unnecessary restraints, as well as understand that violations of law, whether unintentional or flagrant, minor or major, will no longer be tolerated.

The charitable actions of an organization no longer concern simply the consumer. State attorneys general are becoming increasingly involved in the regulation of charities, and the number of cases involving potential fraudulent action has reached a noticeable level. Attorneys general issue the standard warnings and advice for consumers dealing with potentially fraudulent charitable organizations, and aim to protect consumers against such action, as the unsuspecting giver may be unknowingly losing money, rather than voluntarily giving it.

CHARITIES, NONPROFITS, AND THE ATTORNEYS GENERAL

The Charitable Activities Section within the office of Oregon's attorney general is one of the few state attorney general's offices that does keep track electronically of legal actions and court proceedings brought against charities. Approximately 300 cases have passed through the Oregon attorney general's office between January 24, 1985, and June 5, 2006.[1]

Almost two-thirds of those cases have ended with an "Assurance of Voluntary Compliance," an alternative to a lawsuit (see Exhibit 4.7). These cases typically involve fundraisers and individuals engaging in unlawful action, rather than charities. The remaining one-third of cases has been divided, more or less in half, between judgments (contested cases, or cases involving a monetary award, which are rare) and orders (due to an administrative action).

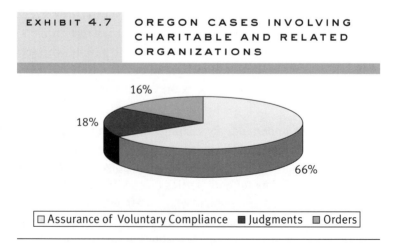

EXHIBIT 4.7   OREGON CASES INVOLVING CHARITABLE AND RELATED ORGANIZATIONS

16%

18%

66%

☐ Assurance of Voluntary Compliance   ■ Judgments   ▨ Orders

Source: State of Oregon, Department of Justice, Charitable Activities Section.

The Pennsylvania Office of Attorney General has seen a total of approximately 94 cases involving charitable organizations, fundraising counsels, and solicitors pass through its office between February 6, 1998, and April 18, 2006, resulting in consent agreements and adjudications. Of those cases, approximately 80 percent have ended in a consent agreement, and a little over 10 percent have ended in adjudication (see Exhibit 4.8).[2]

Typical cases involve charities and nonprofits failing to register, or re-register, with the State of Pennsylvania (where the typical monetary penalty was between $1,000 and $5,000); failing to accurately keep track of the organization's financial activity; and failing to file contracts with organizations, in the required time frame.[3]

The attorney general for Minnesota typically resolves disputes between the state and charities through assurances of discontinuance. Such cases involve illegal activity similar to what has occurred in Pennsylvania: failure to register as a charity, failure to maintain accurate financial records, and so forth. Other illegal activity has focused on the structure and composition of organizations' boards. Some cases are slightly more entertaining. In the matter of Arts Midwest, a nonprofit corporation in Minnesota, the organization failed to submit annual reports to the attorney general's office (an action required by Minnesota law).[4] After the attorney general's office notified the organization twice of this violation, Arts Midwest was withdrawn from the register of charitable organizations in the state. Although the Minnesota Attorney General's Office notified Arts Midwest twice of its violation

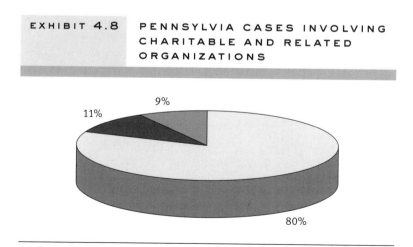

EXHIBIT 4.8   PENNSYLVIA CASES INVOLVING
CHARITABLE AND RELATED
ORGANIZATIONS

9%

11%

80%

Source: Pennsylvania Department of State, Bureau of Charitable Organizations.

and removed it from its registry, Arts Midwest, amazingly enough, continued to operate as a charitable organization, solicitations and all.

In the matter of Centro Cultural de Fargo-Moorhead, also a nonprofit corporation in Minnesota, the organization had, to put it simply, problems controlling its charitable goods.[5] Negligent behavior had resulted in the oversight of such things as the executive director's giving herself a pay raise of $3,000 over seven months in 2005; charging over $600 in personal expenses, to the organization; and charging of over $2,000 in meals, without explanation of the purpose of these meals, to the organization's credit card.

In January 2006, a total of 19 states[6] brought allegations against Newport Creative Communications (NCC), a Massachusetts-based fundraising consultant. According to the states involved, NCC was hired by more than 30 charities to design and send mailings with a sweepstakes component.[7] However, some charities saw their respective promotions as being misleading, in that it led recipients of the mailings to believe that they had already won. The case ended in an Assurance of Voluntary Compliance, with NCC agreeing to change their practices regarding such solicitations and pay $400,000 to the states involved.

Minnesota Attorney General Mike Hatch, in a statement before the Senate Finance Committee in 2005, told the story of Allina Health Systems, registered with his office as a tax-exempt organization under the Internal Revenue Code:

> Allina paid $89,000 for its board members and executives, and their spouses, to travel to the Phoenician Inn in Arizona. The Phoenician Inn boasts a $25 million art collection, marble from the same Italian quarry that Michelangelo used for the Pieta, chocolate for "tuck in" service flown in from Belgium three times per week, and a 22,000 square foot spa. Allina spent over $14,000 on food and alcohol and over $4,500 on golf, tennis, and spas. One dinner alone cost over $5,000. Executives charged the organization for $100 in floral arrangements to decorate their $855 per night suites. When we asked Allina to explain its "business purpose" for the trip, it stated that the trip was designed to inspire discussions about "healthcare reform." . . . On another occasion, Allina paid for its executives and spouses to take a three-day wine tour of Napa Valley, complete with private limousines and hot air balloon rides. On yet another occasion, it sent executives to Monterey, California, where they traveled in limousines and expensed thousands of dollars in meals at the area's most exclusive restaurant. Allina stated that the trip was designed to teach executives how to run a healthcare system with a "moral center."[8]

While the Minnesota cases ending in assurances (there have been several in the last three years) detail some of the Minnesota attorney general's allegations against charities, these assurances typically state that the assurance itself is not a confession, nor is it an acknowledgment of wrongdoing by the organization under investigation. It is interesting that, although the charities must agree to discontinue acts in violation of state laws and suffer a penalty, they do not actually acknowledge any wrongdoing. It would seem that they only acknowledge getting caught. Is it time for charities to step up to the plate and take account for their actions? The answer, quite simply, is yes.

THE SUPREME COURT WEIGHS IN

In 2003, the Supreme Court took action in favor of consumers in the case of *Madigan v. Telemarketing Associates* [538 U.S. 600 (2003)]. The charitable nonprofit corporation VietNow hired for-profit fundraising, telemarketing corporations to solicit donations, which would go to aid Vietnam veterans. Unbeknownst to Illinois consumers, the contract VietNow had with the telemarketing groups maintained that the telemarketers would retain 85 percent of the gross receipts from Illinois donors. According to the opinion written by Justice Ginsburg, "Between July 1987 and the end of 1995, telemarketers collected approximately $7.1 million, keeping slightly more than $6 million for themselves, and leaving approximately $1.1 million for the charity."[9] The Illinois attorney general argued that Illinois donors had been seriously misled to believe that a significant portion of their donations would go to VietNow. The telemarketers argued that restrictions made on charitable solicitation would create restraints on charitable fundraising, and would be in conflict with the First Amendment (which, as determined in *Schaumburg v. Citizens for a Better Environment,* protected the right to engage in solicitations for charities).[10]

The Illinois court ruled in favor of the telemarketers, in the form of a dismissal. However, the Supreme Court ruled otherwise. It explained that while the First Amendment does, in fact, protect the right to solicit for charities, it does not protect against fraud—in this case, the misleading statements provided by the telemarketers, regarding the use of charitable donations. "While bare failure to disclose that information directly to potential donors does not suffice to establish fraud, when nondisclosure is accompanied by intentionally misleading statements designed to deceive the listener, the First Amendment leaves room for a fraud claim."[11] Furthermore, "So long as the emphasis is on what the fundraisers misleadingly convey, and not on percentage limitations on solicitors' fees per se, such actions need not imper-missibly chill protected speech." [12]

FROM THE COURTHOUSE TO THE CHARITY: WHERE TO GO FROM HERE

Obtaining information on legal actions involving charities and nonprofits is difficult, to say the very least. Less than half of state attorneys general keep a record of legal action entered into with charities and nonprofits, and a low number of offices refer those seeking information on nonprofit legal action to their state departments. Here, the question is simple: Are the offices of state attorneys general failing to keep tabs on information that is so important to the consumer and that pertains to an issue that is becoming increasingly sensitive?

Understandably, state attorneys general cannot be expected to maintain detailed databases of every conceivable type of case. That would be impos-sible to ask. Surveys have shown that the departments within the offices of the attorneys general that deal with charities are understaffed and have been for quite some time, and funding for these divisions is lower than it probably could be. [13] Nevertheless, it would seem that very few maintain a database of charities, and whether those few are accessible to the public is another story entirely.

Furthermore, there appears to be a disconnect between the offices of the state departments and the attorneys general, such as when the attorney gen-eral refers information seekers to the state department on legal inquiries, and the state department sends the seeker back to the attorney general.

In a report from the Forum of Regional Associations of Grantmakers and the Council on Foundations, published in 2006, a survey of 16 states was conducted. Out of those 16, only eight had a direct hyperlink from the attorney general's homepage to the charities section of the attorney gen-eral's office; in five states, such a link was found on the Web site for the consumer protection (or similar) division. [14] Needless to say, public access to information on the charitable sector is sparse and difficult to come by.

Should state attorneys general take more of a "Big Brother" approach to the monitoring of charities? Is it even possible for such a thing to be done? Perhaps the attorneys general should not issue warnings before removing charities from the charitable register, for violation of charitable law. Statis-tics on charitable giving are already skewed because of the number of orga-nizations that solicit for donations. In 2000, four unregistered charities based in the state of Virginia received contributions totaling $27,151,663. [15]

If state attorneys general do take the Big Brother approach to regulating charities, several things may happen. First, attorneys general might create for themselves a negative image, seeming too controlling and demanding of the charities. On a related point, the number of charities and nonprofits (or at least newly created ones) may begin to decline, as it may be seen as being too difficult to maintain a nonprofit and keep it in line with state legal requirements. Nonprofits may also view hiring fundraising and solicitation professionals, such as telemarketers, as too risky, since those hired may not measure up to the requirements of state charitable law.

Mike Hatch advocates increased government regulation, explaining that the self-regulation of charities will not suffice, due to what he called the "halo effect"—where nonprofit leaders believe that, because of the goodwill nature of their "mission," they are above and beyond criticism.[16] Furthermore, self-regulation as the only means of keeping watch over charities is undesirable "because boards or trustees often actively participate in the abuses."[17]

Hatch makes several suggestions as to how the federal government can institute legislation and practices that discourage and disallow illegal activity within these nonprofits. He suggests the following:

- Limiting the number of board members who are compensated by the organization

- Promoting efforts to establish legislation that creates basic rules of governance for boards

- Periodically replacing auditing firms, so that nonprofits must "justify their tax-exempt status to the IRS on a periodic basis"

- An increased flow of information between the IRS and attorneys general, whose cases suffer because the IRS is unable to provide the offices with data on organizations

- Congress's limiting how much nonprofits can spend on travel, meals, and accommodations to the rate the U.S. government would pay for those items

- The following of certain procedures to assure that the salaries for nonprofit executives are reasonable

- Stricter regulation of the standards for nonprofit, credit-counseling organizations

- Requiring CEOs to sign IRS 990 forms

- Giving higher penalties for failing to file a 990

- Requiring 990s to "fully disclose the filing organization's relationships with affiliated tax-exempt and nonexempt organizations"[18]

The role of an attorney general, simply put, is to investigate violations of the law, and prosecute those responsible for such violations. What, then, should be the role of nonprofit leadership? The answer is surprisingly simple; leaders in the nonprofit world need to take an active role in making sure organizations abide by the law.

This is not that difficult a task. Many of the charities that have entered into some sort of legal action with a state attorney general have simply broken a law requiring them to file as a charitable organization, or as an organization with permission to solicit in a particular state. Surely charities and nonprofits can find the time to register, and re-register, with the state in order to become, and remain, legal and legitimate. If anything, these cases are the result of forgetfulness on the part of the charity. Many of the cases, such as those in Pennsylvania, could be avoided, by organizations' familiarizing themselves with state charitable law. Nonprofit leaders need to begin taking an active role in preventing such avoidable mishaps, rather than waiting around for them to happen, and *then* dealing with the aftermath, which is usually embarrassing and pricey.

Nonprofit leaders need to realize, if they have not already, that the only way to completely earn the trust of the consumer is to prove that the nonprofit "world"—consisting of nonprofit and charitable organizations, solicitors, professional fundraisers, and other related professions and professionals—can act justly, fairly, and in a manner that is in accordance with state and national law.

Very few people will be willing to give money to a charity if that organization sometimes "misplaces" money that goes to pay an executive board member's personal bills. For example, in March 2004, Oral Suer pled guilty to stealing approximately $500,000 from the United Way of the National Capital Area in Washington, D.C., of which he was a chief executive officer. Suer "admitted to receiving excessive pension payments, pocketing unreimbursed cash advances, and charging the organizations for fraudulent business expenses, including bowling equipment and visits to see his children" who were attending college.[19] As a result of Suer's actions, which were revealed beginning in 2002, private donations declined: during the 2003–2004 fundraising campaign, private donations fell to $38 million, down from over $90 million in 2001.[20]

What, then, are charities to do, to make sure they keep themselves in line with the law? Self-vigilance is almost entirely out of the question. The boards of charities and nonprofits have been unable to maintain a proper composition, as mandated by state law. In fact, as seen in cases from Minnesota, a large number of cases are brought against charities whose boards are made up of the wrong people.

It would appear, however, that perhaps a balance can be struck between tight government regulation of charities and the self-regulation of nonprofits, a concept many believe will just never work. Case studies conducted by the Forum of Regional Associations of Grantmakers and the Council on Foundations, show that in Ohio, New Hampshire, Illinois, and Michigan, effective relationships between charities and state regulators have been formed.[21]

This is not just an opportunity for charities to suddenly stop unlawful practices (although that would be ideal), nor is it a time for the state attorneys general to strictly limit the actions of nonprofit organizations. Rather, this is an opportune time for both parties to work together, to create a common ground and a framework, in which these organizations can be permitted to carry out their business free from harsh or unnecessary restraints, as well as understand that violations of law, whether unintentional or flagrant, minor or major, will no longer be tolerated. The consumer has enough to worry about these days. At least let the consumer rest assured that their philanthropic dollar is being used in a charitable way. Nonprofits must keep in mind the words of Mike Hatch, "[W]hen one organization engages in the types of abuses [he described], confidence in the entire sector is degraded."[22]

■ OTHER SOURCES

J. Cohn, "Uncharitable?" *New York Times,* December 19, 2004: 6:51.

"Annual Survey of State Laws Regulating Charitable Solicitations as of January 1, 2006," *Giving USA Quarterly* 1, Giving USA, 2006.

"Description of Present Law Relating to Charitable and Other Exempt Organizations and Statistical Information Regarding Growth and Oversight of the Tax-Exempt Sector," Joint Committee on Taxation: June 22, 2004.

Department of Justice, State of Orgeon, Charitable Activities Section.

Pennsylvania Department of State, Bureau of Charitable Organizations, http://-www.dos.state.pa.us/char/cwp/view.asp?a=1092&Q=431427&charNav=%7C, June 1, 2006.

"Public Charities Database of Final Legal Actions Against Fundraisers and Charities," (Massachusetts Attorney General's Office: 2006) http://www.ago.state-.ma.us/sp.cfm?pageid=1218, July 17, 2006.

Florida Office of the Attorney General, General Civil Litigation Division, Office of the Assistant Deputy.

Office of the Attorney General, California Department of Justice, http://ag.ca.-gov/.

Office of the Attorney General of Virginia, Antitrust and Consumer Litigation Section.

Office of the Attorney General, Delaware Department of Justice.

Office of the Oklahoma Attorney General, http://www.oag.state.ok.us/.

Charities Bureau, New York State Attorney General, http://www.oag.state.ny-.us/.

Office of the Vermont Attorney General, http://www.atg.state.vt.us/.

State of Minnesota, Office of the Attorney General.

Madigan v. Telemarketing Associates; (Oyez U.S. Supreme Court Multimedia: June 5, 2006. http://www.oyez.org/oyez/resource/case/1572/.

▓ NOTES

1. Department of Justice, State of Oregon, Charitable Activities Section

2. "A consent agreement is a legally enforceable agreement, signed by both parties, settling a matter in which a charitable organization, solicitor, or fundraising counsel admitted to violating one or more provisions of the Pennsylvania Solicitation of Funds for Charitable Purposes Act, 10 P. S. § 162.1 *et seq.,* and agreed to pay an appropriate administrative fine. A consent agreement *does not necessarily prohibit* a charitable organization from soliciting contributions in Pennsylvania. In contrast, an adjudication is a decision and order issued by an administrative law judge, finding that a charitable organization, solicitor or fundraising counsel has violated one or more provisions of the Act after a formal administrative hearing has been held." In addition, the list of violations provided by the Pennsylvania Department of State did not include the full details of each case. Pennsylvania Department of State, Bureau of Charitable Organizations, http://www.dos.state-.pa.us/char/cwp/view.asp?a=1092&Q=431427&charNav=%7C.

3. Ibid.

4. State of Minnesota, Office of the Attorney General.

5. State of Minnesota, Office of the Attorney General.

6. Arkansas, California, Kentucky, Massachusetts, Michigan, Minnesota, Montana, Nevada, New Jersey, North Carolina, Ohio, Oregon, Pennsylvania, South Carolina, Tennessee, Texas, Virginia, Washington, and Wisconsin. State of Minnesota, Office of the Attorney General.

7. State of Minnesota, Office of the Attorney General.

8. Statement of Minnesota Attorney General Mike Hatch, before the Senate Finance Committee (April 5, 2005) http://finance.senate.gov/hearings/testimony/2005test/mhtest040505.pdf, 12.

9. *Madigan v. Telemarketing Associates, Inc.,* 538 U.S. 600, 3 (2003). http://www-.supremecourtus.gov/opinions/02pdf/01-1806.pdf#search=%22opinion%-20of%20the%20court%20madigan%22.

10. Ibid.

11. Ibid.

12. Ibid.

13. D. Biemesderfer and A. Kosaras, "The Value of Relationships Between State Charity Regulators and Philanthropy," 2006. http://www.givingforum-.org/policy/regulators.html, 17.

14. Ibid., p. 18.

15. "Unregistered Commercial Fundraisers Report," Office of the Washington Secretary of State, Charitable Solicitations Program: November 2002. http://www.signature-loans.org/charities/pdfdownloads/commercial.pdf. It is unclear if this data is national, from Washington State, or a combination of the two.

16. Statement of Minnesota Attorney General Mike Hatch, before the Senate Finance Committee, April 5, 2005. http://finance.senate.gov/hearings/testimony/2005test/mhtest040505.pdf, 12.

17. Ibid.

18. Ibid., p. 17.

19. B. Wolverton, "D.C. United Way Leader Sentenced to Jail Time," *Chronicle of Philanthropy Update,* May 17, 2004: 5.

20. Ibid.

21. D. Biemesderfer and A. Kosaras, "The Value of Relationships Between State Charity Regulators and Philanthropy," p. 17.

22. Statement of Minnesota Attorney General Mike Hatch, before the Senate Finance Committee, April 5, 2005: 18.

Money Moves on the Nonprofit Dance Floor: The Consequences of a Faster Tempo

Susan Raymond, PhD, and
Mary Beth Martin, Esq.

> "Will you, won't you, will you, won't you,
> will you join the dance?"
>
> The Lobster-Quadrille
> — Lewis Carroll

One cannot move trillions of dollars anywhere without someone noticing. The reality of the upcoming wealth transfer is not lost on the nonprofit marketplace. That realization has contributed to all manner of nonprofit organizational innovations, to be sure that revenue dance cards are nicely filled once the music starts. And the dance floor is crowded, not only with traditional nonprofits, but with a variety of relatively new entrants.

The trend in the use of private philanthropy to supplement tax-supported institutions is both domestic and international. This has increased competition, but also introduced complexity into the line between the definition of a nonprofit, a for profit, and government.

The federal government has joined the party. Many federal agencies now have affiliated private foundations, which seek philanthropic funds to pursue their work. In seven years, from 1998 to 2004, the National Foundation for the Centers for Disease Control and Prevention more than doubled its annual receipts from private philanthropy, now bringing in more than $10 million per year. This makes the CDC's Foundation one of only 47 foundations in Atlanta with annual revenues in excess of $10 million. Examples of other agencies with affiliated private fundraising entities include the Library of Congress Trust (created in 1925, moved to Web-based fundraising in 1998) and the Fish and Wildlife Service of the Department of the Interior, whose foundation raises in excess of $11 million privately each year.

Local governments have not been far behind. Parks, fire departments, and libraries are all long-time solicitors of private funds to supplement public budgets. Once this was a matter of putting a dollar in the fireman's boot for a chance to climb on the fire truck on Saturday afternoon on Main Street. Today, local government is dancing to the big band sounds of major philanthropy. The Seattle Public Library, for example, has completed a $77.5 million capital and endowment campaign. In Los Angeles, the Library Foundation fundraising effort comes complete with a full list of naming opportunities, including the facilities themselves. In New York City, nearly one in every five dollars spent on the city's parks comes from private sources, not the Parks Department budget.

Public school systems are also energetic competitors on the private philanthropy dance floor. Public universities, of course, have long been recipients of private giving, from alumni and foundations with particular substantive interests. Budget tightening and the increasing costs of education have accelerated this trend. It is estimated that between 75 and 85 percent of the non-tuition operating funds of major public universities comes not from state budget coffers but from private philanthropy. Most public universities have affiliated private foundations to receive these funds, and many have multiple affiliated foundations.

Public K–12 education systems have ventured onto the floor. The combination of state budget cutbacks and court orders for educational equity have left many school systems with little recourse but private philanthropy. The National Association for Public and Private School Foundations estimates that in the early 1990s there were only 1,000 public school–affiliated private foundations. By 2004, that number had increased to 5,000.[1] That would mean that one-third of the nation's school districts have supplemental private funding foundations, raising private philanthropy for their programs and needs. Originally, these foundations raised funds for supplemental programs, like band uniforms, field trips, and after-school activities. Increasingly, they are paying teachers' salaries, to ensure that class sizes do not rise with cutbacks in school budgets.

The trend in private philanthropy support to supplement tax-supported institutions has also brought international institutions onto the nonprofit dance floor. Ted Turner's $1 billion commitment to the United Nations in 1998 created the UN Foundation and the Better World Fund. Together, and by combining Turner money with the philanthropy of other donors, large and small, these organizations have awarded nearly a billion dollars in grants in support of UN activities and projects. Specialized UN agencies also have their private fundraising arms.

The U.S. Fund for UNICEF has been in existence since 1949. It has $75 million in assets, and annually raises nearly half a billion dollars in private contributions to supplement the budget of UNICEF. Of the private money raised, nearly 95 percent is transferred to UNICEF programs and initiatives. UNICEF is the oldest and largest, but far from the only, UN agency swaying to the beat of private philanthropy. The United Nations Fund for Population Activities (UNFPA) raises $2 million annually. The United Nations Development Programme, the United Nations Environmental Programme, and the World Food Programme all have affiliated private U.S. fundraising arms to supplement their government-financed budgets.

There is, of course, a countervailing tendency. With the growth in the number of small nonprofits (80,000 to 90,000 new nonprofits are formed annually), and the consequent competition for resources, larger nonprofits are following the lead of their corporate colleagues and merging. The trend is particularly noticeable in healthcare, where both costs and the structure of reimbursement led to a flurry of mergers in the 1990s. The trend is also seen in the arts, social services, and education.[2] The result does not noticeably thin out the number of dancers on the floor, but it does increase the number of larger participants, further sharpening competition for significant resources.

These trends are all as they should be. Competition brings out the best ideas and the most innovative approaches available among institutions. The nonprofit sector cannot but benefit from such competition.

The inflow of resources implied by the intergenerational transfer of wealth will quicken the tempo for all the dancers. Extremely large amounts of money and the involvement of more personally involved philanthropic leaders will raise the visibility of the sector. The combination of huge pools of resources, sharpened public attention, and skeptical leadership will produce a complex rhythm for nonprofits.

These trends also raise two significant questions: What are the responsibilities of voter-accountable public institutions, and, in turn, what is a nonprofit?

The danger on the first count is obvious. The more successful private philanthropy is in funding public policy priorities, the less likely public budgets are to flow to those policies. When private funds are flowing to tangential areas of public responsibility—band uniforms or stage curtains—the concern is perhaps less worrying. But when funds are flowing to central areas of responsibility—teachers' salaries and textbooks—then there is perhaps greater cause for discomfort.

Public agencies are ultimately accountable to voters for public resource allocations. When resources do not meet public expectations, then there is public discourse and a consequence at the ballot box. When civil society holds public policy and public finance accountable for its decisions, those decisions will reflect public priorities. When civil society does not, either because it is not paying attention or because it has, in effect, given up, it decides to substitute private money for the bother of public discourse and changing public policy. When that happens, the link between public responsibility and citizen accountability can be weakened.

Of course, this is not necessarily so. Often, private resources are infinitely more effective than public resources in solving problems at the community level. But, nevertheless, the combination of public and private resources, as a result not of strategic choice but as a consequence of public weariness over policy disagreements, reflects not "partnership" but resignation.

One example will suffice. In an aging society, there is growing resistance in many communities over the tax costs of public education. It is not uncommon for one budget initiative for public education after another to be turned back as communities age. The dialogue about the importance of education, and public responsibility for education that such resistance engenders, is healthy, whatever the outcome on budget referendum day. Weariness over the debate, and budget frustration, can and do combine. Parents can and do, in effect, withdraw from the discourse to allocate private funds to core educational costs. The educational goals may be achieved, but the high price is the very discourse and debate, as well as the accountability of its result, that is the underpinning of democratically determined public policy. This is, arguably, not healthy.

If the trillions of dollars of resource transfers to the nonprofit sector in this nation come to embody not the robustness of a thriving civil society, but rather the weariness of civil society and its flagging trust in public institutions, then the consequent financial strength of the nonprofit sector will be a pyrrhic victory indeed. Strength will be fleeting as the very roots of nonprofits wither, in tandem with the social compact between what is public and what is private responsibility.

The trends and changes on the philanthropic dance floor raise a second concern. What is a nonprofit? When a nonprofit operates in what is, in effect, an economic market (as is increasingly the case in some areas of healthcare and education), and as a consequence grows to a size that enables dominance in that market, what precisely is "nonprofit" about its role? What precisely is the rationale for its protection from public finance obligations? When a nonprofit is, in effect, raising private funds to finance public policy implementation, why should that nonprofit not be accountable to the very electorate that did, or did not, enable the policy?

These are not trivial issues. The upcoming trillions of dollars of intergenerational transfer of wealth will have a potentially profound impact on the American nonprofit sector. But size has its price. As new nonprofits of all forms and fashions seek to fill their dance cards, and as existing nonprofits seek to better position themselves to be the partners of choice for large philanthropies, questions of appropriateness will be raised. As with all questions, those doing the answering are best served if they anticipate the questions. The nonprofit sector itself must begin immediately to examine the implications of growth and change. That examination must be overt and honest. Where there are weaknesses, where there are inconsistencies between past definitions and future opportunities, where there are conflicts of interest, nonprofit leadership must acknowledge and lead the recognition of problems, as well as lead the search for solutions.

The transfer of wealth is not business as usual on the part of philanthropy. It cannot, therefore, be business as usual on the part of nonprofits. If nonprofit leadership does not openly and energetically examine the consequences and likely reactions that stream from the transfer of wealth, and instead characterizes that transfer as having only a one-dimensional and wholly positive financial effect, then they will have missed the opportunity to be part of solving the inevitable problems that come with any sector, or any industry, awash in resources.

This will be unfortunate. The questions will be raised, and the examination will take place; the transfer of wealth is too large for any other outcome. Failure to lead in raising and resolving those questions, on the part of nonprofits, will only result in leadership by others.

■ **NOTES**

1. S. Carr. "Private Funds Padding Public School Coffers," *Milwaukee Journal Sentinel Online,* November 16, 2004.

2. G. J. MacDonald, "Nonprofit Organizations Seek Strength in Mergers," *Christian Science Monitor,* June 5, 2006.

Index